Department of the Army Pamphlets Published
in the
GERMAN REPORT SERIES

No.	Title	Publication date
20-201	Military Improvisations During the Russian Campaign	Aug 51
20-230	Russian Combat Methods in World War II	Nov 50
20-231	Combat in Russian Forests and Swamps	Jul 51
20-232	Airborne Operations: A German Appraisal	Oct 51
20-233	German Defense Tactics Against Russian Break-Throughs	Oct 51
20-234	Operations of Encircled Forces	Jan 52
20-236	Night Combat	Jun 53
20-240	Rear Area Security in Russia—The Soviet Second Front Behind the German Lines	Jul 51
20-242	German Armored Traffic Control During the Russian Campaign	Jun 52
20-290	Terrain Factors in the Russian Campaign	Jul 51
20-291	Effects of Climate on Combat in European Russia	Feb 52
20-292	Warfare in the Far North	Oct 51

CONTENTS

PART ONE. INTRODUCTION   *Page*
    I. General 1
   II. The Russian Soldier 2
  III. German Adjustments to the Russian Theater of War 3
  IV. Peculiarities of Russian Combat Methods 4
   V. Russian Combat Orders 6

PART TWO. ARMS AND SERVICES

Chapter 1. Infantry

    I. General 7
   II. German Limited-Objective Attacks South of Leningrad (September 1941) 8
  III. Company G Counterattacks during a Snowstorm (November 1941) 15
  IV. Company G Operates in Deep Snow (January 1942) 18
   V. Russian Infantry Attacks a German-Held Town (January 1942) 24
  VI. Company G Struggles Against Overwhelming Odds (March 1942) 32
 VII. Company G Annihilates a Russian Elite Unit (March 1942) . 37
VIII. Company G Recaptures Hill 726 (October 1942) 40
  IX. The 2d Battalion Launches a Limited Counterthrust (November 1942) 44
   X. The 2d Battalion Switches to the Defensive (November 1942) 47
  XI. The 2d Battalion's Stand at Verkhne-Golubaya (November 1942) 50
 XII. The 2d Battalion Holds Out Despite Being Overrun by Russian Armor (December 1942) 55
XIII. Infantry Succeeds Where Armor Failed (December 1942) . 58
XIV. The 2d Battalion's Final Struggle in the Stalingrad Pocket (January 1943) 63
 XV. Sudden Initiation into Russian Winter Combat (February 1943) 65
XVI. Russian Reconnaissance in Force by Tank-Mounted Infantry (October 1943) 68

Chapter 2. Armor

    I. General 74
   II. The Armored Roadblock (June 1941) 76
  III. German Armored Engineers Capture Two Bridges (June 1941) 84
  IV. Russian Tank Trap (July 1941) 91
   V. German Armored Engineers on the Road to Leningrad (August 1941) 92

PART TWO. ARMS AND SERVICES—Continued

Chapter 2. Armor—Continued

	Page
VI. The Struggle for Shelter (December 1941)	100
VII. Seesaw Battle in Subzero Temperatures (January 1942)	103
VIII. The Fedorenko Order (June 1942)	106
IX. Feint, Ambush, and Strike (July 1942)	109
X. Ambush Without Follow-Up (December 1942)	115
XI. Tanks Fail to Eliminate a Bridgehead (June 1944)	117
XII. An Armored Task Force Seizes Two Vital Bridges (August 1944)	118
XIII. Tank Battle Near the Berlin Highway (March 1945)	125

Chapter 3. Engineers

I. General	129
II. A River Crossing that Almost Failed (July 1941)	129
III. The Hidden Bunker in the Stalin Line (July 1941)	138
IV. The Capture of Balta (August 1941)	149
V. Russian Mine-Clearing Methods (July 1942)	163
VI. Russian Excavation Methods (September 1943)	165
VII. The Recapture of Goldap (November 1944)	168

PART THREE. SPECIAL OPERATIONS

Chapter 4. Fighting in Taiga and Tundra

I. General	177
II. A Sabotage Operation Against the Murmansk-Leningrad Rail Line (August 1942)	178
III. German Raid on a Russian Strong Point in Northern Finland (February 1944)	190
IV. The Last German Offensive Operation in Northern Finland (August 1944)	198
V. German Retrograde Movement Through the Taiga (September 1944)	204

Chapter 5. Russian Operations at River Lines

I. General	208
II. Battle Reconnaissance by Infiltration (August 1941)	208
III. A Unique Underwater Bridge (August 1943)	220
IV. The Swamp Bridgehead (June 1944)	228
V. The Oder Crossings (February 1945)	231

Chapter 6. Forest Combat

I. General	236
II. Initiation into Forest Fighting (July 1941)	236
III. Russian Defensive Position near the Edge of a Forest (August 1941)	241
IV. German Defense of a Forest Strong Point (February 1942)	244
V. Russian Infiltration Tactics (October 1942)	248
VI. Russian Attack Through a Forest (November 1943)	254
VII. German and Russian Combat Tricks	259

PART THREE. SPECIAL OPERATIONS—Continued

Chapter 7. Antipartisan Warfare

	Page
I. General	262
II. The First Encounter (June 1941)	264
III. The Forest Camp (December 1942)	268
IV. Attack on a Partisan Headquarters (June 1943)	274
V. Operation QUARRY (January–March 1944)	281

MAPS

Map No.		Page
1.	General Reference Map of European Russia	Frontispiece
2.	Advance from Romanovka to Slutsk	9
3.	Hill 747 Northeast of Rzhev	16
4.	Fighting East of Toropets	19
5.	Defense of Khristishche	25
6.	Defense of Village T North of Olenino	33
7.	Defense of Village S Northwest of Olenino	38
8.	Attack on Hill 726 North of Olenino	41
9.	The 2d Battalion's Moves During the Stalingrad Fighting	44
10.	Counterthrust from Verkhne-Buzinovka	46
11.	Defense of Verkhne-Buzinovka	46
12.	Defense of Verkhne-Golubaya	51
13.	Fighting North of Bolshaya Rossoshka	51
14.	The Struggle South of Verkhniy Kumskiy	59
15.	The Advance from Konstantinovka to Krasnogorka	65
16.	Skirmish North of Kiev	68
17.	A Russian Tank Obstructs German Advance in Southern Lithuania	77
18.	The Two Bridges Across the Dvina	84
19.	The Seizure of Zhlobin	90
20.	Approach to Leningrad	92
21.	German Defense of Berestovaya	100
22.	Fighting West of Kursk	103
23.	German Advance to the Resseta River	110
24.	German Armor at the Foothills of the Caucasus Mountains	114
25.	Russian Bridgehead on the Dnestr	116
26.	German Counterthrust in Southern Poland	119
27.	German Defense of the Kuestrin-Berlin Highway	127
28.	Bridge Construction Across the Dvina at Ulla	130
29.	Demolition of a Russian Bunker on the Bank of the Dnestr	138
30.	The Capture of Balta	149
31.	Russian Mine Clearing in the Voronezh Salient	164
32.	Russian Tunnels Dug South of Lake Ladoga	167
33.	The German Attack on Goldap	169
34.	General Reference Map for "Fighting in Taiga and Tundra"	177
35.	The Sabotage Company's Route to the Murmansk-Leningrad Rail Line	182
36.	Assault on Hill 858 East of the Litsa River	191
37.	Situation in the 307th Regiment's Sector	198
38.	The 307th Regiment's Route of Withdrawal	203
39.	Russian Cross-River Reconnaissance Along the Lower Dnepr	210
40.	Russian Attempts to Cross the Upper Donets South of Belgorod	219

Map No.		Page
41.	Russian Bridgehead on the Pripyat	228
42.	Russian Crossings South of Frankfurt an der Oder	231
43.	Forest Fighting in Latvia	237
44.	Russian Forest Positions Near Kanev in the Ukraine	240
45.	German Defense of a Forest Strong Point Southwest of Moscow	245
46.	Russian Forest Force Southeast of Rzhev	249
47.	Russian Attack North of Kiev	254
48.	Partisan Resistance in Southern Lithuania	265
49.	Elimination of a Partisan Force in the Bryansk Area	271
50.	Attack on a Partisan Headquarters in the Lepel-Borisov Area	275
51.	Antipartisan Operations Near Kerch in the Crimean Peninsula	282

ILLUSTRATIONS

No.		
1.	German Patrol Returning With Prisoners and Wounded Comrades	11
2.	German Sentry Using Large Wash Tub to Protect Himself Against Icy Wind	17
3.	German Sentry in Sheepskin Coat Near Moscow, December 1941	23
4.	German Supply Column Returning From the Front, January 1942	30
5.	German Foxhole Near Rzhev, February 1942	35
6.	German Reconnaissance Patrol Near the Don, 1942	43
7.	German Sentries Near the Don, 1942	49
8.	German Infantry Fighting Russian Tanks, 1942	57
9.	Russian T-34 in Action	70
10.	German Columns Advance Past Immobilized Russian Tanks, July 1941	75
11.	German 50-mm. Antitank Gun in Position	79
12.	Russian KV Tank Demolished by the Germans, July 1941	83
13.	German Tank Attacks With Mounted Infantry, 1942	96
14.	German 88-mm. Gun Crew Keeping Warm, Winter 1942	105
15.	German Tanks Attack With Luftwaffe Support, 1942	111
16.	Two German Tiger Tanks Meet Near a Forest, 1944	126
17.	German Advance Through Ukrainian Wheat Field During Attack on Stalin Line, July 1941	131
18.	Construction of a German Ponton Bridge, 1941	136
19.	The Russian Bunker in the Stalin Line (Dnepr Bridge in the Center)	140
20.	Closeup View of the Russian Bunker	147
21.	Russian Position in the Ukraine, August 1941	151
22.	German Ponton Bridge, 1941	159
23.	German Bunker in the Taiga	174
24.	German Bunkers on the Kandalaksha Front, 1944	186
25.	German Ski Company in the Tundra, May 1944	193
26.	German Patrol Reports in Lapland, 1942	195
27.	German Infantry, 1944	202
28.	Russian POW's, 1941	211
29.	Russian Infantry Mopping Up While German Tank Burns, 1943	221
30.	German Assault Gun Attacks Behind Smoke Screen	225
31.	German 88-mm. Gun Knocks Out Russian Tanks	233
32.	German River Crossing, 1942	239
33.	German 20-mm. Antiaircraft Gun Used in Ground Fighting, 1942	243
34.	German Armored Infantry Advancing Through Forest	250

No.		Page
35.	German Assault Gun Advances Ahead of Infantry, 1942	253
36.	German Tanks Rumbles Through Kiev	258
37.	German Motorized Column Takes a Break on the Road to Minsk, July 1941	263
38.	German Poster Warns of Death Penalty for Any Partisan or Anyone Assisting Him, August 1941	269
39.	German Soldier Searching a Captured Russian Partisan	279
40.	German Supply Dump in Russia	285

(Most of the illustrations are from the collection of captured German combat paintings now in the custody of the Chief of Military History, Special Staff, U.S. Army; the others are U.S. Army photos from captured German films.)

PART ONE
INTRODUCTION

I. General

Proper combat training for officers and enlisted personnel is essential to military victory. The objective of peacetime training must be to improve their efficiency so that they can achieve optimum performance in time of war. This will be attained if every soldier knows how to handle his weapon and is fully integrated into his unit and if every leader is able to master any situation with which he might be faced. The better their preparation for war, the fewer improvisations commanders and soldiers will have to introduce in combat.

Every tactician and instructor recognizes the validity of these principles and tries to instill them in his trainees in the most realistic manner. Yet even the best-trained German troops had to learn many new tricks when war broke out and when they were shifted from one theater to another. In each instance they were faced with problems for which they were not sufficiently prepared. In unusual situations field commanders were sometimes compelled to violate certain regulations before they could be rescinded or modified by higher authority.

The preceding observations give an indication of the problems involved in preparing the German field forces for an encounter with an opponent whose pattern of behavior and thinking was so fundamentally different from their own that it was often beyond comprehension. Moreover, the peculiarities of the Russian theater were such that German unit commanders were faced with situations for which there seemed to be no solution. The unorthodox Russian tactics with which the Germans were not familiar were equally disturbing, and Russian deception and trickery caused many German casualties. Several months of acclimatization were often necessary before a unit transferred to Russia was equal to the demands of the new theater. Occasionally a combat efficient unit without previous experience in Russia failed completely or suffered heavy losses in accomplishing a difficult mission that presented no problems to another unit familiar with the Russian theater, even though the latter had been depleted by previous engagements. This fact alone proved how necessary it was to disseminate the lessons learned in Russia, since this was the only method by which inexperienced troops could be spared the reverses and heavy casualties they would otherwise suffer during their commitment against Russian troops. To meet this need for training literature, a series of pamphlets and instructions based on German combat experiences in Russia was issued in 1943–44.

II. The Russian Soldier

The Germans found, however, that to be acquainted with Russian tactics and organization was useful but by no means decisive in achieving victory in battle. Far more important was the proper understanding of the Russian soldier's psyche, a process involving the analysis of his natural impulses and reactions in different situations. Only thus were the Germans able to anticipate Russian behavior in a given situation and draw the necessary conclusions for their own course of action. Any analysis of the outstanding characteristics of the Russian soldier must begin with his innate qualities.

a. Character. The Slav psyche—especially where it is under more or less pronounced Asiatic influences—covers a wide range in which fanatic conviction, extreme bravery, and cruelty bordering on bestiality are coupled with childlike kindliness and susceptibility to sudden fear and terror. His fatalistic attitude enables the Russian to bear extreme hardship and privation. He can suffer without succumbing.

At times the Russian soldier displayed so much physical and moral fortitude that he had to be considered a first-rate fighter. On the other hand, he was by no means immune to the terrors of a battle of attrition with its combination of massed fire, bombs, and flame throwers. Whenever he was unprepared for their impact, these weapons of destruction had a long-lasting effect. In some instances, when he was dealt a severe, well-timed blow, a mass reaction of fear and terror would throw him and his comrades completely off balance.

b. Kinship With Nature. The Russian soldier's kinship with nature was particularly pronounced. As a child of nature the Russian instinctively knew how to take advantage of every opportunity nature offered. He was inured to cold, hot, and wet weather. With animal-like instinct he was able to find cover and adapt himself to any terrain. Darkness, fog, and snowdrifts were no handicap to him.

Even under enemy fire he skillfully dug a foxhole and disappeared underground without any visible effort. He used his axe with great dexterity, felling trees, building shelters, blockhouses, and bunkers, and constructing bridges across waterways or corduroy roads through swamps and mud. Working in any weather, he accomplished each job with an instinctive urge to find protection against the effect of modern weapons of destruction.

c. Frugality. The frugality of the Russian soldier was beyond German comprehension. The average rifleman was able to hold out for days without hot food, prepared rations, bread, or tobacco. At such times he subsisted on wild berries or the bark of trees. His personal equipment consisted of a small field bag, an overcoat, and occasionally one blanket which had to suffice even in severe winter weather. Since he traveled so light, he was extremely mobile and did not depend on the arrival of rations and personal equipment during the course of operations.

d. Physical Fitness. From the outset of the Russian campaign the German tactical superiority was partly compensated for by the greater physical fitness of Russian officers and men. During the first winter, for instance, the German Army High Command noticed to its grave concern that the Russians had no intention of digging in and allowing operations to stagnate along fixed fronts. The lack of shelter failed to deter the Russians from besieging German strong points by day and night, even though the temperature had dropped to $-40°$ F. Officers, commissars, and men were exposed to subzero temperatures for many days without relief.

The essentially healthy Russian soldier with his high standard of physical fitness was capable of superior physical courage in combat. Moreover, in line with the materialistic concepts of communism, the life of a human being meant little to a Russian leader. Man had been converted into a commodity, measured exclusively in terms of quantity and capability.

III. German Adjustments to the Russian Theater of War

Conversely, the German troops were ill prepared for a prolonged campaign in Russia. An immediate readjustment and a radical departure from the norms established in the western and central European theaters of war became necessary. As a first adjustment to local conditions the German Army revised the standards for selecting lower echelon commanders. Their average age was lowered and the physical fitness requirements were raised. Staff cars, riding horses, and every piece of excess baggage had to be left behind whenever a German unit had to go into action against Russian forces. For weeks at a time officers and men had no opportunity to change their underwear. This required another type of adjustment to the Russian way of life, if only to prevail in the struggle against filth and vermin. Many officers and men of the older age groups broke down or became sick and had to be replaced by younger men.

In comparison with the Russian soldier, his German counterpart was much too spoiled. Even before World War I there was a standing joke that the German Army horses would be unable to survive a single night in the open. The German soldier of World War II had become so accustomed to barracks with central heating and running water, to beds with mattresses, and to dormitories with parquet floors that the adjustment to the extremely primitive conditions in Russia was far from easy. To provide a certain amount of comfort during a term of service extending over several years was perfectly justifiable, but the German Army had gone much too far in this respect.

The breakdown of the supply system and the shortage of adequate clothing during the winter of 1941–42 were the direct outgrowth of German unpreparedness. The extraordinary physical fitness of the Russians, which permitted them to continue the struggle without let-up throughout the biting-cold winter, caused innumerable German casualties and thereby shook the confidence of the troops.

IV. Peculiarities of Russian Combat Methods

During the course of the war the Russians patterned their tactics more and more after those of the Germans. By the time they started their major counteroffensives, their methods of executing meticulously planned attacks, organizing strong fire support, and establishing defensive systems showed definite traces of German influence. The one feature distinguishing their operations throughout the war was their total disregard for the value of human life that found expression in the employment of mass formations, even for local attacks. Two other characteristics peculiar to the combat methods of the Russians were their refusal to abandon territorial gains and their ability to improvise in any situation.

Infantry, frequently mounted on tanks and in trucks, at times even without weapons, was driven forward wave upon wave regardless of the casualties involved. These tactics of mass assault played havoc with the nerves of the German defense forces and were reflected in their expenditure of ammunition. The Russians were not satisfied at merely being able to dominate an area with heavy weapons or tanks; it had to be occupied by infantry. Even when as many as 80 men out of 100 became casualties, the remaining 20 would hold the ground they had finally gained whenever the Germans failed to mop up the area immediately. In such situations the speed with which the Russian infantry dug in and the skill with which the command reinforced such decimated units and moved up heavy weapons were exemplary.

A quick grasp of the situation and instantaneous reaction to it were needed to exploit any moment of weakness that was bound to develop even after a Russian attack had met with initial success. This was equally true in the case of a successful German attack. Under the impression that they had thoroughly beaten and shattered their Russian opponents during an all-day battle, the Germans occasionally relaxed and left the followup operation or pursuit for the next morning. On every such occasion they paid dearly for underestimating their adversary.

The conduct of the Russian troops in the interim periods between major engagements deserved careful analysis because it provided clues to what had to be expected during the initial phase of the coming battle. The gathering of information was complicated by the fact that Russian commanders put so much stress on concealing their plans during the buildup phase for an attack and during the preparation of a defensive system. The effectiveness of secrecy and adaptation to terrain was forcefully demonstrated in the shifting and regrouping of forces. While the speed with which Russian commanders effected an improvised regrouping of large formations was in itself a remarkable achievement, the skill with which individual soldiers moved within a zone of attack or from one zone to another occasionally seemed unbelievable. To see a few soldiers moving about in the snow at great distance often meant little to a careless and superficial observer. However, constant observation and an accurate head count often revealed surprisingly quick changes in the enemy situation.

In view of the alertness of the Russian infantryman and the heavily mined outpost area of his positions, a hastily prepared reconnaissance in force by the Germans usually failed to produce the desired results. Under favorable circumstances the patrol returned with a single prisoner who either belonged to some service unit or was altogether uninformed. The Russian command maintained tight security, and the individual soldier rarely knew his unit's intentions. The resulting lack of information with regard to Russian offensive plans gave no assurance, however, that strong Russian forces would not launch an attack at the same point the very next day.

To celebrate major Soviet holidays Russian sharpshooters usually tried to break the standing marksmanship scores and on those occasions German soldiers had to be particularly on the alert. In general, however, Russian attacks were likely to take place on any day, at any time, over any terrain, and under any weather conditions. These attacks derived their effectiveness mainly from the achievement and exploitation of surprise, toward which end the Russians employed infiltration tactics along stationary fronts as well as during mobile operations. The Russians were masters at penetrating the German lines without visible preparation or major fire support and at airlanding or infiltrating individual squads, platoons, or companies without arousing suspicion. By taking advantage of the hours of darkness or the noon rest period, the weather conditions and terrain, or a feint attack at another point, the Russian soldiers could infiltrate a German position or outflank it. They swam rivers, stalked through forests, scaled cliffs, wore civilian clothing or enemy uniforms, infiltrated German march columns—in short, suddenly they were there! Only through immediate counteraction could they be repelled or annihilated. Whenever the Germans were unable to organize a successful counterthrust, the infiltrating Russians entrenched themselves firmly and received reinforcements within a few hours. It was like a small flame that rapidly turns into a conflagration. Despite complete encirclement Russian units which had infiltrated German positions could hold out for days, even though they suffered many privations. By holding out, they could tie down strong German forces and form a jumpoff base for future operations.

V. Russian Combat Orders

In contrast to the steady stream of propaganda poured out by the political commissars whose language abounded in flowery phrases and picturesque expressions designed to stimulate the Russian soldier's morale and patriotism, the combat orders of lower-echelon commanders were very simple. A few lines drawn on a sketch or on one of their excellent 1:50,000 maps indicated the friendly and hostile positions, and an arrow or an underscored place name spelled out the mission. As a rule such details as coordination with heavy weapons, tanks, artillery, tactical air support, or service units were missing, because more often than not the mission had to be accomplished without such assistance.

On the other hand, it would be unjust not to mention that these details were considered with utmost care by the intermediate and particularly by the higher echelon command staffs. Whereas in the early stages of the campaign captured Russian division and regimental orders often showed a tendency toward stereotype thinking and excessive attention to detail, during the later phases the Russian staff work improved considerably in this respect.

PART TWO
ARMS AND SERVICES

Chapter 1

Infantry

I. General

Hitler's plans for the invasion of Russia called for the destruction of the bulk of the Russian Army in western European Russia. A rapid pursuit was then to be launched up to a line extending approximately from the Volga to Archangel. Along this line, Asiatic Russia was to be screened from the European Continent by the German Army.

The execution of the operation was to be entrusted to three army groups. Army Group Center was to rout the Russian forces in White Russia and then pivot northward to annihilate the armies stationed in the Baltic area. This objective was to be achieved in conjunction with Army Group North which was to thrust from East Prussia in the general direction of Leningrad. Meanwhile, Army Group South was to attempt a double envelopment south of the Pripyat Marshes and crush the Russian formations defending the Ukraine before they could withdraw across the Dnepr. Here, Kiev was to be the first major objective, the seizure of the highly industrialized Donets Basin the next one. Once the northern and southern wings had made sufficient progress, all efforts were to be concentrated on the capture of Moscow, whose political and economic importance was fully recognized. The entire campaign was to be over before winter; the collapse of the Soviet Government was anticipated at an early stage of the campaign.

The description of the course of the actual operations is not within the scope of this study. However, knowledge of the planning on which the invasion was based does afford a better understanding of the series of actions involving Company G of a German infantry battalion during the crucial winter of 1941–42. This unit helped to guard the life lines of the two German armies holding the Vyazma–Rzhev salient west of Moscow (secs. III, IV, and VI–VIII).

The infantry actions included in this chapter stress fighting under poor weather conditions, particularly in subzero temperatures, in the heart of European Russia. It was under such adverse conditions, which hampered armored operations, that German infantry battalions and companies demonstrated their capabilities and combat efficiency.

A series of five other actions describes the struggle of the 2d Battalion of a German infantry regiment that fought to the bitter end in the Stalingrad pocket during the winter of 1942-43 (secs. IX-XII and XIV). The remaining examples have been selected to complete the picture of German and Russian small infantry units fighting under unusual weather and terrain conditions.

II. German Limited-Objective Attacks South of Leningrad (September 1941)

After its lightning advance through the Baltic States during the early days of the Russian campaign Army Group North arrived at the gates of Leningrad, where the Russians fiercely contested every inch of ground. During the late summer of 1941 the Germans were slowly forging a ring of steel around the strongly fortified city. In mid-September the 490th Infantry Regiment was given the mission of eliminating Russian centers of resistance approximately 15 miles south of Leningrad in the area north of the Izhora River between Romanovka and Slutsk. In the path of the regiment's advance stood an unknown number of Russian bunkers and defense positions established on the hills dominating the Izhora Valley. These positions had to be neutralized in order to secure the German lines of communication during the thrust on Slutsk. Late on 13 September the regiment crossed the river south of Gorki and spent the night in that village. The attack against the Russian-held hills north of the river was to start the next day, with the 1st and 2d Battalions advancing along the river valley and the 3d protecting the flank to the north (map 2).

Very little was known about either the terrain or the Russian fortifications in the area. The German maps, as well as previously captured enemy maps, were either inadequate or inaccurate. For this reason, the commander of the 3d Battalion decided to conduct careful terrain reconnaissance before attacking. The reconnaissance took the entire morning, and it was not until noon that the attack of the 3d Battalion against the Russian bunkers east of Gorki finally got under way. Attached to the forward elements were three demolition teams equipped with flame throwers and shaped charges. Only a few minutes were required to dispose of the first Russian bunker. While the engineers were preparing to attack the next bunker, two Russian howitzers in a cornfield west of Vilosi went into action.

SMALL UNIT ACTION

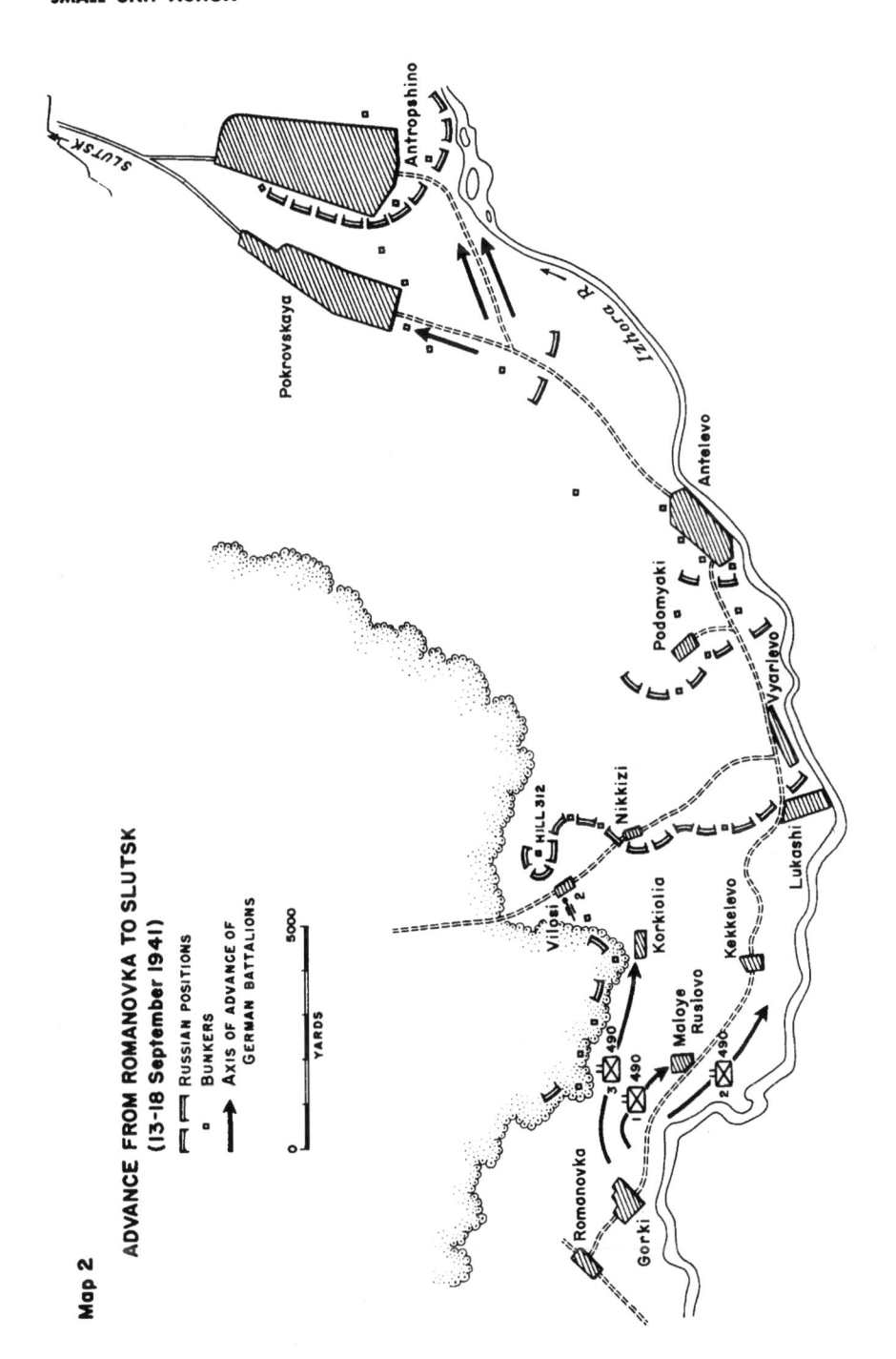

Map 2

ADVANCE FROM ROMANOVKA TO SLUTSK
(13-18 September 1941)

The regimental artillery was on the alert and destroyed the two howitzers and a nearby ammunition dump. By 1600 the demolition teams had captured the second bunker and were preparing to attack a third, which they presumed to be the last. Half an hour later this bunker was in German hands. The engineers were just about to withdraw and take a well-deserved rest when the 1st Battalion advancing farther to the south, discovered two additional bunkers, one of which was about 1,000 yards southwest of Vilosi. The demolition teams destroyed both bunkers in short order, thus paving the way for the 3d Battalion's advance toward Hill 312 northeast of Vilosi. Continuing its attack, the 3d Battalion made some slight gains in the late afternoon of 14 September, but halted at 2015 after darkness set in and withdrew to Vilosi for the night. The other two battalions had made only little headway during the day, and spent the night of 14–15 September at the eastern edge of Vyarlevo. During the night Russian aircraft scattered bombs over widely separated areas, including some positions held by their own troops.

The seizure of strongly fortified Hill 312, scheduled for the next day, promised to be an arduous task. Although H-hour had originally been set for 0600, the attack had to be postponed until afternoon because the morning hours were needed for thorough terrain reconnaissance by two patrols sent out by the 3d Battalion.

One of the patrols, led by Lieutenant Thomsen, was to reconnoiter the hills between Korkiolia and Lukashi to determine whether and in what strength they were occupied by the Russians. The second patrol, under Sergeant Ewald, was to reconnoiter the area north of Hill 312 to determine the enemy's disposition and strength, and to probe for weak spots in his defense.

Patrol Thomsen was stealthily advancing southeastward from Korkiolia when it was suddenly intercepted and pinned down. In the ensuing exchange of fire the patrol was able to identify a number of Russian bunkers and field positions and to relay the necessary target data to the 3d Battalion CP. A short time later these Russian strong points were destroyed by the accurate fire of the regimental artillery. After having completed its mission, Patrol Thomsen returned to battalion headquarters.

By noon no word from Patrol Ewald had been received by the commander of the 3d Battalion. Since he could not postpone the attack on Hill 312 any longer, he ordered Lieutenant Hahn, the commander of Company I, to seize the hill.

At 1230 Hahn assembled the assault force, which consisted of Company I plus a machinegun and a mortar platoon, a demolition team

GERMAN PATROL, returning with prisoners and wounded comrades.

consisting of two engineers equipped with flame throwers and shaped charges, and an artillery observer. Since Sergeant Ewald's patrol had not returned, only the two platoons led by Lieutenant Borgwardt and Sergeant Timm were available for the attack. In extended formation, the assault force advanced through the woods west and northwest of Vilosi and reached a point north of Hill 312 apparently without attracting the enemy's attention. From there, Lieutenant Hahn identified a bunker on top of Hill 312 and two positions on its northern slope. The fortifications were held in strength. Before he was able to conclude his observations, the enemy spotted the Germans, fired on them, and pinned them down.

The artillery observer attached to the assault force called for direct howitzer fire, whereupon the bunker received two hits which, however, appeared to do little damage. Hahn reported the situation to battalion headquarters and was ordered to continue the attack.

Platoons Borgwardt and Timm were to skirt Hill 312 and approach its base through the dense thicket that extended southward from the forest edge to the hill. Platoon Borgwardt went to the right, Platoon Timm to the left. The latter was to support Borgwardt's advance up the hill and then dispose of the obstinate bunker on the crest of the hill as soon as Borgwardt entered the two slope positions. While the two platoons were moving out, the attached machinegun and mortar platoons went into position at the edge of the forest north of Hill 312. The howitzers gave the signal to attack by firing six rounds at the enemy bunker on top of Hill 312. Company headquarters personnel had to act as covering force since an enemy relief thrust was to be expected at any time.

Again the fire of the howitzers failed to put the bunker out of action. While the shells were exploding on and around the bunker, Borgwardt's men stealthily worked their way up the hill, creeping toward the two Russian positions whose occupants' attention was diverted by machinegun and mortar fire from the edge of the woods north of the hill. Platoon Borgwardt suddenly broke into the positions and caught the Russians completely by surprise.

While Borgwardt's men were engaged in seizing the two positions, Platoon Timm followed them up the hill and captured the bunker with the help of the engineers, whose flame throwers and shaped charges succeeded where the artillery had failed. Just as the operation seemed to have been brought to a successful conclusion, the personnel who had remained at the edge of the forest north of Hill 312 were attacked from behind by a force of about 50 Russians. Hahn ordered the newly arrived Patrol Ewald to hold off the Russians while the rest of the assault force followed the elements that had captured the hill. Upon arriving at the summit they immediately set up their weapons, took the Russians under effective fire, and repulsed their attack. From the top of the hill, Hahn saw the 1st Battalion, now no longer subject to flanking fire from Hill 312, penetrate the Russian positions west of Nikkizi. He immediately established contact with the battalion commander and made preparations to defend the hill against a potential Russian counterattack. This precaution had to be taken, for within the hour the artillery observer on top of the hill noticed Russian forces assembling for a counterattack in the woods north and northeast of Hill 312. However, the Russians lost all enthusiasm for an attack after the German artillery lobbed a few well-aimed shells into their midst.

After the capture of the hill on the afternoon of 15 September, the 3d Battalion continued its advance on the left of the 490th Infantry Regiment. Russian resistance was light, and the battalion had little difficulty in occupying Podomyaki since the Russians had evacuated the fortified position west of the village and had withdrawn to Antelevo.

On the morning of 17 September the 3d Battalion prepared to advance from the northwest toward Antelevo, which the Russians appeared to be defending its strength. The Russian positions west and north of the village were situated on high ground dominating the terrain over which the battalion had to advance; to the south and east Antelevo was protected by the Izhora River. At dawn a reconnaissance patrol of Company I identified two concrete bunkers as well as field emplacements in and around Antelevo. The northern and western sections of the village were held by one Russian battalion. German howitzers and antitank guns took the bunkers under fire, though only with little effect. Once again demolition teams were needed to destroy the enemy fortifications with shaped charges. The flame throwers, which previously had proved so effective, could no longer be used since the supply of flame-thrower fuel had been exhausted.

By an unexpected stroke of luck, the reconnaissance patrol managed to capture a Russian outpost whose telephone was still connected to the CP of the Russian regimental commander at Antelevo. The German battalion commander immediately interrogated the captured Russian telephone operator and obtained the latter's code name. His next step was to put his knowledge of Russian to the test. Using the code name of the Russian telephone operator, he called the Russian regimental commander. The latter was apparently misled, but did not divulge anything of value except that he was determined to hold Antelevo.

When the German officer became more insistent in his quest for additional information, the suspicions of the Russian commander were aroused, and he changed his tone. The German then tried a more direct approach and made an outright demand for the surrender of the Russian regiment at Antelevo. This was curtly rejected.

The commander of the 490th Infantry Regiment thereupon decided to mass his forces and seize Antelevo by direct assault. During the afternoon of 17 September he assembled the 1st and 3d Battalions west and north of the village, respectively, and launched an attack against the enemy stronghold after a strong artillery preparation. Again the demolition teams performed their task in an exemplary manner and quickly put one Russian bunker after another out of action. The Russians had apparently considered these particular bunkers impregnable, for once they were destroyed the enemy infantry fled in wild disorder, abandoning most of its equipment. By nightfall Antelevo was securely in German hands.

With the fall of Antelevo, Russian resistance seemed to disintegrate all along the regiment's route of advance, except for a brief encounter at the road fork south of Antropshino. There the Russians attempted to stop the regiment along prepared positions, but failed to do so. After this delay the German forces fanned out and reached Slutsk on 18 September, the 3d Battalion via Pokrovskaya and the 1st and 2d via Antropshino. Upon its arrival in Slutsk the regiment established contact with the 121st Infantry Division, which had previously captured the town.

A number of lessons may be learned from this operation. First, all regimental units had to conduct thorough terrain reconnaissance since their maps and those captured from the Russians were frequently either inadequate or inaccurate. Whenever one of the battalion commanders failed to reconnoiter the terrain thoroughly, his unit was in danger of being ambushed by the Russians.

The Germans were able to take the Russian bunkers with a minimum loss of time and men by employing skilled demolition teams. Each member of these teams had been thoroughly trained and was well versed in his task.

The capture of the Russian outpost on the morning of 17 September might have provided the Germans with information about Russian intentions and troop dispositions, had it been properly exploited. The battalion commander showed a lack of good judgment by using his average knowledge of Russian in an attempt to extract information from the Russian regimental commander. This was clearly a task for an expert interpreter who was skilled in methods of interrogation.

The Russians were fighting a delaying action during which they often failed to take advantage of the favorable terrain and of their prepared positions. The flight of the Antelevo garrison was indicative of how easily the Russians became demoralized when they were confronted by an unexpected situation. When the German demolition teams blew up the bunkers with shaped charges, the Russians panicked and instinctively took to flight, as happened so often during the early months of the campaign.

III. Company G Counterattacks During a Snowstorm (November 1941)

This action is typical of the fighting in the late autumn of 1941, when Russian resistance began to stiffen west of Moscow and the ill-equipped German troops had to rally all their energy to continue the advance toward the Russian capital.

In November 1941 the 464th Infantry Regiment of the German 253d Infantry Division was occupying field fortifications about 60 miles northeast of Rzhev. On the regiment's right flank was Hill 747 (map 3). Since the hill afforded an extensive view of the German rear area, the Russians had made repeated attempts to capture it in an effort to undermine the position of the 464th Infantry Regiment. The hill had changed hands several times, but was now occupied by the Germans. The presence of heavy weapons including assault guns, as well as reports of repeated reconnaissance thrusts, gave rise to the belief that the Russians were preparing for another attack against the hill. Accordingly, the regimental commander withdrew Company G from the sector it was holding and committed it on the regiment's right flank.

After reporting to battalion headquarters around noon on 15 November, Lieutenant Viehmann, the commander of Company G, accompanied by his platoon leaders, undertook a terrain reconnaissance. A heavy snowfall set in. As the group was returning from the reconnaissance mission, submachine gun and mortar fire was heard from the direction of Hill 747. The company commander attached little importance to this at the time. However, upon arriving at the battalion CP he learned that the Russians had taken advantage of the snowstorm and had seized the hill without artillery or mortar support in a surprise raid. An immediate counterattack by German troops failed to dislodge the Russians.

Viehmann thereupon received orders to recapture the hill in a surprise attack to be launched at 2200. Regimental headquarters attached a medium mortar platoon and a light howitzer platoon to the company and promised artillery support. Viehmann formed three assault parties and moved them into jumpoff positions close

**HILL 747 NORTHEAST OF RZHEV
(15 November 1941)**

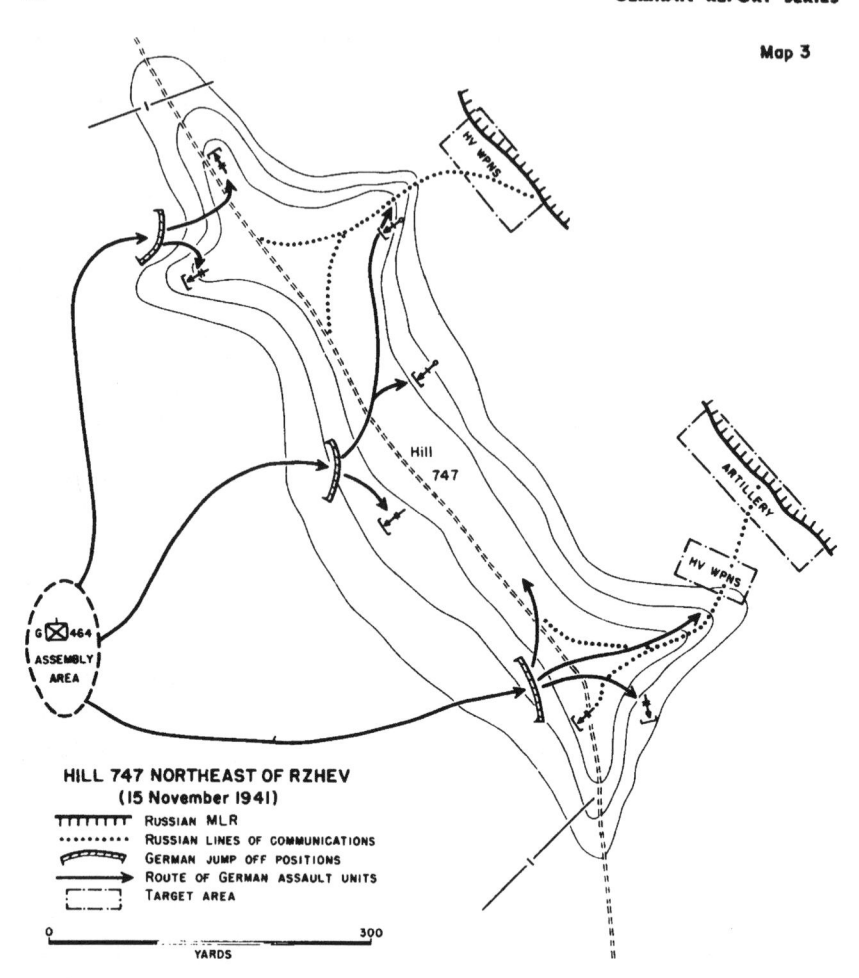

⊥⊥⊥⊥⊥⊥	Russian MLR
....	Russian lines of communications
⌒⌒⌒	German jump off positions
──▶	Route of German assault units
⌐ ⌐	Target area

0 — 300 YARDS

to the Russian line under cover of darkness. The infantry company to the right was to divert the attention of the defending force at the time of the actual attack, while the unit to the left was to support the attack with its fire. Artillery and heavy weapons were to open fire on specified areas at prearranged flare signals.

The German assault parties occupied their jumpoff positions without attracting the attention of the defending Russians. The party in the center, led by Viehmann, was only about 35 yards from the nearest Russian position. Close observation of the Russian defenses and the actions of individual soldiers indicated that a German attack was not anticipated. The Russian sentries were shivering from the cold and were by no means alert. Rations and supplies were being drawn. Not far from Viehmann's observation point a Russian detail was unloading furs and felt boots from a sled.

At 2200 the German assault parties, shouting loudly, broke into the Russian position. The attack confused the Russians, who dropped everything and attempted to make their way to the rear. Their escape, however, was prevented by the two assault parties that, at the beginning of the attack, had skirted either side of the hill and severed the Russian lines of communications. Unaware of the fighting, the Russian heavy weapons and artillery remained silent throughout the

GERMAN SENTRY using large wash tub to protect himself against icy wind.

attack. When the signal flare went up, the German artillery and heavy weapons opened fire, laying a barrage on the Russian-held side of the hill. Two Russian machineguns covering each flank put up fierce resistance before being silenced in the hand-to-hand fighting.

After 45 minutes Hill 747 was completely in the hands of the Germans; their former MLR had been reoccupied and communications established with adjacent units. About 60 prisoners, 7 medium mortars, 5 heavy machineguns, 3 antitank guns, and large quantities of ammunition were taken. In the morning 70 Russian dead were found on the hill. Of the five German casualties, only one was severely wounded.

The manner in which the Russians exploited the snowstorm in carrying out a surprise attack without artillery or mortar support was typical of Russian infantry combat methods in wintertime.

The Russians launched their attack before winter clothing had been issued; some of the men wore only thin summer uniforms. As a stimulant, each Russian soldier was issued five tablets which had an effect similar to that of alcohol and a large ration of sugar cubes. In addition, the men were promised a special liquor ration upon completion of their mission. The sugar and tablets were presumably issued to counteract the discomfort caused by the temperature of 16° F. However, once the effects of these stimulants wore off, the men began to feel the cold acutely and their senses became numbed, as was observed in the case of the Russian sentries. During the German assault to retake Hill 747 the Russian defenders appeared to be as susceptible to the cold as were the Germans. This must be considered an isolated case, however, since the Russian soldiers were generally able to endure extremely low temperature. At the same time it indicates that some of the Russian units were insufficiently prepared for winter combat and had to improvise protective measures to overcome the rigors of the unexpectedly early winter weather.

IV. Company G Operates in Deep Snow (January 1942)

On 13 January Company G of the 464th Infantry Regiment was ordered to provide protection against Russian partisan raids on the division's supply line, which led from Toropets via Village M to Village O (map 4). To this end the company was reinforced by two heavy machineguns, two 80-mm. mortars, and one antitank platoon.

On the evening of 14 January the company, mounted in trucks, reached Village O, 5 miles east of Village M. Upon its arrival at Village O, a supply unit, which was fleeing eastward toward Rzhev before the powerful Russian offensive, indicated that strong contin-

SMALL UNIT ACTIONS

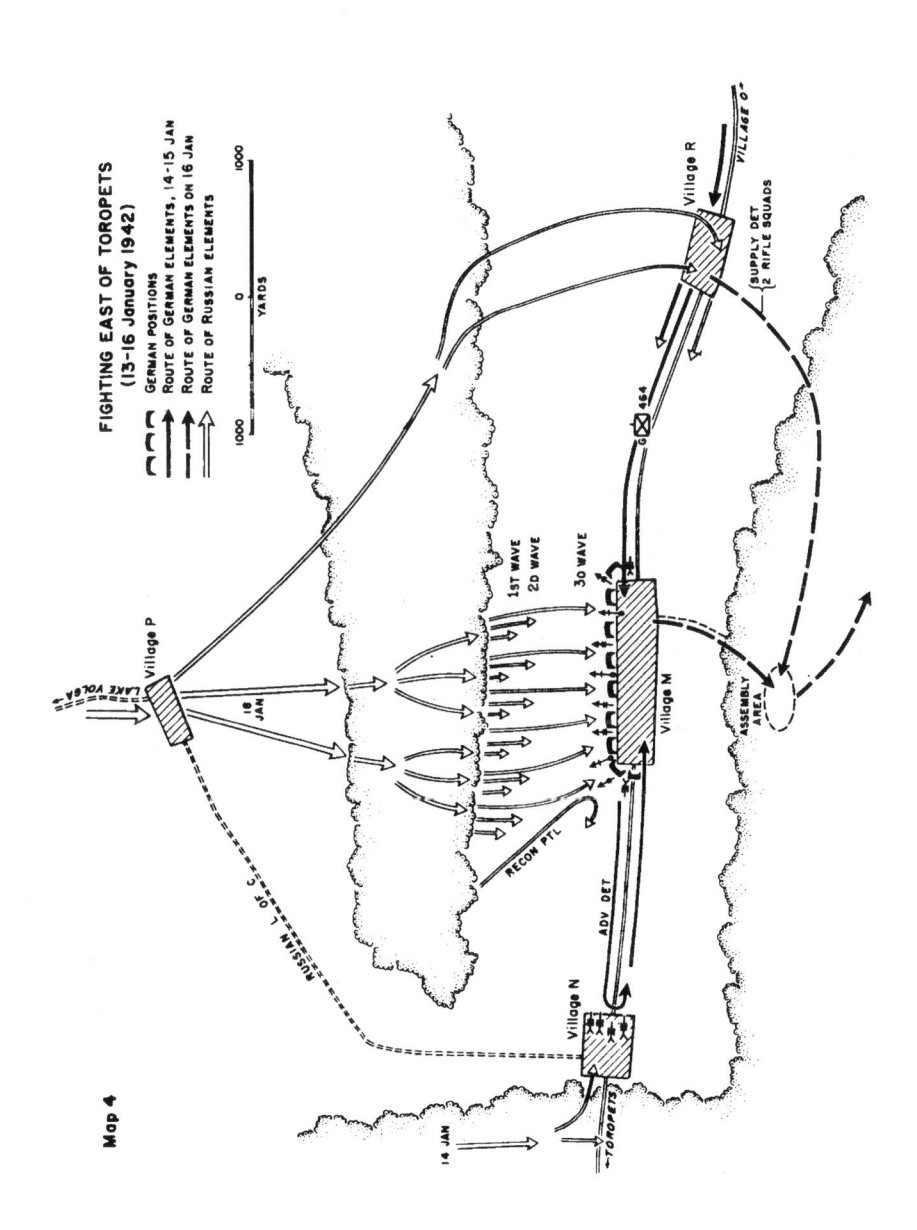

Map 4

FIGHTING EAST OF TOROPETS
(13-16 January 1942)

German positions
Route of German elements, 14-15 Jan
Route of German elements on 16 Jan
Route of Russian elements

gents of Russian troops from the north had cut the German supply route in the forest west of Village N. Using civilian labor, the Russians had constructed a road at least 30 miles long that led south through the large forest bypassing Toropets to the east. The company commander, Lieutenant Viehmann, decided to establish local security in Village O, spend the night there, and continue westward on foot the next morning in order to see what was going on. During the night a few Russian civilians slipped out of the village, established contact with the Russian troops, and supplied them with intelligence regarding the German dispositions.

At dawn on 15 January, after posting security details, the company started out and arrived in Village M without having made contact with the Russians. As the company's advance element approached Village N, the Germans noticed a large group of soldiers in German uniform standing in the road, beckoning to them. That these soldiers were not Germans became evident when the antitank gun moving up behind the advance element was suddenly fired upon. The company's other antitank guns covered the advance element's withdrawal to Village M, where it rejoined the main body of the company. The prime mover of the lead gun was lost during this action. The Russians, however, did not follow up their attack.

In Village M the company set up hasty defenses against an attack from the north and west and tried to determine the strength and intentions of the opposing Russian force. From a vantage point in Village M it was possible to observe the eastern edge of Village N, where the Russians were building snow positions and moving four antitank guns into position. There was an exchange of fire but no indication of an impending Russian attack. During the hours of darkness Company G built snow positions along the western and northern edges of Village M, while the aforementioned supply unit occupied Village R, about one mile east of Village M, and took measures to secure it, particularly from the north.

During the night of 15–16 January reconnaissance patrols reported that the Russians were continuing their defensive preparations in Village N and that their line of communications was the road leading north from there.

On 16 January between 0400 and 0500 a 50-man Russian reconnaissance patrol approached the northwest corner of Village M on skis. Although the Russian patrol had been detected, it was allowed to come very close before it was taken under fire. Approximately 10 men of the patrol escaped and three were taken prisoner; the rest were killed before they could reach the German position.

SMALL UNIT ACTIONS

According to the statements of the three prisoners, two Russian divisions were moving south toward Village M. On 16 January Villages M and R were to be captured. What the prisoners either did not know or refused to tell, was that the Russians, attacking in force across frozen Lake Volga, had broken through the German positions west of the 253d Infantry Division 2 days before and had pushed on to the south. Thus, Viehmann was unaware of the true German situation.

Since the Russians in Village N remained passive, Viehmann decided to concentrate on defending his village against an attack from the north. The deep snow caused some difficulties; for instance, machineguns had to be mounted on antiaircraft tripods so that a satisfactory field of fire could be obtained.

About 0800 on 16 January the company's observation post identified three Russian columns moving south toward the forest north of Village M. Except for antitank guns these columns did not seem to be equipped with heavy weapons. Around 1000 the first Russians appeared at the southern edge of the forest, some 1,000 yards from the German defensive positions. At 1020 the Russian center and right-wing columns attacked with antitank guns and infantry. Just a short time before this attack Company G had dispatched two rifle squads to Village R to reinforce the supply unit there, since the Russian left-wing column was headed in that direction.

The first wave of Russian infantry, some 400 men strong, emerged from the forest on a broad front. It was evident that the 3-foot snow was causing them great difficulty. The concentrated fire of the German heavy weapons succeeded in halting the attack after it had advanced about 200 yards.

After a short while a second, equally large wave emerged from the forest. It advanced in the tracks of the first and carried the attack forward, over and beyond the line of dead. The Russian antitank fire became heavier, being directed against the German machinegun positions, which the Russians had spotted. As a result, several machineguns were destroyed; some changed their positions frequently in an effort to dodge the Russian fire. The Russians advanced an additional 200 yards, then bogged down under the effective German small arms fire. They sustained heavy losses which, however, were compensated for by the reinforcements pouring down south into the forest from Village P. Viehmann estimated that the Russians committed the equivalent of two regiments in this action.

By 1100 the Russian left-wing column had reached a point 150 yards from the German positions in Village R, where the terrain was more favorable for the attacker than that north of Village M. The supply unit and the two rifle squads defending Village R could no longer be reinforced because the road from Village M was under constant Russian fire.

Realizing that his position would become untenable within the next few hours, Viehmann ordered his men to prepare to evacuate Village M. A few men with minor wounds were detailed to trample a path through the deep snow from Village M toward the forest to the south in order to facilitate a quick withdrawal. The troops in Village R were also to withdraw to the same forest if pressed too heavily by the Russians.

The members of the third Russian assault wave emerged from the forest unarmed. However, they armed themselves quickly with the weapons of their fallen comrades and continued the attack. Meanwhile, Village R was taken and the Russians closed in on Village M from the east. The Germans were now very low on ammunition, having expended almost 20,000 rounds during the fighting.

About 1300 Company G, after destroying its mortars and antitank guns, evacuated Village M. Viehmann planned to make contact with the German troops in Village O by withdrawing through the forest south of Village M. He ordered the evacuation of the wounded, then withdrew with the main body of the company, and left behind a light machinegun and an antitank gun to provide covering fire and to simulate the presence of a larger force. After the gun crews had expended all the ammunition, they destroyed the breech operating mechanism of the antitank gun and withdrew toward the forest. About halfway there they were fired on by the Russians who had meanwhile entered Village M. The retreating Germans managed to escape without losses because the Russians did not pursue them into the forest.

During the next 3 days the company marched—with almost no halts for rest—through the deep snow that blanketed the dense forest, relying heavily on a compass in the absence of familiar landmarks. On 19 January, after bypassing Village O, which was found to be occupied by the Russians, it finally reestablished contact with the 253d Infantry Division. Only then did the company learn that all forces on the German front south of and parallel to Lake Volga had been withdrawn in the meantime.

In this action deep snow hampered the movements of both the attacking Russians and the defending Germans. Only by trampling a path in the snow before its withdrawal from Village M, did Company G avoid being trapped by the Russians.

The appearance of a Russian reconnaissance patrol in German uniform was a frequent occurrence; however, the number of disguised

GERMAN SENTRY in sheepskin coat near Moscow, December 1941.

Russians encountered on 15 January in Village N was unusually large.

As so often happened during the winter of 1941–42, the Russians attacked in several waves on a given front, each successive wave passing over the dead of the preceding and carrying the attack forward to a point where it, too, was destroyed. Some waves started out unarmed and recovered the weapons from their fallen comrades.

V. Russian Infantry Attacks a German-Held Town (January 1942)

While the German troops west of Moscow tried to weather the Russian winter offensive and maintain their precarious lines of communication in the Rzhev-Velikiye Luki area, Marshal Timoshenko's forces launched a strong attack against Army Group South. In mid-January 1942 they attacked the German positions along the Donets River between Kharkov and Slavyansk and achieved a deep penetration near Izyum. The Russians smashed through the weakly held German positions and advanced westward, attempting simultaneously to widen the gap by attacking southward. In that direction the Russian objectives were Slavyansk and the industrial Donets Basin, whose capture would lead to the collapse of the German front in southern Russia.

The German troops along the Donets River had not expected a Russian winter offensive since the opposing forces were believed to be weak and incapable of launching one. Because of the shortage of winter equipment, the Germans had been forced to leave only outposts along the Donets River and in isolated villages, while their main forces occupied winter quarters far to the rear. In most instances the defending units were unable to delay the progress of the Russian offensive because the attacking troops simply bypassed them.

Toward the end of January the temperature dropped to −50° F. The snow was about 3 feet deep. The weather was clear and a biting east wind prevailed.

There was light Russian air activity, with fighters and light bombers intervening occasionally in the ground fighting. The Lufwaffe rarely made an appearance.

Timoshenko's forces were at full combat strength, well armed, appropriately equipped for winter combat, and fed adequate rations. By contrast, the German units were at 65 percent of T/O strength and short of winter clothing and equipment, but their rations were plentiful.

By defending the town of Khristishche against attacks from the north, northeast, and east, the 1st Battalion of the German 196th Infantry Regiment was to block any further Russian advance along the road to Slavyansk (map 5). To the south, reconnaissance patrols were to maintain contact with a few strong points located in nearby villages. To the west the battalion was to keep in close contact with the adjacent unit of its regiment. Snow positions had been established at the edges of Khristishche because it was impossible to dig in the frozen soil. The battalion's field of fire extended up to

SMALL UNIT ACTIONS

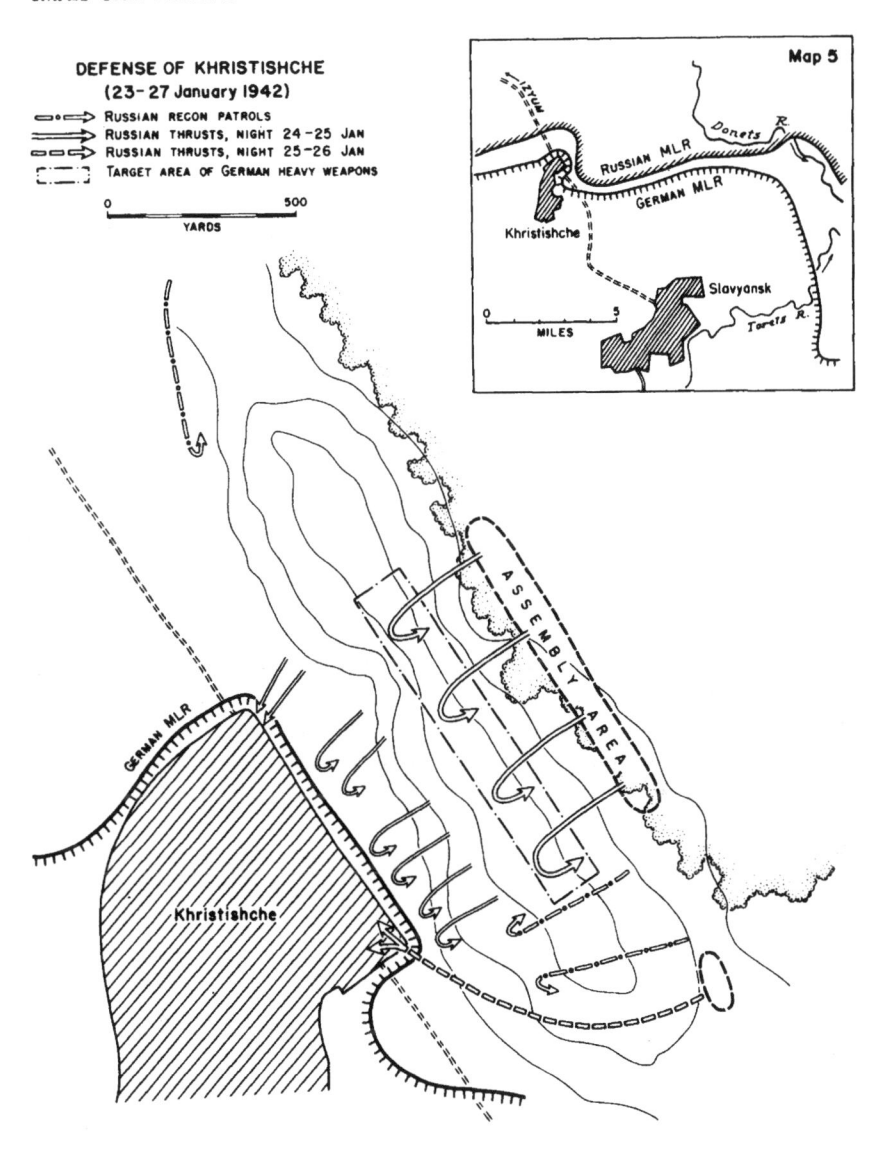

DEFENSE OF KHRISTISHCHE
(23–27 January 1942)

- ⇨ RUSSIAN RECON PATROLS
- ⇨ RUSSIAN THRUSTS, NIGHT 24–25 JAN
- ⇨ RUSSIAN THRUSTS, NIGHT 25–26 JAN
- ▭ TARGET AREA OF GERMAN HEAVY WEAPONS

0 — 500 YARDS

Map 5

2,200 yards north and south. To the east lay a long ridge, beyond which there was a large forest held by strong Russian forces.

During the night of 23–24 January a Siberian rifle regiment with twenty-four 76.5-mm. guns, advancing westward, reached a point 1 mile northeast of Khristishche. It fired on a German reconnaissance patrol, which withdrew southwestward leaving behind one wounded man, who disclosed to the Russians that there were two German regiments in and around Khristishche.

On the morning of 24 January a Russian reconnaissance patrol in platoon strength attempted to approach Khristishche, but was almost completely wiped out by German machinegun fire and snipers. Russian reconnaissance patrols looking down from the hill observed lively movement in the town, but made no attempt to advance any farther during daytime.

According to information obtained from a subsequently captured Russian officer, the Siberian rifle regiment received the following order on 24 January:

> The Germans have been beaten along the entire front. They still cling to isolated villages to retard the victorious Russian advance.
>
> Khristishche is being defended by severely mauled German units, whose morale is low. They must be destroyed so that the Russian advance to Slavyansk can continue.
>
> At 2115 on 24 January two battalions of the regiment will attack Khristishche without artillery preparation and will advance to the western edge of the town. The 3d Battalion will follow behind the 1st and 2d Battalions and clear the village of all Germans. Then the 3d Battalion will occupy the northeastern edge of Khristishche on both sides of the road leading to Izyum, facing southeast. Reconnaissance patrols will probe in the direction of Slavyansk. One ski company* will reinforce each assault battalion. The ski units will enter Khristishche without permitting anything to divert them from this objective. During the day preceding the attack the battalion and regimental artillery and mortars will fire for adjustment on all important targets. However, the Germans must not be led to expect our attack.

Throughout 24 January the positions of the 1st Battalion of the German 196th Infantry Regiment were hit by intermittent fire from light artillery and heavy mortars. Apparently this fire was directed by Russian observers on the ridge northeast of Khristishche.

At dusk the Germans increased their vigilance. In the snow trenches the sentries, dressed in white parkas, were doubled and posted at intervals of approximately thirty feet. Observation was made very difficult by the east wind, which blew snow into the men's faces. The sentries were relieved every 30 minutes.

At 2115 the sentries of Company C observed rapidly approaching figures near the boundary between their sector and that of Company B. They tried to open fire with their machineguns but found them frozen. Finally, one sentry was able to give the alarm by firing his

---

*For T/O and E of a Russian ski company see chart on p. 27.

T/O & E of a Russian Ski Company

Officers and Men	Weapons	Personal Equipment	Organizational Equipment
1 captain	1 submachinegun each	Padded winter uniform, fur cap with ear flaps, felt boots with leather soles, white parkas, skis and poles.	
1 first lieutenant	1 pistol each		
3 commissars	1 signal pistol each		
	3 hand grenades each		
12 sergeants and corporals	1 automatic rifle each with 150 rounds of ammo.	do	
	3 hand grenades each		
95 privates	1 rifle each with fixed bayonet	do	
	3 hand grenades each (15 snipers had rifles with telescopic sights).		
Wire Team:			
1 corporal	1 submachinegun each	1 spade and 1 intrenching tool each.	2 field telephones and pack reels of cable.
4 privates	3 hand grenades each		
117 officers and men			

carbine. By this time Russian assault troops on skis had been observed along the entire battalion front firing carbines and signal pistols and throwing hand grenades. The only German machinegun which would fire was the one that had been kept indoors.

The Russian surprise raid did not proceed as planned because the attackers were unable to jump over the 4-foot snow wall on skis and because most of them were not immediately ready to fire since they carried their weapons slung across their backs. The Russians were therefore repulsed, except for those who penetrated into the extreme north end of the town. Twenty-five Russians occupied the first house but were wiped out within 5 minutes by hand grenades.

Meanwhile, the German mortars and infantry howitzers laid down a barrage on the ridge northeast of the town. Two Russian battalions, which had just gained the ridge, were caught in the barrage and turned back.

The 1st Battalion took 43 prisoners, including some wounded. Over a hundred Russians lay dead in and around the German positions. The Germans had lost 2 dead, 8 wounded, and 3 suffering from frostbite.

Throughout the night the Germans heard loud cries and shouting from the forest, followed by submachinegun and rifle fire. Russian prisoners subsequently stated that the commissars assigned to the platoons and companies were trying to reorganize their units. They were unsuccessful in this attempt until the following morning (25 January), by which time several Russian soldiers had been shot and the regimental commander replaced.

That same morning a Russian combat patrol of 60 men approached Khristishche from the north but was wiped out some 500 yards from the German positions. In the afternoon two Russian reconnaissance patrols of 30 men each, supported by 3 machine gunners and 20 snipers, advanced toward the town from the southeast in single file. They were stopped halfway to their objective by German small arms fire. Approximately 20 men ran back over the hill, only to be stopped by their commissars and shot for cowardice. The intervening hours before darkness passed without incident.

The Russian troops built snow positions at the edge of the forest, set up observation posts and combat outposts on the crest of the hill, and dug emplacements for their artillery and mortars. Each squad built a shelter hut with tree trunks and branches, on top of which snow was packed. These shelters were built close together in an irregular pattern. The infantry howitzers and heavy mortars received five extra issues of ammunition, which were stored in nearby shelters.

That night a Russian combat patrol of 50 men under the command of an officer approached Khristishche from the east. The patrol was armed with 8 submachineguns, 2 pistols, 2 signal pistols, 38 automatic rifles, 2 light machineguns, each with 500 rounds of tracer ammunition, and 8 hand grenades per man. Most of the men wore padded winter uniforms and felt boots with leather soles; those, however, who could speak German were dressed in German uniforms. The patrol was to occupy the first houses and then send a message to the rear, where a reinforced company was kept in readiness to follow up the patrol's attack and to occupy Khristishche.

About 0130, while an icy east wind was blowing, five figures approached the two German sentries near the eastern corner of the town and called out from a distance, "Hello, 477th Regiment! Hello, comrades!" The Germans, who because of the whirling snow could see only about 60 feet ahead, challenged them from a distance of 30 feet with "Halt! Password!" The answer was "Don't fire! We are German comrades!" They continued to advance. The sentries now noticed a number of men about 50 feet behind the 5 soldiers who were approaching. Again they called "Password, or we fire!" Again the answer was "Don't shoot! We are German comrades!" Meanwhile the 5 Russians in German uniforms had approached to within 20 feet, whereupon they hurled hand grenades, which wounded 1 German sentry. The other fired his carbine to give the alarm, but in doing so was shot by the Russians, who immediately headed for the first house, followed by the main body of the combat patrol.

The Russians tossed hand grenades into the first house just as the men of the German squad which occupied the building ran out the back door without suffering any casualties. Throwing hand grenades and firing carbines and machineguns from the hip, the German infantrymen tried to stop the Russians who closed in from three sides. The German squad was pushed back to the second house, and the Russians immediately occupied the first one, set up two machineguns, and opened fire on M Company men, who were coming up on the double.

The Russians threw hand grenades and explosives through a window into the second house in order to wipe out the German squad occupying this house. At first this attempt was unsuccessful, but when the house caught fire that German squad was forced to evacuate. It got outside through a damaged wall on the far side of the house. By this time the commander of Company M had taken charge of the situation and had launched a counterthrust with company headquarters personnel, reserve squads, and the squad that had initially occupied the first house. Throwing hand grenades and firing their weapons on the run, the counterattacking Germans drove the Russians from Khristishche within a few minutes. Eight Russian enlisted men and one commissar

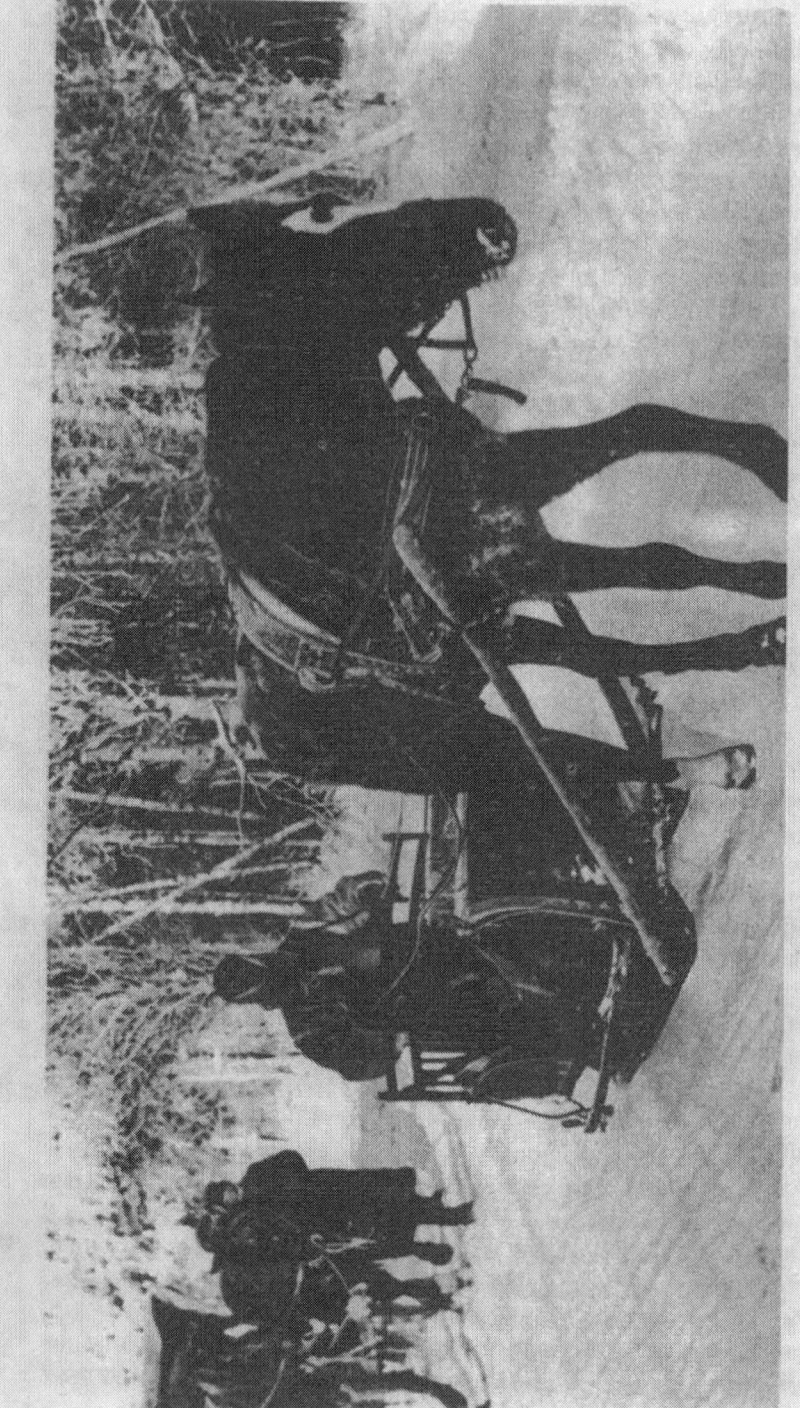

GERMAN SUPPLY COLUMN returning from the front, January 1942

manned two machineguns in the first house, where they resisted to the last man.

Upon noticing the signal equipment that the Russians had left behind in the first house, the German company commander correctly concluded that a Russian main force was assembled outside the village, waiting for the signal to advance. He called for artillery support against the suspected Russian jumpoff positions. The artillery fire began a minute later and probably prevented the Russian company from following up the attack. The remainder of the night passed quietly.

On the morning of 26 January the sun shone brightly, and the east wind continued to blow across Khristishche. Quiet reigned until 1000, when the Russian artillery started to shell the northeastern part of the town. Harassing fire continued until 1500.

At 1100, as the battalion commander was making his rounds of the German positions, a sentry from Company C reported that he had observed some suspicious movements on the forward slope of the hill east of Khristishche. A few Russian corpses which had been lying there had already vanished that morning, and he believed that the small piles of snow some 200 yards east of his post had increased in size.

The battalion commander observed the forward slope of the hill with binoculars for 1 hour, although a cold wind was blowing. He discovered a number of Russians hiding in the deep snow and cautiously piling up snow in front of them to increase their cover. The German sentries fired their carbines at every suspicious-looking pile of snow; no further movements were observed.

Russian prisoners subsequently stated that 1 Russian platoon of 40 men had been ordered to approach the town under cover of darkness and to dig into the snow. After daybreak this platoon was to push further toward the town in order to launch a surprise attack against it at nightfall. The platoon maintained wire communication with the rear.

Despite the bitter cold, the Russians remained in the snow for about 10 hours without being able to raise their heads or shift their bodies. Yet not one of them suffered frostbite.

On the basis of previous experience, the Russian commander ordered a mass attack without artillery support for that night (26–27 January). The fact that there were snow flurries and a strong east wind, may have induced him to make this decision.

The Russians assembled 3 battalions, totaling 1,500 men, for the attack. Two battalions were echeloned in the first assault wave, while the third battalion followed about 350 yards behind. The Russian regimental command post remained at the edge of the forest. Each company had 20 submachineguns, 35 automatic rifles, 10 rifles with telescopic sights, 8 heavy machineguns (drum fed), 5 light mortars, 12 pistols, and 2 signal pistols, as well as a number of rifles with fixed bayonets. Each man was issued three hand grenades and an ample supply of ammunition. All men wore padded winter clothing and felt boots.

At 0330 the Russian regiment started its attack. Any noise that the approaching Russians might have made was drowned out by the howling wind. The battalions advanced in close formation without leaving any intervals between units. The companies marched abreast in columns of three's and four's, with an interval of 5 to 10 paces between them. Without commands the Russians marched in close order to within 50 yards of the German positions and then began their assault amid wild shouting.

Only a few Russians broke into the German position; they were greeted with such a devastating hail of fire from the alert defenders that the dense Russian columns were mowed down, row after row. Nevertheless, those who survived attacked again and again.

Then the German artillery fire hit the Russian reserve battalion, which was completely dispersed. After half an hour the impetus of the attack had spent itself. Within two or three yards of the German positions the enemy dead or wounded had piled up to a height of several feet. The Russians suffered about 900 casualties in the engagement.

Khristishche remained in German hands because the garrison was alert and had learned to take proper care of its weapons.

VI. Company G Struggles Against Overwhelming Odds (March 1942)

The following action shows a Russian regiment attacking eastward in an attempt to cut off some German units and link up with friendly forces moving in from the opposite direction. The attack methods employed by the Russian infantry showed that the troops were inadequately trained. The infantry units emerged from their jumpoff position in a disorderly manner, having the appearance of a disorganized herd that suddenly emerged from a forest. As soon as the Germans opened fire, panic developed in the ranks of the attack force. The infantrymen had to be driven forward by three or four officers with drawn pistols. In many instances any attempt to retreat or even to glance backward was punished with immediate execution. There was virtually no mutual fire support or coordinated fire.

Typical of Russian infantry tactics was the tenacity with which the attack was repeated over and over again. The Russians never

Map 6

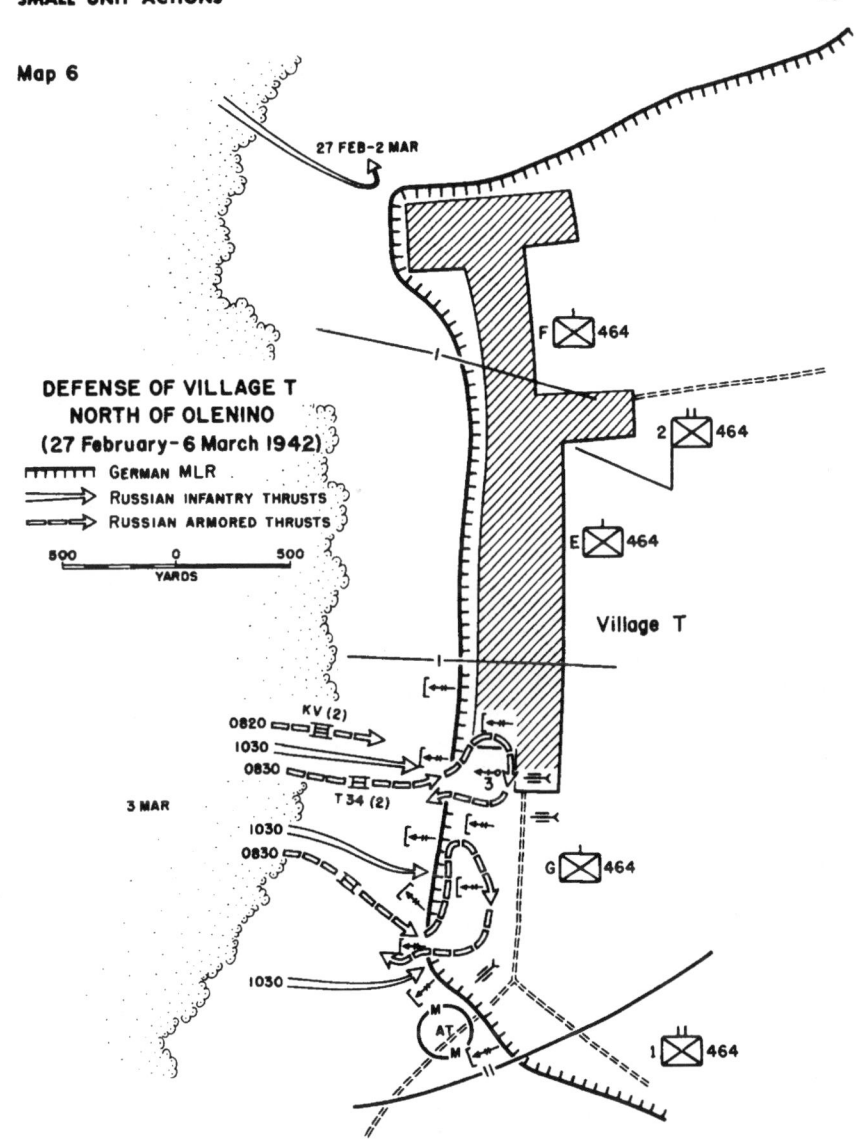

**DEFENSE OF VILLAGE T
NORTH OF OLENINO
(27 February – 6 March 1942)**

⊥⊥⊥⊥⊥ German MLR
⟹ Russian infantry thrusts
⇢⇢⇢ Russian armored thrusts

500 0 500
YARDS

abandoned ground which they had gained in an attack. Frequently, isolated Russian soldiers would feign death, only to surprise approaching Germans by suddenly coming to life and firing at them from close range.

In February 1942 the 2d Battalion of the 464th German Infantry Regiment occupied snow positions without bunkers or dugouts along the western edge of Village T, situated north of Olenino near the rail line leading from Rzhev to Velikiye Luki (map 6). German reconnaissance patrols probing through the forest west of that village had been unable to establish contact with the Russians. Toward the end of February a reconnaissance patrol ascertained the presence of Russian forces in the forest. Subsequent information obtained from local inhabitants indicated that the Russians were being reinforced for an attack.

From 27 February to 2 March, detachments, consisting of about 80 Russians each, attacked daily in the same sector and at the same time. The attacks took place about 1 hour after sunrise and were directed against a point at the northwest edge of Village T. Every one of them was unsuccessful, the attacking Russians being wiped out before they could reach the German position.

On the evening of 2 March a Russian deserter reported that his infantry regiment, supported by six tanks, would attack Company G's sector, which was south of the village. To strengthen the defense of his sector the company commander, Lieutenant Viehmann, placed three 37-mm. antitank guns behind the MLR and planted antitank mines across the road leading southwestward. Although his unit was understrength, Viehmann ordered each platoon to form a reserve detachment of 10 men for a possible counterthrust.

At daybreak on 3 March two Russian heavy tanks of the KV type, painted white to blend with the landscape, were spotted standing at the edge of the forest about 500 yards in front of Company G's sector. At 0820 Russian aircraft bombed the village, while the two tanks, about 150 yards apart, advanced another 100 yards, stopped, and opened fire at the most conspicuous German fortifications. At 0830 four more Russian tanks, this time T34's, emerged from the forest. They paired off, penetrated the right and center of Company G's MLR, and rolled up the stretch between the two points of penetration. Encountering no effective resistance, they pushed deeper into the German defensive position while providing mutual fire support. The three German 37-mm. antitank guns proved ineffective against the T34's and were quickly knocked out, as were a number of German heavy weapons. However, without immediate infantry support the Russian tanks were incapable of achieving any further results.

It was not until 2 hours later that approximately 300 Russian riflemen attacked from the forest, while the two KV tanks stood still and the T34's roamed at will through the depth of the German defensive position. Hampered by the deep snow, the infantry had to bunch up and advance along the tank tracks, offering easy targets during their slow movement. Despite the loss of many of their heavy weapons, the German defenders mustered sufficient strength

GERMAN FOXHOLE near Rzhev, February 1942

to repel the Russian attack and to force the infantry to withdraw into the forest, the tanks following soon afterward.

A short time later the four T34's reappeared. This time each tank carried a rifle squad. Additional infantry supported the attack. When the T34's re-entered the German MLR three of them were eliminated by German infantrymen who threw antitank mines into their paths. The Russian foot infantry elements advanced 350 yards from the forest's edge before being pinned down by German mortar fire. The one tank that remained intact quickly withdrew into the forest, followed by the Russian infantry. Throughout the day the two KV's remained in the German outpost area and fired on everything that moved within the German position.

Russian prisoners taken during the fighting stated that the riflemen mounted on tanks had been ordered to establish themselves within the German defensive position to support the Russian infantry's attack. These statements were confirmed when it was discovered that a number of small Russian detachments had infiltrated the German outpost area, from where they refused to be dislodged despite the severe cold. After dark, German combat patrols were finally able to move out and liquidate them.

All was quiet on 4 March. The next day the Russians resumed the attack all along the 2d Battalion sector with a force estimated at 2 to 3 infantry regiments and supported by 16 tanks. While the Russian artillery confined itself to harassing the German rear area, the mortars laid down intensive fire, whose effect was insignificant because of the deep snow. Severe fighting continued unabated until evening. After dark the Russians broke into the southern part of Village T at several points. By that time severe losses in men and materiel had greatly weakened the defending force. Nevertheless, the Germans held the northern part of Village T until the morning of 6 March, when they withdrew to a new position 2 miles farther east.

In this engagement the Russians demonstrated extraordinary skill in approaching through the snow-covered forests without attracting the attention of the Germans. They permitted small German reconnaissance patrols to pass at will to create the impression that the forest was clear.

The four limited attacks that preceded the main assault were either feints or reconnaissance thrusts in force. By repeating them against the same sector on 4 subsequent days, the Russians probably intended to divert German defense forces to that point.

During the main assault the teamwork between Russian tanks and infantry was inadequate. In this particular engagement the Russian infantry showed little aggressiveness, and the tanks had to advance alone to break up the German defense system before the infantry jumped off. Actually, the long interval between tank and infantry attacks had precisely the opposite effect. It is true that the Russian tank attack threw the German defense into temporary confusion, because the 37-mm. antitank guns were ineffective against the T34's and KV's and the German infantry lacked experience in combatting tanks at close range. Moreover, the two KV tanks acted as armored assault guns and prevented all movements within the German position. These often-used tactics were successful as long as the Germans did not have antitank guns whose projectiles could pierce the armor of these tanks. However, by the time the Russian infantry launched its attack two hours later, the defenders were able to overcome their initial fear of the giant KV tanks and to rally sufficient strength to frustrate the Russian infantry attack. When the Russian armor attacked for the second time, the German infantry knew how to cope with it effectively.

As in many other instances, the lower echelon Russian commanders revealed a certain lack of initiative in the execution of orders. Individual units were simply given a mission or a time schedule to which they adhered rigidly. This operating procedure had its obvious weaknesses. While the Russian soldier had the innate faculty of adapting himself easily to technological innovations and overcoming mechanical difficulties, the lower echelon commanders seemed incapable of coping with sudden changes in the situation and acting on their own initiative. Fear of punishment in the event of failure may have motivated their reluctance to make independent decisions.

The Russian troops employed in this action seemed to be particularly immune to extreme cold. Individual snipers hid in the deep snow throughout day or night, even at temperatures as low as −50°F. In temperatures of −40° F. and below, the German machineguns often failed to function, and below −60° F. some of the rifles failed to fire. In these temperatures the oil or grease congealed, jamming the bolt mechanism. Locally procured sunflower oil was used as a lubricant when available, as it guaranteed the proper functioning of weapons in subzero temperatures.

VII. Company G Annihilates a Russian Elite Unit (March 1942)

During March 1942 Russian pressure from the north and west forced the Germans to make a limited withdrawal northwest of Rzhev. In late March the 2d Battalion of the German 464th Infantry Regiment, including Company G, established defensive positions in

Map 7

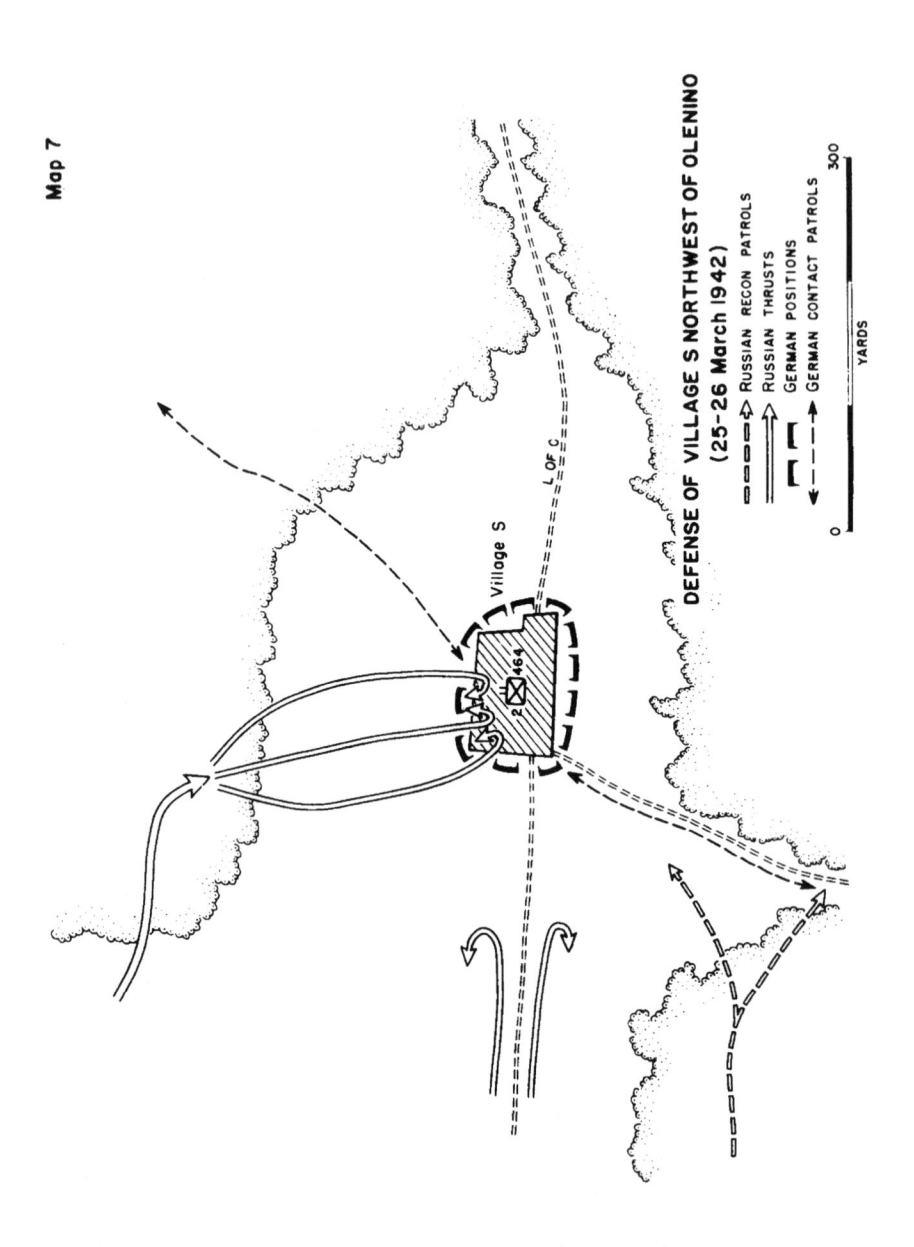

DEFENSE OF VILLAGE S NORTHWEST OF OLENINO
(25-26 March 1942)

⇢⇢⇢ RUSSIAN RECON PATROLS
⇒ RUSSIAN THRUSTS
⊏⊐ GERMAN POSITIONS
←--→ GERMAN CONTACT PATROLS

0 — 300
YARDS

Village S, about 12 miles northwest of Olenino. The village was situated on level ground and was faced by forests to the north, east, and south (map 7). The terrain to the west was open, permitting the defenders to detect at an early moment the approach of any Russian forces coming from that direction. Since the German forces in the area were not strong enough to establish a continuous defense line, the village was organized for perimeter defense. The battalion constructed snow positions above the ground, excavation of the frozen soil being impossible, and maintained contact with adjacent units by sending patrols through the forests around the village. On 25 March the low temperature was −44° F. and 3 feet of snow covered the ground. On that day the 2d Battalion repelled several attacks from the west, inflicting heavy losses on the Russians, who then intensified their patrol activity.

Before dawn on 26 March a reconnaissance patrol sent out by Company G returned from the forest bordering Village S to the north without having encountered enemy troops. The distance from the edge of the forest to the defense perimeter measured approximately 150 yards. Half an hour after the return of the German patrol 100 Russians suddenly emerged from the forest and attacked Company G at the northwestern part of the defense ring. The Russians participating in the attack were armed with submachineguns and moved on skis, which made the small force exceedingly mobile in the snow-covered terrain. In addition, every third man carried a frangible grenade in his pocket, presumably for the purpose of setting fire to the village. Several Russians literally blew up when their frangible grenades were struck by bullets and exploded. Because of the severe cold some of the German machineguns failed to function, and the Russians succeeded in penetrating the German positions.

Half an hour later Company G counterattacked in order to eliminate the penetration. The Russians fought tenaciously, and there was violent hand-to-hand combat. By 1200 Company G had recaptured the positions. Eighty-nine Russians were killed and nine, including two seriously wounded, taken prisoner. All of the attackers were NCO candidates who had been promised battlefield promotions if they captured Village S.

While Company G was mopping up the area, brief hand-to-hand fighting suddenly flared up at two points where prostrate Russians, suddenly coming to life, jumped to their feet and assaulted the German soldiers.

This example illustrates how effectively the Russian riflemen exploited the terrain when approaching the enemy, even in deep snow and extreme cold. The attack was conducted skillfully and silently, and fullest use was made of the element of surprise. The entire assault force rushed out of the forest and attacked in a single wave. However, when the surprise attack did not result in the immediate capture of the village but led to a struggle for the German positions, the operation lost its tactical value since the Russian unit had gone into battle without any support. Instead of breaking off the engagement and withdrawing, the Russians continued fighting until their entire force was wiped out.

This action, however, does not lend itself to generalization since a special Russian unit composed of noncommissioned officer candidates was involved. Except for the resistance offered to the German advance in the summer of 1941 by certain Russian elite formations, no other Russian units had fought so violently and tenaciously.

During World War II the training status of different Russian units showed such great variations that generalizations based on the performance of individual units are not permissible. As in any other army, there were both good and indifferent units among the innumerable divisions which opposed the Germans. Training courses at Russian service schools were conducted with great thoroughness, and even senior officers were subjected to the rigors of the ordinary training schedule. Training was not limited to the achievement of military proficiency; it was constantly overshadowed by political indoctrination designed to imbue every soldier with the ideological principles involved in the life-and-death struggle.

VIII. Company G Recaptures Hill 726 (October 1942)

During the spring and summer of 1942 the Germans strengthened the Rzhev salient and eliminated Russian forces that had gained a foothold west of the Vyazma-Rzhev rail line. The salient gradually became one of the strongest defense lines the Germans had built in Russia. In the early autumn Marshal Zhukov launched an offensive against the Rzhev salient to divert German forces from the Stalingrad front and to eliminate this potential threat to the Russian capital. In this action, which is the last one in the series concerning the fighting west of Moscow, Company G resisted the onslaught of fresh Russian troops who had recently arrived from training centers in Siberia.

In mid-September Russian infantry supported by tanks seized Hill 726, some 10 miles north of Olenino. Once the Russians had wrested it from the Germans, they withdrew their tanks and left an infantry company of about 75 men to defend the newly won position. This hill now constituted a dent in the German MLR and afforded a

SMALL UNIT ACTIONS

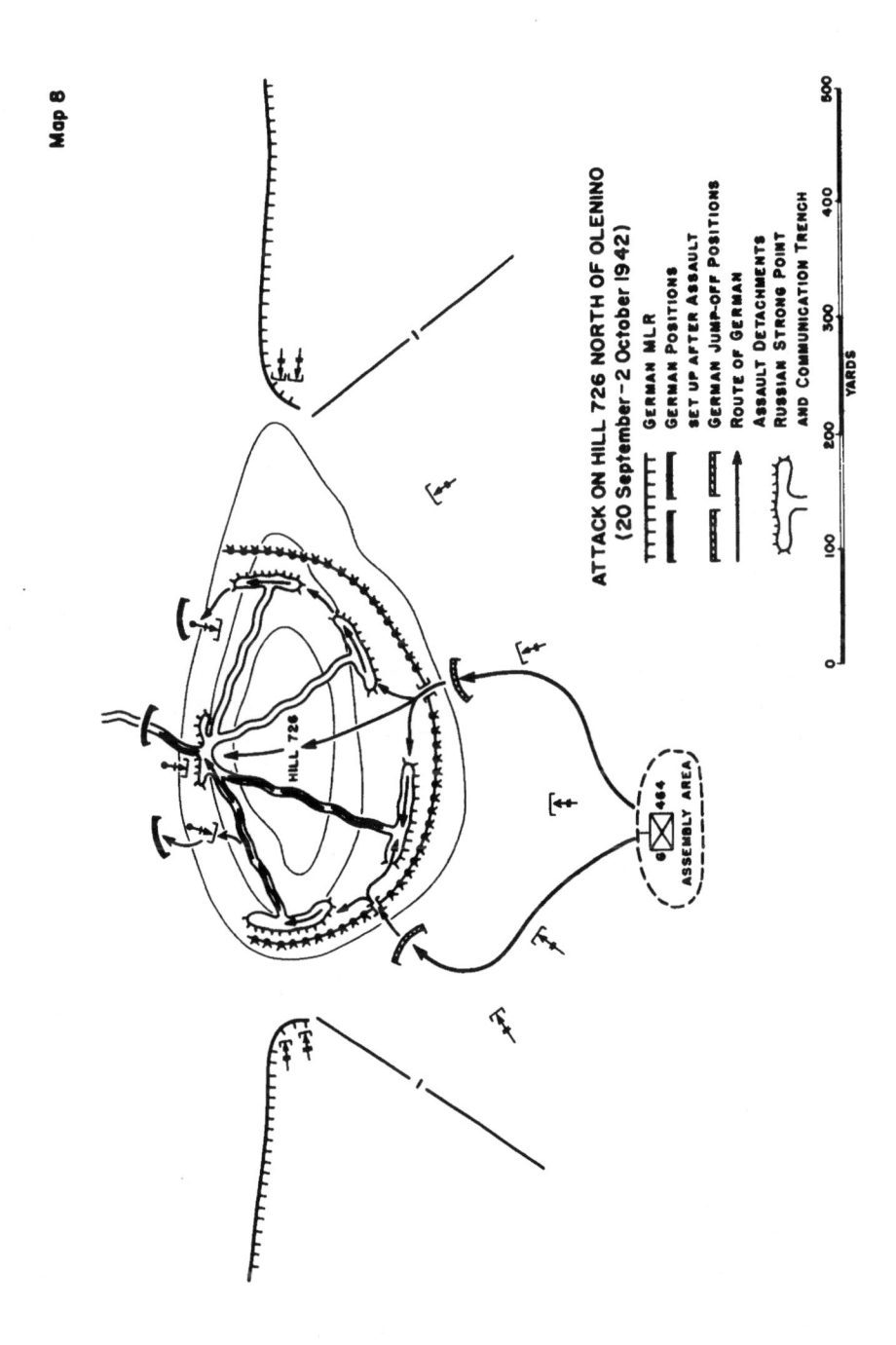

Map 8

ATTACK ON HILL 726 NORTH OF OLENINO
(20 September – 2 October 1942)

⊤⊤⊤⊤⊤⊤	GERMAN MLR
▬▬▬▬▬	GERMAN POSITIONS SET UP AFTER ASSAULT
▭▭▭▭▭	GERMAN JUMP-OFF POSITIONS
⟶	ROUTE OF GERMAN ASSAULT DETACHMENTS
⌒	RUSSIAN STRONG POINT AND COMMUNICATION TRENCH

0 100 200 300 400 500
YARDS

sweeping view of the German rear area, thus hampering movements. Its rapid recapture was of vital importance to the Germans (map 8).

The Russian defense system on the hill was not organized in a continuous line, but rather in the form of strong points. The positions were quite deep, afforded overhead cover, and were so well camouflaged that they could be detected only at very close range. The communication trenches leading to the rear were deep enough only for crawling. All machineguns were emplaced so as to deliver only frontal fire. Mortars were emplaced on the reverse slope of the hill, and large quantities of ammunition and hand grenades had been stored in the strong points. A belt of wooden mines—to which German detectors did not respond—extended almost completely around the hill. Gaps had been left in the mine belt to permit passage of friendly patrols. Before the attack German reconnaissance patrols were able to identify these lanes.

Company G made five or six attempts to retake Hill 726, but failed; in each case the attack was halted at the very beginning because of heavy casualties incurred from mines and massed mortar fire. The Russians defended the hill with extreme tenacity. The company commander, Captain Viehmann, observed that the Russians confined their activity to the hours of darkness. During the day their positions appeared deserted. Russian reconnaissance patrols were very active, but only between midnight and dawn.

Viehmann decided to launch a surprise attack at dusk on 2 October. He selected 30 men who, together with two flame thrower teams, were to make up the assault detachments. Six machineguns were to follow directly behind. After seizure of the hill, an intrenching team was to move in with previously prepared barbed wire obstacles, set them up on the reverse side of the hill, and establish defensive positions. All men in the assault detachments were equipped with submachineguns and issued an ample supply of hand grenades. They were familiar with the terrain, including Hill 726 itself and the Russian MLR.

Under cover of darkness and unnoticed by the Russians, the assault troops moved from their assembly area into the jumpoff positions. At the scheduled time the two companies along the flanks of the German MLR facing the right and left sides of the hill as well as the machineguns located on the southern slope poured fire into the Russian positions. While the German troops in the MLR diverted the enemy's attention by sudden shouting, the assault elements attacked and penetrated the Russian mine belt through two previously identified gaps.

The defending Russians were taken completely by surprise. The

SMALL UNIT ACTIONS

GERMAN RECONNAISSANCE PATROL near the Don, 1942.

fire and shouting coming from all sides confused them as to the true direction of the attack. They were further thrown off balance by the German flame throwers, despite the fact that the latter failed to function after only a few bursts.

Nevertheless, the Russians did not give way to panic or abandon their positions, but struggled to the bitter end. After about an hour of hand-to-hand fighting the entire hill was in German hands, as were 20 Russian prisoners. The initial German objective, to cut Russian communications to the rear, had been achieved early in the attack. The Russian MLR was thereby out of contact with the defenders on the hill, who apparently were not alert enough to summon assistance from the rear before being cut off.

Once the hill was taken, the Germans immediately dispatched two listening sentries to points about 30 yards in the front of their lines, set up barbed wire obstacles, and otherwise prepared their defensive positions. Within 2 hours a continuous line of wire entanglements stretched across the crest of the hill.

About an hour after the completion of these defenses one of the sentries reported the approach of about 40 Russians. All intrenching work was immediately suspended and the defense positions were quickly manned. Soon thereafter the second sentry confirmed the report of the first. The gap in the wire obstacle line which had until then been left open for the men stationed at the listening post was closed.

At a given signal the Germans opened fire just as the screaming Russians began their counterattack. Rushing headlong into the wire entanglements, which they had failed to spot in advance, the Russians were cut down by German defensive fire concentrated on that zone. Only three of the attackers were able to regain the safety of their jumpoff position.

The next day the Russians directed heavy harassing fire against Hill 726, but made no further attempts to conduct a concerted infantry attack.

IX. The 2d Battalion Launches a Limited Counterthrust (November 1942)

The Battle of Stalingrad has often been referred to as the turning point in the German campaign in Russia. It was at Stalingrad that the Germans lost the initiative, never to regain it except for a few brief periods. The Russian strategy that led to the recapture of the city called for a double envelopment to trap the German Sixth Army in an area of 50 square miles. The initial blow was struck from the north, where three armored and two Russian cavalry corps annihilated three Italian and Hungarian divisions and crossed the Don at Serafimovich. One of the Sixth Army units thrown into the battle to stem the Russian advance was a German infantry battalion, whose fate is described in the following series of actions.

In mid-November 1942 the 2d Battalion of the German 132d Infantry Regiment occupied defensive positions on the bluffs along the west bank of the Don River near Sirotinskaya (map 9). The battalion's 3 rifle companies averaged 50 to 60 men, while the strength of the heavy weapons company was approximately a hundred men. The combat efficiency and morale of the battalion, which had been fighting in Russia since the beginning of the campaign in June 1941, were high. On the evening of 18 November the 2d Battalion was alerted for movement on the 19th, and during the night it was relieved by a reserve unit. Before the regiment started its movement, the 3d Battalion was dissolved because of insufficient manpower and its remnants were transferred to the other two battalions. No additional reinforcements were available.

The 1st and 2d Battalions covered the distance of 25 miles from Sirotinskaya to Verkhne-Buzinovka on foot and by truck. Although the movement was slowed down by a light snowfall, both battalions arrived at Verkhne-Buzinovka on the evening of 19 November. At the time of their arrival, weak German service elements were defending the northern and northwestern outskirts of the village in the face of heavy enemy pressure.

At dawn on 20 November the two battalions launched a counterattack, which was preceded by a heavy artillery preparation. The 2d Battalion, on the right, was to thrust to the north across a wide, overgrown ravine, while the 1st Battalion was to drive along the road leading northwest toward Platonov (map 10). The 1st Battalion's attack was to be supported by assault guns.

As always when they were on the defensive, the Russians proved to be tough opponents. Small detachments forming nests of resistance in the numerous depressions and recesses of the ravine were so well dispersed and concealed that the German artillery fire could have little effect. As a result, the 2d Battalion had to form small assault detachments to get the attack under way. The German machinegun and mortar teams worked together systematically. First, the high trajectory fire of the mortars drove the Russian soldiers from their concealment, then the machineguns pinned them down, and finally the men armed with submachineguns and hand grenades finished them off. As soon as a nest of resistance on one side of the ravine was neutralized, a Russian position on the other side was taken under flanking fire. Simultaneously, other German assault detach-

Map 10

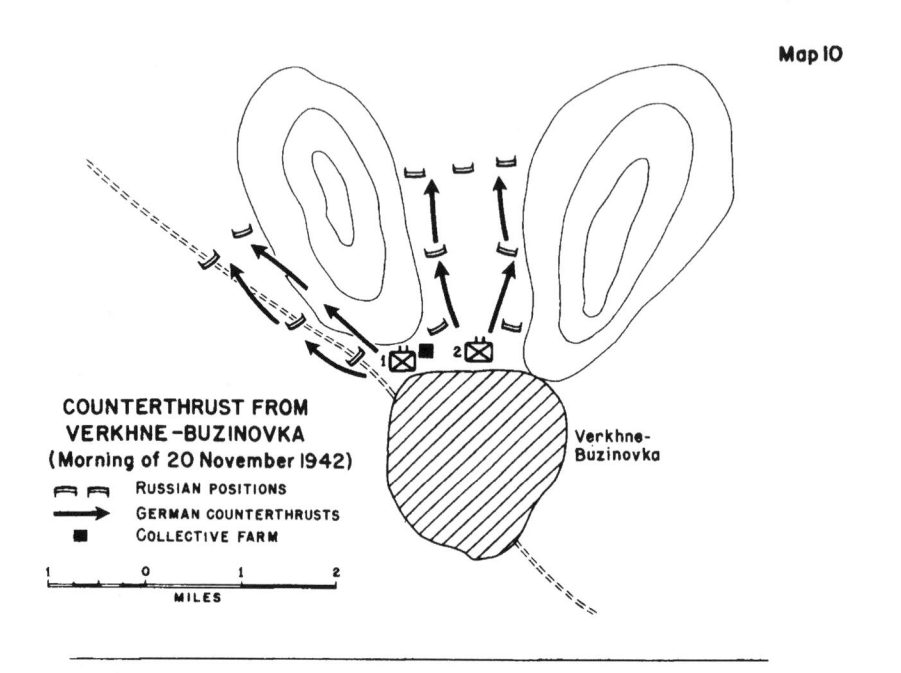

**COUNTERTHRUST FROM
VERKHNE-BUZINOVKA**
(Morning of 20 November 1942)

⌐⌐ RUSSIAN POSITIONS
→ GERMAN COUNTERTHRUSTS
■ COLLECTIVE FARM

MILES

Verkhne-Buzinovka

Map 11

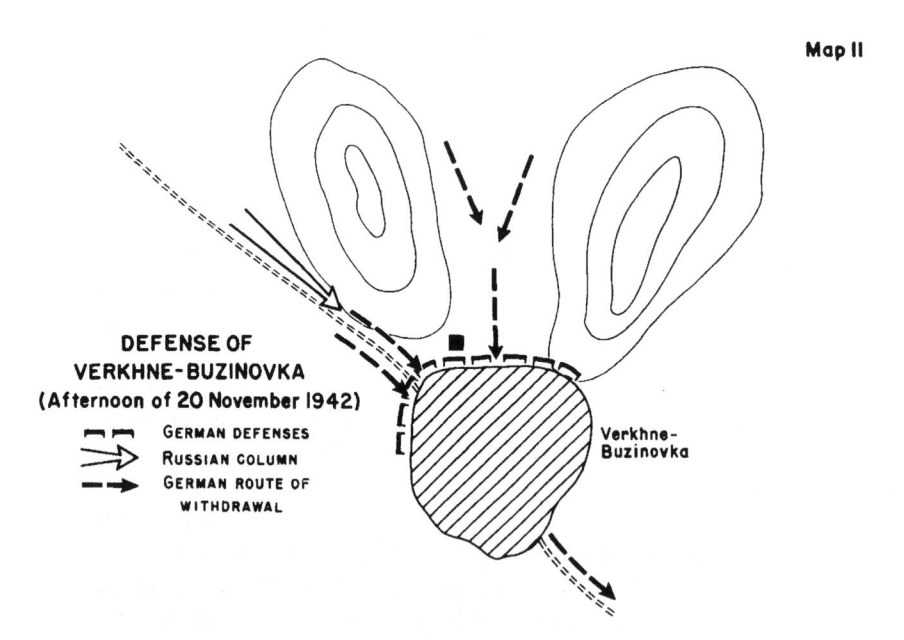

**DEFENSE OF
VERKHNE-BUZINOVKA**
(Afternoon of 20 November 1942)

⌐⌐ GERMAN DEFENSES
⇨ RUSSIAN COLUMN
⇢ GERMAN ROUTE OF
   WITHDRAWAL

Verkhne-Buzinovka

ments worked their way forward across the bottom of the ravine, where the defenders were pinned down. By alternating punches, as does a boxer, the Germans slowly but surely pushed their opponents back approximately 2 miles. Toward noon the Russians abandoned the ravine altogether and withdrew northward. Their casualties had been heavy, and no less than 80 men had been taken prisoner. The enemy forces opposing the 1st Battalion joined the withdrawal, giving way to German pressure.

X. The 2d Battalion Switches to the Defensive (November 1942)

Toward 1300 on 20 November a long Russian march column consisting of infantry, cavalry, and artillery quietly approached the village along the road from Platonov. The column marched in close order without any advance guard. Surprised by the overwhelming strength of the approaching Russian forces, the two German battalions hastily took the most essential countermeasures. Using every possible means of concealment, the rifle companies split up into assault detachments and, abandoning the terriar they had captured during the morning, worked their way back to the edge of Verkhne-Buzinovka as rapidly as they could. As soon as a detachment arrived at the outskirts of the village, it was assigned the position it was to defend (map 11). Every available officer was given charge of a sector a few hundred yards in width. Being arbitrarily designated, some of these sectors comprised elements from several different units since there was no time to assemble the troops in their respective companies or work out a defense plan.

When the Russian column had approached to within 1,600 yards of the village, the German artillery, assault guns, and heavy infantry weapons opened fire with devastating effect. The stunned and confused Russians had great difficulty in getting off the road, which was soon blocked with burning vehicles and littered with debris. The German battalions thus gained an hour's respite during which they were able to close the gaps in their MLR at the outskirts of the village, place ammunition next to each weapon, set up a wire communication network, and extend their flank protection along the western edge of the village.

This incident was typical of the first phase of the Russian counteroffensive west of Stalingrad, during which higher headquarters, both German and Russian, often lost contact with their subordinate units. Caught in the tidal wave of Russian forces converging upon Kalach from the northwest, individual German units were still launching local counterattacks. They acted according to orders long superseded, ignorant of the fact that enemy forces had driven past them and that they were cut off. On the other hand, the Russians, equally ignorant of the general situation and of the exact front-line demarcations, advanced in the general direction of the northern arm of the pincers in massed columns without security or reconnaissance detachments, apparently under the impression that they were crossing territory that had already been mopped up by their predecessors.

After they had recovered from the surprise assault on their march column, the Russians assembled their forces for an attack on Verkhne-Buzinovka. At 1430, under cover of heavy artillery concentrations, wave after wave of massed Russian infantry began to descend upon the outskirts of the village. The collective farm occupied by a platoon of Company F was the first German outpost to change hands. The German regimental commander realized that Verkhne-Buzinovka could not be held for any length of time. He was aware, too, that a daytime withdrawal would undoubtedly result in heavy casualties for the Germans, whose escape route to the southeast passed through several miles of wide-open terrain, where the withdrawing rifle companies would be exposed to merciless enemy fire for at least half an hour. There was no choice but to attempt to hold Verkhne-Buzinovka until nightfall. For the remainder of the afternoon, the defending force dispensed with aimed fire and turned its entire fire power to setting up a barrage. Heavy and light machineguns, mortars, even submachineguns and carbines laid down a curtain of fire which was heaviest around the collective farm, where the Russian infantry was assembling for the continuation of its attack. The 105-mm. guns were moved up to the northeast edge of the village. With all German artillerymen who could possibly be spared being used as riflemen, machine gunners, or ammunition carriers, the officers, aided by a few enlisted men, fired rapid salvos at a range of 250–350 yards. After 30 to 40 rounds had been fired from the same emplacement, a prime mover, waiting under nearby cover, moved the gun to another position, where it was quickly readied for action.

At the same time, the regimental commander initiated a ruse, which was to be highly successful. On the premise that the Russian soldiers were usually underfed and therefore hungry and greedy, the German cooks were ordered to prepare lentil and pea soup from the stocks of legumes that had been left in one of the buildings. The legumes were emptied into large pots filled with water and placed over fires in front of the first houses the Russians would reach upon entering Verkhne-Buzinovka. Next, the Germans opened some mail bags containing packages from Germany addressed to a headquarters

GERMAN SENTRIES near the Don, 1942.

unit that had recently departed, and emptied their contents onto the streets of the village. By twilight the situation had become so critical that the Russians were expected to enter the village at any moment. The two German battalions now began their withdrawal. Platoon by platoon the companies disengaged and withdrew. The self-propelled assault guns and artillery pieces continued to fire at point-blank range and did not move out until just before the last rifleman. Then they drove straight to the southeast edge of the village, where the previously withdrawn companies had collected and established a provisional defense line. It was now that the ruse proved effective. The Russian soldiers, who at first had followed close behind the withdrawing German detachments, hesitated when they smelled the aroma of hot soup and saw all the packages on the ground. The temptation proved too much for them, and there was a general rush for the unexpected treat. The resulting delay enabled the German battalions to assemble their companies and carry out an orderly withdrawal from Verkhne-Buzinovka without being subjected to enemy pressure.

When a pocket comes into existence the situation of the encircled forces is usually confused. The individual units are temporarily on their own, facing almost unsurmountable difficulties. In such situations a determined and resourceful leader who does not hesitate to improvise and resort to ruses will be able to inflict heavy losses on the enemy, gain valuable time, and preserve the combat strength of his unit for further action.

XI. The 2d Battalion's Stand at Verkhne-Golubaya (November 1942)

The two battalions marched through the entire night. At 0200 on 21 November the company commanders were ordered to inform their men that the German Sixth Army had been encircled. While heavy snow was falling, the battle-weary troops halted along the road on which drifts were beginning to accumulate. The men realized the seriousness of the situation but were not dejected. The idea that the ring around the Sixth Army might not be broken did not occur to them at the time. They knew that difficult days and weeks lay ahead, but their confidence remained unshaken. On 22 November there was only isolated small-scale fighting, during which the two battalions withdrew to Verkhne-Golubaya where they arrived at 2300. Orders received from higher headquarters stipulated that the village was to be defended and that the enemy advance was to be delayed at Verkhne-Golubaya at least until the following evening.

SMALL UNIT ACTIONS

Map 12

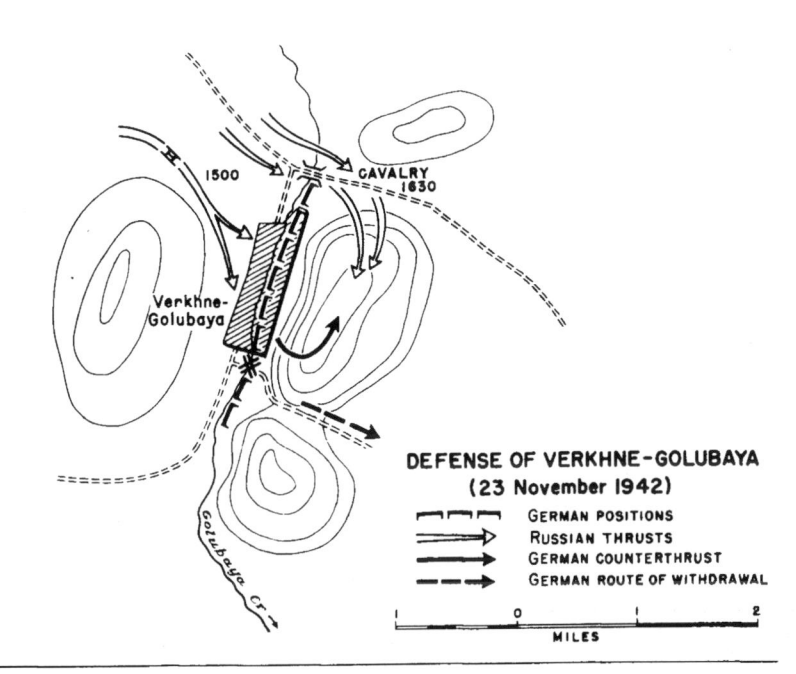

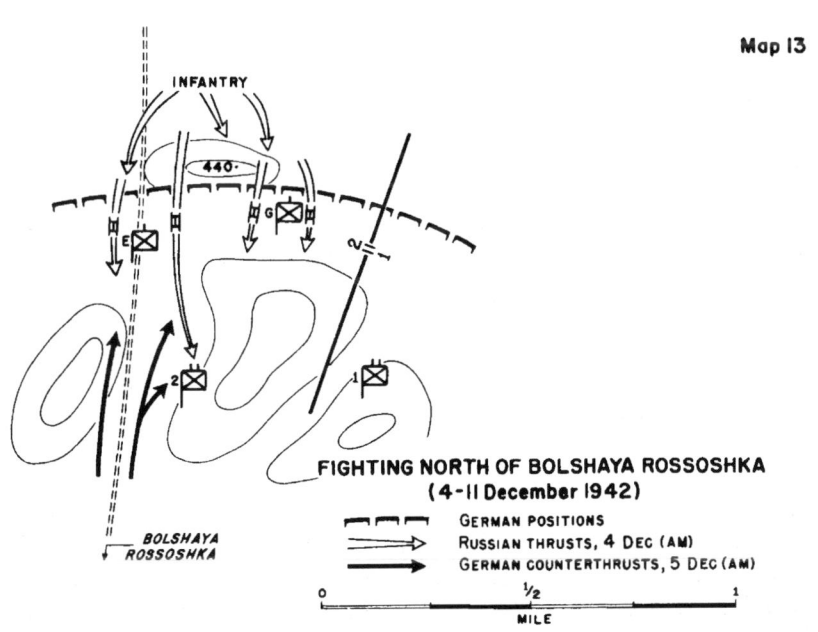

DEFENSE OF VERKHNE-GOLUBAYA
(23 November 1942)

- GERMAN POSITIONS
- RUSSIAN THRUSTS
- GERMAN COUNTERTHRUST
- GERMAN ROUTE OF WITHDRAWAL

MILES

Map 13

FIGHTING NORTH OF BOLSHAYA ROSSOSHKA
(4-11 December 1942)

- GERMAN POSITIONS
- RUSSIAN THRUSTS, 4 DEC (AM)
- GERMAN COUNTERTHRUSTS, 5 DEC (AM)

MILE

At this time Sixth Army headquarters attempted to tighten its control over all German units in the Stalingrad pocket. In its effort to direct the employment of every unit, Sixth Army occasionally issued orders that went into too much detail and did not take the local situation sufficiently into account. The commander of the 2d Battalion, for instance, had selected the gently ascending hill west of Verkhne-Golubaya for establishing a defense position. Higher headquarters, however, ordered him to move his unit to the east bank of Golubaya Creek, as unfavorable a line for setting up a defense position as could be found in that area (map 12). The section of the village west of the creek obstructed the battalion's field of fire. The maneuvering space between the houses lining the east bank of the river and the steep slope adjacent was only about 200 yards in width. Also disadvantageous was the 800-yard gap between the 2d Battalion and the nearest German unit, which was committed northeast of the village. By noon of 23 November reconnaissance patrols had established contact with that unit, but the gap remained open.

A Russian force, consisting of 2 infantry battalions, 10 T34 tanks, and 2 cavalry troops approached Verkhne-Golubaya around noon. The 2d Battalion was exhausted from the recent fighting and hasty withdrawal and, despite the fire power delivered by its heavy weapons emplaced on the hills to the east, was unable to prevent the Russian infantry from gradually infiltrating the western section of the village.

Toward 1500 the 10 Russian tanks emerged from behind the hill situated west of Verkhne-Golubaya and drove straight toward the village. The Germans destroyed four, but the other six managed to penetrate the western section. In the bitter struggle that followed the 2d Battalion sustained extremely heavy losses. At dusk the German riflemen and machine gunners were handicapped by poor visibility, whereas the Russians were able to observe every German movement against the light background of the steep, snow-covered slope behind the village.

The struggle soon developed into a fire fight across Golubaya Creek. Two Russian tanks that had ventured too close to the creek were knocked out by German tank demolition teams which had to wade through the icy water to accomplish their mission. The situation reached a critical stage around 1630, when about 120 Russian cavalrymen outflanked the German positions from the north and rode toward the hill east of the village, thus threatening to cut the escape route of the German units still holding out in the village and of the heavy weapons section on the ridge of the hill. The commander of Company G, the right flank unit and a battalion staff officer, who happened to be at the company's CP at the time, were the first to realize the danger. They took immediate action without awaiting orders from battalion headquarters. Having gotten hold of every man they could find, they led their group to the top of the hill by the quickest route without taking cover or using concealment. On the hill the detachment of about 30 men was hastily organized for a counterthrust. The supply of ammunition was pitifully low. There were only 8 to 10 rounds of carbine ammunition per man, a machinegun with 80 rounds, 2 submachineguns with 20 rounds each, and a total of 6 hand grenades.

No time was to be lost, since the enemy was closing in fast. The German detachment advanced in extended formation. The Russians, dismounting at the foot of the hill, started to move up. Darkness was falling when the clash occurred, the opposing elements having approached to within 20 yards of each other. Shouting "Hurrah!" at a given signal, the German detachment fired a few rounds and threw the six hand grenades in the direction of the enemy. The Germans then sought cover and took their time in directing well-aimed small arms fire at the enemy. The Russians, surprised by the suddenness with which the Germans struck, suffered considerable losses since they had advanced in close formation. The initial random fire led them to believe that they were facing a strong German force, while the deliberate fire that had followed pinned them down and helped the Germans to save their ammunition.

This resolute German counterthrust, carried out by a few men without an adequate supply of ammunition, had succeeded in intercepting the Russian enveloping movement. Both officers and six of the men were wounded, but reinforcements and ammunition reached the detachment on the hill within the hour. Under the protection afforded by the detachment, the battalion was able to break off the engagement in Verkhne-Golubaya that same night and withdraw to the southeast without further incident.

The fighting at Verkhne-Golubaya demonstrated once again that the selection of a defense line solely on the basis of map study by a higher headquarters rarely takes all terrain features into account. In the above instance, the German position lacked depth and space for maneuver. The heavy machineguns, for example, which had been emplaced halfway up the slope of the hill east of the village, could not be shifted to alternate positions because movement by any crew member was conspicuous against the white background. In view of the narrowness of the battle position, the battalion and company commanders were unable to organize an effective defense of the village because their only choice was to establish their CP's either in the MLR, where they could not see what was happening on the wings of their units, or on top of the hill, from where they were unable to exercise proper control. As a result, German losses were heavy, with each company losing one-quarter to one-third of its strength and much of its equipment. This was all the more regrettable because the losses had been sustained in a relatively insignificant defensive action. Had it not been for the hill detachment's well-timed counterthrust, the consequences might have been disastrous for the battalion.

The mistakes made by Sixth Army headquarters in this instance were typical of those made during the second phase of an encirclement. The Sixth Army had decided to shorten the defense perimeter in accordance with an integrated plan. During this phase isolated units which had been fighting at outposts within the pocket gradually established contact with their neighbors. The defense lines solidified, even though the front was not continuous. In many instances, however, the planning was too hasty and superficial; units were ordered to occupy sectors as if the front were a continuous line. At Verkhne-Golubaya, for example, higher headquarters made the mistake of designating a sector from a map without on-the-spot reconnaissance, thus denying the lower echelon commanders any exercise of initiative. Moreover, since every man would be needed for the defense of the pocket to whose outer boundary his unit was gradually converging and which had to be held as long as possible, the 2d Battalion commander should have been allowed to use his own judgment in order to hold casualties to a minimum.

The last week of November was marked by several minor engagements similar to the one at Verkhne-Golubaya. During their gradual eastward withdrawal across the Don toward Stalingrad, the German units repeatedly became involved in bitter fighting that flared up suddenly. In the process they slowly drew closer to one another and began to form a continuous front. The troops were subjected to extreme hardships, spending cold nights without sleep, making difficult marches without adequate rations, and fighting without sufficient ammunition against a far superior enemy. Often the soil was frozen so solid that the men were unable to dig in. This difficult period was the acid test of whether or not a unit had *esprit de corps* and discipline. Some newly organized divisions, which had recently arrived from Germany, showed early signs of disintegration. Men who lost their leaders discarded their weapons, plundered ration dumps, stole alcoholic beverages, and staggered aimlessly over the snow-covered paths. Stragglers and isolated service troops roamed around as fugitives from discipline. On the other hand, the older, seasoned regiments—and they represented the majority—continued to give a good account of themselves, even after their officers had become casualties. Those noncommissioned officers who had participated in innumerable engagements since the crossing of the Bug River in June 1941 formed the backbone of resistance. In units that still had their officers the comradeship between officers and enlisted men became closer than ever. The company commanders did their best to provide the men with food and shelter and set an example of endurance and courage. Once Sixth Army assumed control over all personnel in the pocket, it disbanded those units whose combat value was doubtful and distributed their personnel, as well as any excess service troops and stragglers, to reliable regiments, where high morale and strict discipline prevailed and which could exercise a beneficial influence on the troops assigned to them.

XII. The 2d Battalion Holds Out Despite Being Overrun by Russian Armor (December 1942)

In early December the 2d Battalion reached the Kergachi Hill area, where it was to remain until the end of the Stalingrad pocket (map 13). Although available maps indicated that the Kergachi Hills dominated the area, the terrain was actually fairly level, thereby exposing the battalion to enemy observation. The hills, whose elevation averaged 400 feet, did not appear very prominent on the vast plateau west of the Volga. There were no trees, shrubs, or inhabited localities which might have provided the defending force with adequate cover or concealment. The battalion's situation with regard to strength is illustrated by Company G. Of the 55 men who had departed from Verkhne-Buzinovka, only 25 remained fit for combat. The company was subsequently reinforced by 30 men from a veterinary unit, a few riflemen from the disbanded 376th Infantry Division, and 26 Romanians, so that its strength in early December approximated 90 men. Company G was committed on the 2d Battalion's right flank and ordered to defend a 500-yard sector. The German MLR was established as an almost straight line of foxholes. Each squad, consisting of 6 to 10 men, occupied 3 to 4 foxholes situated close to one another for mutual support. Each center of resistance had a machinegun, of which Company G had a total of six. Approximately 60 yards behind the MLR the company commander emplaced his 3 light mortars. Ammunition was a critical item. During the first week of December each man was allotted 400 rounds, but this allowance had to be cut to 80 rounds during the following week.

The 2d Battalion occupied a particularly important sector since the Kergachi Hills blocked access to the Rossoshka Valley from the northwest. By driving through this valley the Russians could split the pocket in two. It was therefore not surprising that the battalion soon became involved in some of the bitterest fighting in the pocket.

a. The First Day. During the night of 3–4 December the noise of engines and tracked vehicles coming from the valley north of Hill 440 betrayed the assembly of a Russian armored force. Ammunition shortage limited the German artillery's interference with the enemy concentration to only weak harassing fire. At dawn the following morning, while a dense fog blanketed the area, 40 T34's accompanied by a few KV's were seen driving directly toward the 2d Battalion's position. From then on things began to happen with incredible speed. Within a few minutes the Russian tanks overran Company G's MLR and drove adjacent Company E from its positions. Some Russian infantrymen, moving up behind the armor, occupied the foxholes formerly held by Company E and fired into Company G's flank, while others made a frontal attack against Company G's MLR. The Russian armored force fanned out and broke through the German lines in massed formation. About 10 tanks drove to the 2d Battalion's CP, overran the heavy weapons of Company H emplaced in the vicinity, smashed the battalion's communication center located in a bunker, and took up positions in a depression east of the road leading to Bolshaya Rossoshka. Ten other tanks stopped near Company E's former CP and kept the terrain west of the road under fire. Another group of 10 tanks roved across the depth of Company G's battle position, while the remaining tanks tried to annihilate this company by rolling over the foxholes and firing at everything in sight.

Company G was in an extremely precarious situation with enemy armor and infantry to its front, on its left flank, and in its rear. A steady stream of fire poured from the tanks as they crisscrossed over the foxholes. Only on its right did the company still maintain contact with friendly elements. Despite the many adverse factors, the company held out until evening. This was possible because the ground around the narrow, carefully dug foxholes had frozen so hard that the walls withstood the pressure of the Russian tanks. Russian infantry, advancing hesitantly and halfheartedly, was pinned down at a distance of 200 yards by bursts of machinegun, aimed carbine, and well-placed artillery fire from the 1st Battalion sector on the right. Two of the T34's were destroyed by German riflemen who fired shaped charges at the tanks just after they had rolled over a group of foxholes. As a result, the other Russian tanks became more cautious in their movements.

GERMAN INFANTRY fighting Russian tanks, 1942

Despite the tremendous superiority of the Russian forces, Company G still held its position at 1500, as darkness was settling over the area. The majority of the Russians withdrew to Hill 440 and established a hedgehog defense. During the night the left wing platoon of Company G emerged from its foxholes and attacked the Russian detachment that was occupying the foxholes formerly held by Company E. Without firing a shot the German platoon took the Vodka-happy Russians by surprise, overwhelmed them, and reoccupied 200 yards of the former German MLR. In the early hours of 5 December a German reserve battalion which had shrunk to only 80 infantrymen and 8 Mark IV tanks moved up and assembled approximately 1,300 yards south of Hill 440. At dawn that German force counterattacked northward astride the road leading from Bolshaya Rossochka to Samofalovka. This counterattack was no less successful than the Russian operation of the preceding day. At the very outset six T34's were put out of action. The Russian forces on Hill 440 withdrew to the north and the 2d Battalion reoccupied all its former positions. Some hundred prisoners and a sizeable quantity of supplies and equipment fell into German hands.

Thus ended the first engagement near Hill 440. Once again an experienced infantry unit had demonstrated that a seemingly hopeless situation can be mastered provided the men do not give way to panic.

b. The Second Russian Attack. On 8 December the Russians launched another powerful attack at the same point, but this time they announced their intentions with a 1-hour artillery preparation. The situation developed in a fashion similar to that of 4–5 December. Again a strong combined arms team, this time with infantry mounted on tanks, penetrated the weakly held German MLR south of Hill 440. Although accurate German small-arms fire did inflict heavy casualties on the tank-mounted Russian infantry, the 2d Battalion was overrun and isolated, except for one contact point on the right wing. Despite heavy odds the battalion held out until nightfall brought an end to the enemy attack. The German counterattack the next morning jumped off from the ravine near the 1st Battalion's CP and drove the Russians from the former German positions. Five Russian tanks were destroyed during this action.

On 11 December weaker Russian forces launched one more attack against the 2d Battalion s MLR, but during their approach they were stopped by two German tank destroyers stationed at the exit of the ravine in the 1st Battalion sector.

The situation then remained unchanged until after Christmas. In the 2d Battalion's sector the Russians limited their operations to minor diversionary attacks, their main effort being directed against the 1st Battalion. Their repeated attempts to break through the German positions were, however, unsuccessful, even though on many occasions the Germans averted disaster by only a narrow margin.

XIII. Infantry Succeeds Where Armor Failed (December 1942)

Toward the end of November 1942 the German Fourth Panzer Army with headquarters at Zimovniki, due east of Rostov, was responsible for organizing and directing the relief thrust on Stalingrad. By 27 November, under the command of the LVII Panzer Corps, the reinforced 6th Panzer Division was moving toward Stalingrad via Kotelnikovo, while advance elements of the 23d Panzer Division were preparing to join the advance.

In the steppe north of Kotelnikovo the Russians had deployed a cavalry corps on the right and an infantry corps on the left in order to protect the approaches to Stalingrad. Behind these two corps and

SMALL UNIT ACTIONS

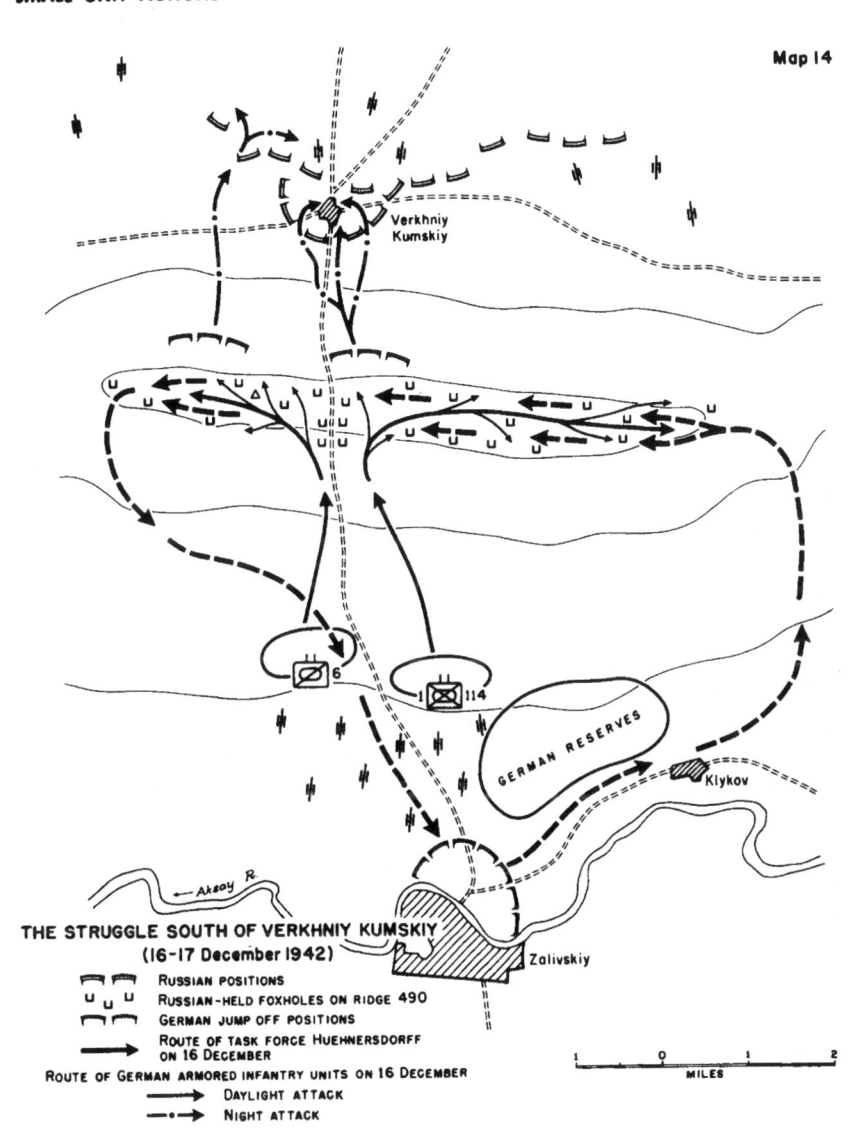

Map 14

THE STRUGGLE SOUTH OF VERKHNIY KUMSKIY
(16-17 December 1942)

⊓⊓ ⊓⊓ RUSSIAN POSITIONS
U U U   RUSSIAN-HELD FOXHOLES ON RIDGE 490
⊓⊓ ⊓⊓ GERMAN JUMP OFF POSITIONS
━━━▶ ROUTE OF TASK FORCE HUEHNERSDORFF ON 16 DECEMBER
ROUTE OF GERMAN ARMORED INFANTRY UNITS ON 16 DECEMBER
━━━▶ DAYLIGHT ATTACK
━‧━▶ NIGHT ATTACK

north of the Aksay River loomed the powerful Russian Third Tank Army, often called Tank Army Popov after its able commander.

During the first half of December the German relief force steadily battled its way northeastward. With 200 tanks and self-propelled assault guns, the 6th Panzer Division, the 23d Panzer Division covering its right flank, overran the Russian cavalry and infantry corps, and by 12 December forward elements crossed the shallow river bed of the

Aksay against only weak opposition and established a bridgehead opposite Zalivskiy (map 14).

About 8 miles north of the river the Russian tank army was concentrating its forces in the town of Verkhniy Kumskiy. When the 6th Panzer Division continued northward and drove into the village during the afternoon of 12 December, the Russian armored forces reacted violently. A furious tank battle ensued during which the village repeatedly changed hands in the following 24 hours. When it became apparent that the Russians were gradually concentrating numerically superior forces, including motorized infantry and scores of antitank guns, the Germans quickly withdrew to the Aksay. The Russians, however, had suffered such heavy tank losses that they did not pursue, but rather contented themselves with establishing defensive positions along Ridge 490, which stretched across the steppe about 2 miles south of Verkhniy Kumskiy.

By 16 December the two panzer divisions had repaired most of their disabled tanks. On orders from army, an armored task force composed of elements from both panzer divisions was to launch a flanking attack against the Russian-held ridge. The intrenched Russian motorized infantry forces were to be rolled up from east to west.

Composed of one tank regiment and one armored infantry battalion of the 6th and one tank company of the 23d Panzer Division, Task Force Huehnersdorff, so named after its commander, moved out from Zalivskiy and ascended the gentle slopes of the Aksay Valley via Klykov. After reaching the eastern end of the enemy-held ridge the tanks began to move westward along the crest of the ridge without encountering opposition. The Russian infantrymen, hiding in their deep foxholes and narrow trenches in groups of two to four men, permitted the tanks to pass over them. However, as soon as the German armored infantry at the tail end of the column had passed them, the Russians fired antitank grenades at the lightly armored vehicles at point-blank range, inflicting heavy losses. Repeatedly, the tanks had to stop and come to the assistance of the armored infantrymen who tried to flush out the Russian nests of resistance. But even the tanks were ineffective against the Russian infantrymen, who were so well concealed by the tall, brown steppe grass that they could not be discovered by the tankers or infantrymen from their armored vehicles. In most instances the German soldier was hit by a sniper's bullet before he ever got close to his hidden opponent. German planes were as powerless as the tanks, whose ineffectiveness in this situation was only too obvious. Although the lead tanks were able to reach the opposite end of the ridge by midafternoon, the majority of the Russians were still in their positions. Having failed in its mission and

SMALL UNIT ACTIONS

suffered considerable losses, the task force had no other choice but to return to the bridgehead.

This experience induced the commander of the 6th Panzer Division to revise his plans for the next day. Not tanks but infantrymen on foot would have to dislodge the enemy from the ridge. He formed an assault force that same night (16/17 December) and assembled it north of the bridgehead directly in front of the armored artillery regiment.

The left wing was formed by the seasoned 6th Armored Reconnaissance Battalion, the right by the 1st Armored Infantry Battalion of the 114th Infantry Regiment (Mechanized). The two battalions were reinforced by engineer assault detachments, flame-thrower teams, and mine-clearing details. The tanks and remaining armored infantry elements were assembled in the rear between Zalivsky and Klykov, where they stayed in reserve, ready to follow up the assault force.

At 0800 on 17 December the massed guns of the artillery regiment opened fire. As the hail of shells came down on the ridge it obliterated the Russian observation post. The dried-out steppe grass burned fiercely and reddish clouds of dust enveloped the whole ridge, depriving the Russians of all visibility. After a short time, however, the fires died out because a light snowfall prevented them from spreading.

Meanwhile, the first German assault wave moved up to the ridge. When a signal flare was set off to indicate it was entering the Russian defensive positions, the artillery fire was shifted. The assault detachments had opened a gap at the center of the ridge. The difficult task of ferreting out the enemy force dug in on the ridge had thus begun.

Several squadrons of German dive bombers, flying in relays, came over and headed in the direction of Verkhniy Kumskiy, where they blasted Russian artillery positions, silencing one battery after another. Directly overhead, Messerschmitts and Ratas tangled in dogfights, during which three of the Russian fighters were shot down near the ridge.

Paying little heed to the air action, the assault forces fanned out from the initial point of penetration and moved forward. Machine gunners and sharpshooting riflemen stalked the hidden Russians like game and fired well-aimed bullets at anything that moved. Whenever Russians from a nearby foxhole returned the fire, they were silenced by a well-placed hand grenade. The fortified positions were neutralized by the flame-thrower teams. Whenever a particularly fanatic Russian force could not be flushed out by the assault troops, they fired a signal flare to pinpoint the target for the German artillery pieces and mortars.

By noon the reconnaissance battalion had cleared all enemy forces from its zone of action, and an hour later the armored infantry battalion had done likewise on the eastern part of the ridge. An attack on Verkhniy Kumskiy could be envisaged. Reconnaissance patrols reported that the village and the slopes facing it to the north were occupied by strong Russian forces. As the patrols approached Verkhniy Kumskiy, they encountered hostile fire from all directions. German reconnaissance planes identified numerous antitank guns and dug-in tanks along the outskirts and in well-concealed positions in the hills. Russian tanks were observed to be moving toward the village from the west.

During the rest of the afternoon the Russian positions and gun emplacements in and around the village were shelled by German artillery. Until nightfall dive bombers, flying in waves, made low-level attacks against tank concentrations, dug-in tanks, and batteries of antitank guns. After darkness the armored infantry units resumed their northward drive. With special assault detachments leading the way, infantrymen felt their way along routes that had been reconnoitered during the daylight hours. The smoldering ruins of bombed and shelled houses in the village illuminated the area and facilitated orientation. Like phantoms, the assault detachments crept up to the first houses and observed Russian field kitchens preparing rations. This was the ideal time for a surprise raid!

Upon a given signal the German assault detachments stormed the village from three sides. Seized by panic, some surprised Russians ran for their lives. Many were too stunned to move and were taken prisoner as the German infantrymen pursued the disorganized remnants into the hills to the north. The Russian tanks tried to make a dash to the north in order to escape the approaching German tank-demolition teams, but many failed to get started in time and were destroyed. Scores of Russian antitank guns and disabled tanks, as well as a great store of heavy equipment, fell into German hands.

The Russian stronghold of Verkhniy Kumskiy was thus taken by the Germans at the cost of negligible losses. Where a task force of almost two tank regiments had failed the day before, an armored reconnaissance and an armored infantry battalion achieved a decisive success. Without this success, the relief thrust on Stalingrad would have bogged down much earlier than it eventually did, and the men in the pocket would have lost all hope.

XIV. The 2d Battalion's Final Struggle in the Stalingrad Pocket (January 1943)

The third and final phase of the operations along the periphery of the Stalingrad pocket began immediately after Christmas 1942. At that time the pocket had a diameter of approximately 22 miles. The life expectancy of the encircled Sixth Army depended on its ability to defend this perimeter. If the Russians succeeded in breaking through the German ring at any point, they would split the encircled army into smaller pockets, capture the remaining airfields, and thus cut off the supply by airlift. Ration and ammunition dumps would fall into their hands, and the German resistance would crumble. Although sporadic fighting might continue, such isolated German resistance would merely have nuisance value and could be eliminated in the course of mopping-up operations.

This explains the ferocity with which both sides fought to gain a decision. The stakes were high, and the Germans needed cool-headed leaders. Whereas German unit commanders could envisage the possibility of a voluntary withdrawal during the first and second phases of the encirclement, defense in place was mandatory during the third. At this stage Russian front-line propaganda took over. On New Year's Day Russian psychological warfare teams went to work. Night after night loudspeakers blared forth speeches by German refugees speaking from a studio in Moscow, who read appeals, ostensibly from German mothers and wives, imploring their loved ones to give up the fight. German prisoners, who had been confined in model Russian camps, were sent back across the lines to their former units to report the excellent treatment they had received.

The prospect of relief from the outside had meanwhile grown dimmer. Nevertheless, the men in the pocket refused to give up hope, even though there was every indication that the Sixth Army was doomed. Living conditions in the pocket went from bad to worse. The German infantrymen had to stay in their foxholes, exposed to snow and rain, extreme cold, and sudden thaw. Again and again the rations had to be cut. At first every man was issued one-third of a loaf of bread per day, then a quarter, and later a fifth. This monotonous diet was occasionally supplemented by a few slices of sausage and a meat broth obtained by boiling horse meat. Only the wounded were given half a bar of chocolate and some brandy immediately after the evacuation to revive their spirits.

Constant Russian pressure resulted in a steadily growing number of casualties. The 2d Battalion's combat strength diminished gradually. When the Russians resumed their large-scale attacks early in

January 1943, the battalion had only 3 officers and about 160 men left. In mid-January the executive officer was killed in close combat during a German counterattack. On the following day the battalion commander committed suicide as the result of a nervous breakdown. On 19 January the battalion's last remaining officer, a platoon commander of Company G, launched a final desperate counterthrust and led the last 13 men of the battalion to their death. A few days later, at the beginning of February 1943, the battle of Stalingrad came to an end.

XV. Sudden Initiation Into Russian Winter Combat (February 1943)

After they had liquidated the Stalingrad pocket, the Russians launched a powerful counteroffensive which quickly carried them westward. At the beginning of February Soviet tanks took Slavyansk against virtually no German opposition since the entire sector had been stripped of German troops except for a few service units. In an effort to stem the tide the XL Panzer Corps, including two panzer and one infantry divisions, was moved up from the south and ordered to drive the Russians back across the Donets River.

Typical Russian winter weather prevailed in the Konstantinovka area south of Slavyansk. Blankets of deep snow covered road and countryside alike, and the temperature reached a low point of $-49°$ F. at night. Such conditions alone were enough to tax to the utmost the fortitude and hardiness of even the fittest German soldier.

The 679th Regiment of the 333d Infantry Division, forming part of the XL Panzer Corps, had not seen previous combat in Russia. Upon detraining at the railhead in Konstantinovka at 0400 on 12 February, the 3d Battalion received orders to launch an immediate thrust toward Kramatorskaya (map 15). The battalion assembled, and the forward elements started to move out without delay. At 0800, after having advanced barely a mile east of the Torets River, the battalion point ran straight into an oncoming Russian tank force. After a brief clash the German detachment was annihilated and the advance party put to rout. Deeply impressed by this sudden turn of events, the main body of the German battalion, which was just then moving out of Konstantinovka, began to waver and was seized by an acute case of tank jitters.

The regimental commander realized that he had to act immediately. Fear of tanks had gripped the battalion, suddenly converting gallant troopers into quivering cowards. What could he do? The overall situation was none too favorable since the 2d Battalion was not due

Map 15

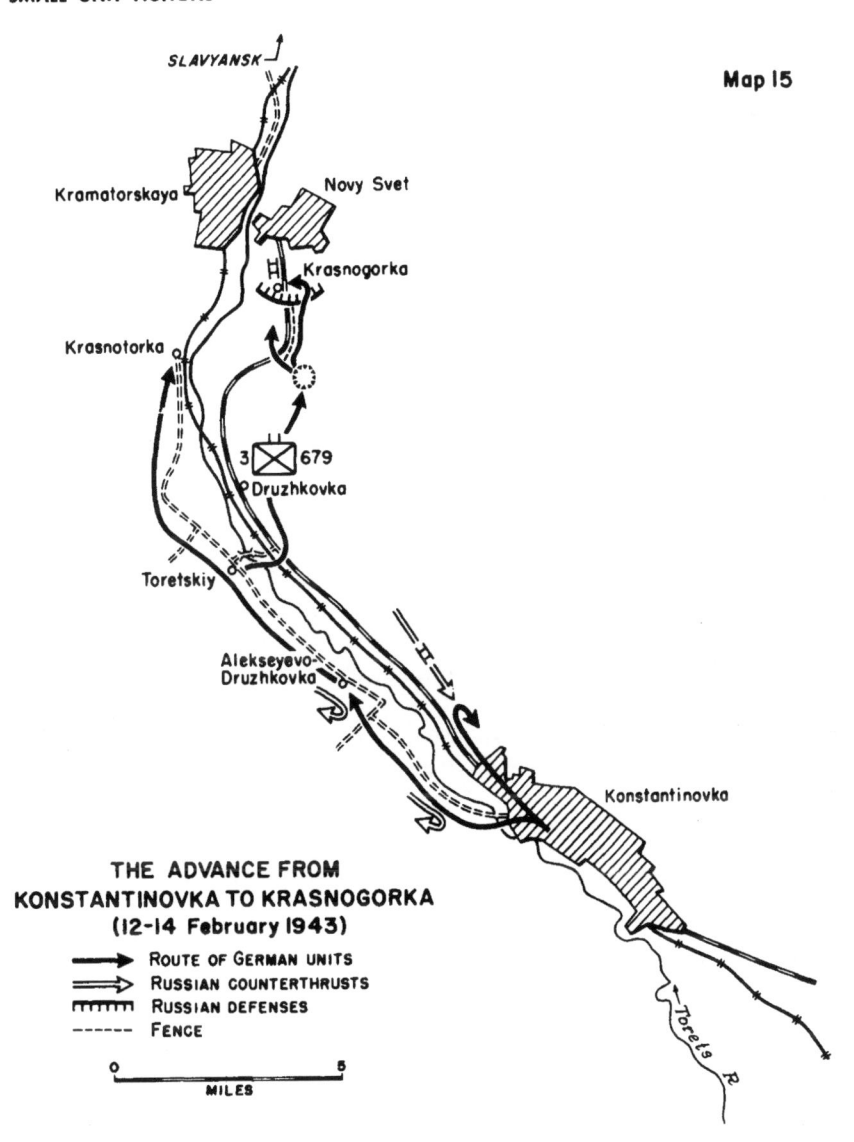

THE ADVANCE FROM KONSTANTINOVKA TO KRASNOGORKA (12-14 February 1943)

- ➡ ROUTE OF GERMAN UNITS
- ⇨ RUSSIAN COUNTERTHRUSTS
- ⊓⊓⊓⊓ RUSSIAN DEFENSES
- ------ FENCE

0 — 5 MILES

to arrive for 12 hours and the 1st Battalion would take at least another 24 hours.

When the regimental commander discovered that a self-propelled gun was undergoing repairs in Konstantinovka, he immediately commandeered it. Realizing that the danger of encountering enemy tanks was greatest east of the Torets, he chose the road running along the west bank as the new axis of advance.

The regimental and battalion commanders mounted the assault gun and proceeded to lead the advance northward. The men were heartened by the sight of their two commanders speeding northward along the new route without encountering enemy opposition. They quickly regained confidence and, falling in behind their leaders, moved forward with new courage. Against light enemy resistance the battalion fought its way to Alekseyevo-Druzhkovka, and during the night the newly arrived 2d Battalion closed up and moved into the same town.

On 13 February, as a result of the previous day's experience, the regimental commander decided to employ the 2d Battalion as lead element in order to condition the unit to combat in Russia. In an effort to simulate greater strength all motorized vehicles were ordered to follow the lead battalion in plain view of the enemy. This deception could be used only because enemy interference from the air was not expected.

Toward evening the 2d Battalion arrived at Krasnotorka without major incident. During the night, however, the battalion suffered heavy casualties from frostbite when the battalion commander, who was unfamiliar with the severe Russian winter weather, ordered sentries to be posted in the open outside the village. The deception, however, had been successful, judging by an intercepted Russian radio message in which the enemy command was warned that strong German motorized formations were advancing toward Kramatorskaya.

The regimental commander moved the 1st Battalion, the last one to arrive, to Toretskiy with orders to capture Krasnogorka the next day. At dawn the 1st Battalion crossed the river, passed through Druzhkovka, and moved into a hollow about 2 miles south of Krasnogorka. The cross-country march in deep snow was exhausting because the motorized equipment constantly bogged down and had to be pulled out by wreckers. Nevertheless, the battalion arrived in its jumpoff position by 1000.

The situation facing the battalion commander was exasperating. Ahead of him lay strongly defended Krasnogorka, from where a few enemy tanks were firing in his direction. Between him and his objective loomed a vast expanse of snow that was more than 3 feet deep. Despite promised support from a medium artillery battery, a direct frontal assault on the town was bound to fail and involve heavy casualties. From afar off the Russians could observe the individual German soldiers cautiously inching their way forward, their silhouettes clearly outlined against the white background, and could pick them off at will. Although the regimental commander shared his apprehensions, the attack had to be launched and Krasnogorka had to be taken.

The only landmark that broke the monotony of the flat landscape was a high, snow-covered fence extending for about 2 miles along the right side of the road from the turn to the village. This fence, which actually looked more like a wall of snow, might conceal the troops while they worked their way toward the objective in single file, hugging the fence until they reached Krasnogorka. Although far from an ideal solution to the problem of carrying out a frontal assault on the village, this plan was the only apparent way out. To deceive the Russian garrison and divert its attention, one company was to be echeloned in depth and advance on Krasnogorka on a wide front on the left side of the road. While this company was launching its diversionary attack, the rest of the battalion crept to within 500 yards of the objective. The Russians fell for this ruse and concentrated the fire of their multibarrelled rocket launchers, self-propelled guns, and mortars on the single company, which was promptly pinned down. Meanwhile, the main assault force continued its advance along the snow fence, infiltrated into Krasnogorka, and seized it in short order. Because of the deep snow, the battalion took 2 hours to cover the 2-mile stretch along the fence. The Russians were taken completely by surprise and beat a hasty retreat to Kramatorskaya. A few days later the regiment, committed as a unit for the first time, followed up this initial success by seizing Slavyansk after overcoming stiff Russian resistance.

One of the lessons to be learned from the above action is that infantry units lacking combat experience against tanks should not be committed without adequate support from antitank weapons. Unless this precaution is taken, the strength of the unit will be uselessly dissipated and its morale will suffer unnecessarily.

The regimental commander had to make several decisions which were in contradiction to standing operating procedures and had to introduce improvisations that fulfilled the needs in unexpected situations. When he and the battalion commander mounted the assault gun and drove ahead of the column, they contravened all standing regulations. This daring exploit, assisted by a good measure of luck, helped to turn a dispirited unit into an aggressive one.

In this instance the Russians let themselves be deceived too easily. They had obviously failed to obtain essential reconnaissance information and grew panicky when the Germans suddenly launched the *coup de main* on Krasnogorka.

XVI. Russian Reconnaissance in Force by Tank-Mounted Infantry (October 1943)

Early in October 1943, the German 196th Infantry Regiment occupied defensive positions within a forest about 20 miles north of Kiev. Although both flanks were well protected, the positions themselves were vulnerable because the soil was loose and sandy. The Germans neglected to plant antipersonnel mines but did lay antitank mines across roads leading toward their main line of resistance. Behind the MLR they erected roadblocks, covered by dug-in 50-mm. antitank guns.

The ground sloped gently upward in the direction of the Russian MLR, which was then located along the crest of a flat ridge about 2,000 yards north of the German MLR (map 16).

On 5 October the Russians made the first of a series of forward moves. These movements remained undetected until German observers discovered that the ground had been broken in the vicinity of Advance Position A. Later in the day Russian artillery fired smoke shells on such known German targets as the forester's house and the road intersections. German artillery and mortar fire against the Russian forward positions was ineffective. The patrols that probed the enemy during the night were repulsed.

During the following 2 days the Russians moved their positions forward over 500 yards to Position B. Again the movements remained unobserved because the intermittent rain restricted visibility. Heavy German mortar fire succeeded only in drawing more violent Russian mortar and artillery fire on the road intersections near the fringes of the forest. As German night patrols probed forward, they began to encounter Russian patrols in increasing numbers.

By 10 October the Russians had succeeded in establishing themselves along Advance Position C, only 500 yards from the German MLR. Under the protective cover of mortar and artillery fire, reinforced German reconnaissance patrols were sent out during the day to determine the strength and disposition of the Russian forces and positions and to occupy the latter, should they be found deserted. However, after advancing scarcely 100 yards the patrols came under such heavy mortar fire that they were forced to turn back with heavy casualties.

When the weather cleared, the Germans were able to observe all three Russian advance positions, but could not spot any further movement. During the night the Russian positions were placed under harassing mortar and infantry weapon fire. While three German patrols were being driven off in front of Position C, numerous Russian reconnaissance parties infiltrated the intermediate area and at some points approached to within a few yards of the German main line of resistance.

For the next three nights the Russians were busy digging in along Advance Position C. Heavy rains helped to dampen the noises of their intrenching activities. Shortly after dusk on 12 October, a German patrol finally succeeded in reaching the fringes of Position C. After having spotted some hasty intrenchments, all of which appeared deserted, the Germans were driven back to their lines by three Russian patrols which, supported by nine light machineguns, suddenly appeared from nowhere.

Heavy rains fell again in the evening of 13 October. At 2300 the Russians began to rake the entire German sector with a savage artillery barrage which lasted two hours. Over the din of the exploding shells the sound of approaching tanks could be distinguished in the German forward area. However, the tank noise soon faded away, giving every indication that the armor had been withdrawn.

Toward noon of the next day, in a driving rain, a 3-man German patrol succeeded in crawling into the forward Russian positions. They were still deserted and gave the appearance of having been occupied for only a very short time. The Germans concluded at once that these were dummy positions. Unknown to the members of the patrol at the time was the fact that they had been closely observed by the Russians, who nevertheless permitted them to reconnoiter the positions unmolested, feeling certain that their true intentions would not be revealed.

Meanwhile, the Russians were proceeding with preparations for their reconnaissance mission inside the German lines.

During the afternoon of 14 October, a 20-man patrol, including an officer and two noncommissioned officers, was selected from a Russian rifle company which had been resting in a village behind the lines. These men were all specially selected, veteran fighters familiar with the terrain since all of them had originally come from the Kiev region. Each man was provided with 2 days' rations, 1½ days' ammunition supply, and 6 hand grenades. The officer was issued a two-way radio. He and his noncommissioned officers carried submachineguns while the rest of the men were armed with automatic rifles. After reaching a trench in the vicinity of Position A, the patrol was met by a Russian officer who briefed them as follows:

> You will move out and proceed to Advance Position C where you will join four tanks that have been dug in. Tomorrow you are to mount the tanks, advance on the German positions facing us, pene-

RUSSIAN T-34 in action.

trate them, and drive into the wooded enemy rear area. Nothing should be allowed to delay your forward progress since everything depends on lightning speed. Knock down whatever gets in your way but avoid any prolonged encounter. Remember your primary mission is to gain information about German positions, how they are manned, and where the enemy artillery, mortars, and obstacles are emplaced. Don't stop to take prisoners until your return trip; one or two will suffice. You must create fear and terror behind the enemy lines and then withdraw as swiftly as you came.

Late that same evening the patrol moved out toward the German lines. Despite enemy harassing fire it reached the tanks in Position C at 0100. The tanks, with their crews inside, had been dug in by engineers and were well camouflaged. The entrances to the pits sloped upward toward the rear.

The infantry patrol was now split into squads of five men and each squad was assigned to a tank. The men were ordered to dig in close to their tanks, maintain absolute silence, and remain covered, especially after daybreak.

At dawn all was quiet and well concealed. A light haze hovered over the area in the early morning hours and toward afternoon turned into fog, limiting visibility to about 300 yards. At approximately 1600 an officer suddenly came up from the direction of the Russian MLR and ordered the patrol to mount at once. The engines were quickly started and, as the camouflage nets were removed, the infantrymen jumped on their respective tanks. Within a matter of minutes the tanks backed out of their pits, formed a single column to the front, and raced toward the German line at top speed. After the tanks had overrun several trenches, the first German soldiers could be seen. However, none of them made any attempt to fire but scrambled for cover at the unexpected sight of the tanks.

Having penetrated the center of the German MLR the tanks moved cross-country through heavy underbrush before taking to the road. As they neared the forester's house, a German water detail was spotted running for cover in great haste. The tanks upset two ration trucks that were blocking the road and sped deep into the German lines. About 1,000 yards beyond the forester's house the Russians suddenly turned half-right and followed the road leading into the woods. After proceeding another 1,000 yards they approached a crossroad and decided to stop. Enjoying a commanding view of the road intersection, the Russians dismounted and prepared all-around defenses right in the midst of the German positions, hardly 700 yards away from the regimental CP. The tanks formed the core of the position; the infantrymen dug in around the cluster of armor. The Russian officer quickly established radio contact with his lines and exchanged messages.

Before long German infantry assault and combat engineer platoons, equipped with close-combat antitank weapons, moved in from two directions and surrounded the Russians. However, they could approach no closer than 150 yards from the tanks because the sparsely wooded forest afforded the Russians excellent observation and permitted them to fire at everything that moved. Finding themselves pinned down, the Germans sent a detail to the left flank of their MLR for one of the 50-mm. antitank guns. Since the static gun was dug in and had to be pulled by hand, its arrival would be delayed. Finally, at 1800, two self-propelled assault guns from division moved into position to the south of the tanks, opened fire, and wounded a number of Russian riflemen.

Leaving their wounded behind, the Russians within 10 minutes mounted their tanks and sped off in a northerly direction toward their own lines with tank guns blazing in all directions.

Darkness was setting in when the 50-mm. antitank gun detail spotted the approaching Russian tanks. The German crew had no opportunity to fire their piece and barely succeeded in getting off the road. They remained under cover until the last Russian tank had passed. After quickly pulling their gun into position the Germans fired at the rear tank and scored a direct hit, killing two of the mounted infantrymen.

When it had become quite dark the Russian lead tank turned its headlights on and, with the other three tanks following closely behind, sped unmolested across the German main line of resistance. After they reached open terrain the Russians dimmed the lights and raced northward into the night in the direction of their positions.

This was a daring Russian undertaking, meticulously prepared and executed with boldness and speed. However, it was crowned with success primarily because of the inadequacy of the German antitank defenses. The Russians must have been aware of the sparse minefields and the shortage of self-propelled antitank guns.

The Russians spent a great deal of time on preparations by allowing themselves an interval of several days between their advances from Position A to B and from B to C. Then there was still another interlude of several days before the tanks moved into position; finally, two more days elapsed before the action was actually launched.

The Russians were extremely adept in carrying out and concealing large-scale intrenching activities, such as the digging of tank pits.

In making their positions appear totally deserted during the daytime and by creating dummy positions which patrols were purposely induced to reconnoiter, the Germans, if not completely misled, were at least left in doubt as to the true Russian intentions.

Still another safeguard that the Russians used again and again to insure maximum surprise was to move up their infantry at the latest possible moment, usually not until the night preceding an operation. In this manner they eliminated the possibility of capture by enemy patrols and the potential disclosure of their plans.

Three weeks after the action just described, the Germans discovered how skillfully the Russians had camouflaged the approach movements of their tanks. A Russian prisoner told of how the tanks were moved forward, masked by the noise of the artillery barrage. Since this concealment was not fully adequate they went a step further. By initially sending six tanks and then immediately withdrawing two the Russians strove to create the impression that all tanks had been pulled back. This ruse was employed with complete success.

That the Russians decided to stop at the road crossing seemed a blunder. The ensuing loss of time might well have led to the annihilation of the patrol had the Germans employed their assault guns from the north rather than from the south and had they been able to block the roads leading northward to the MLR with mines and antitank guns. Why the Russians suddenly stopped and dug in is not specifically explained. The stop, however, did permit them to establish radio contact. It is therefore reasonable to assume that in this instance, as in so many others, the Russian lower echelon command lacked the imagination and initiative necessary to continue the action beyond its immediate scope.

Chapter 2

Armor

I. General

In 1941 the Russian armored command was in the process of reorganizing and converting to new equipment. Only selected personnel were assigned to this arm of the service, and the outdated heavy and light tanks were being replaced with medium models, primarily T34's, which mounted a 76-mm. gun and were exceptionally fast and powerful.

Before 1941 the principal function of the Russian tank unit was to support the infantry. The successes achieved by German armor during the blitzkrieg in Poland, France, and the Balkans led the Russians to a reevaluation of their doctrine affecting armor, and the Russian planners turned to the idea of using armor in a strategic role along the German lines.

During this transitional period the Russian armored command was suddenly confronted with the German invasion. The first year of the war saw the Russians suffering heavy losses in desperate attempts to stem the tide which threatened to engulf them while at the same time they were trying to carry through fundamental changes in their armored tactics and equipment.

In hastily passing from one stage to the next, Russian armored tactics and techniques developed along lines that seemed, at least to the German foe, entirely unorthodox. It was this very unorthodoxy that baffled the Germans and enabled the Russians to achieve successes, which began to sap the German strength long before Russian armor reached its full effectiveness. At the beginning of the campaign the Russians were forced to commit their armor piecemeal, usually in units no larger than a regiment. By early 1942 the independent tank brigade appeared on the field of battle, and eventually the Russians organized armored armies.

The T34 was constantly improved during the war years, particularly with regard to its radio and sighting equipment, its armor, and, above all, its armament, which was eventually changed to an 85-mm. gun.

The technological improvements in Russian tanks were the result of many factors. The developments in German armor were without doubt

SMALL UNIT ACTIONS

GERMAN COLUMNS advance past immobilized Russian tanks, July 1941 known to the Russians, sometimes even in the blueprint stage. Captured German tanks became available early in the war, as did the latest United States and British thought on tank design. Of all the factors involved, it was perhaps the delivery of materiel under lend-lease agreements that had the most important impact on Russian tank construction.

The imbalance which resulted from the simultaneous effort to attain both technical perfection and tactical skill was most obvious in the conduct of battle by the small unit. In one action the Russians might demonstrate a conspicuous lack of flexibility, while in another they might prove masters in maneuvering mobile units. The records show instances where tank strength was woefully wasted, and, on the other hand, an example of how a single Russian tank tied down an entire German combat team for 48 hours.

In the actions selected for the purpose of this study there is no pattern that lends itself to generalization. If they do convey a unified impression, it is that the Russian is aware of the need for constant changes in armored tactics to keep in step with technological improvements, and that he is extremely flexible in the application of these tactics. He is a master of camouflage. He will dig in his tank as readily as he digs in an antitank gun, and will usually succeed in removing it after it has been bypassed. He seeks ever to preserve mobility. He will hit and run; he will hit and stay; he will use his tanks as decoys, for traps, in ambush. He will always do the unexpected. The Russian tanker, who knew his native soil better than he knew his field manuals, eventually drove the German invaders all the way back to Berlin.

The following small unit actions show clearly the way in which the Russians overcame their early mistakes and developed an effective fighting force. In these examples of armored combat, descriptive details are fewer than in infantry engagements at a similar level. This comparative lack of detailed information reflects the very nature of tank warfare, which takes place at a rapid pace and therefore offers fewer clues to permit a reconstruction of events. The absence of details, however, in no way diminishes the intrinsic value of the material presented.

II. The Armored Roadblock (June 1941)

When Germany launched her attack against Russia on the morning of 22 June 1941, Army Group North jumped off from positions along the border separating East Prussia from Lithuania. On D plus 1 the 6th Panzer Division, which was part of Army Group North,

SMALL UNIT ACTIONS

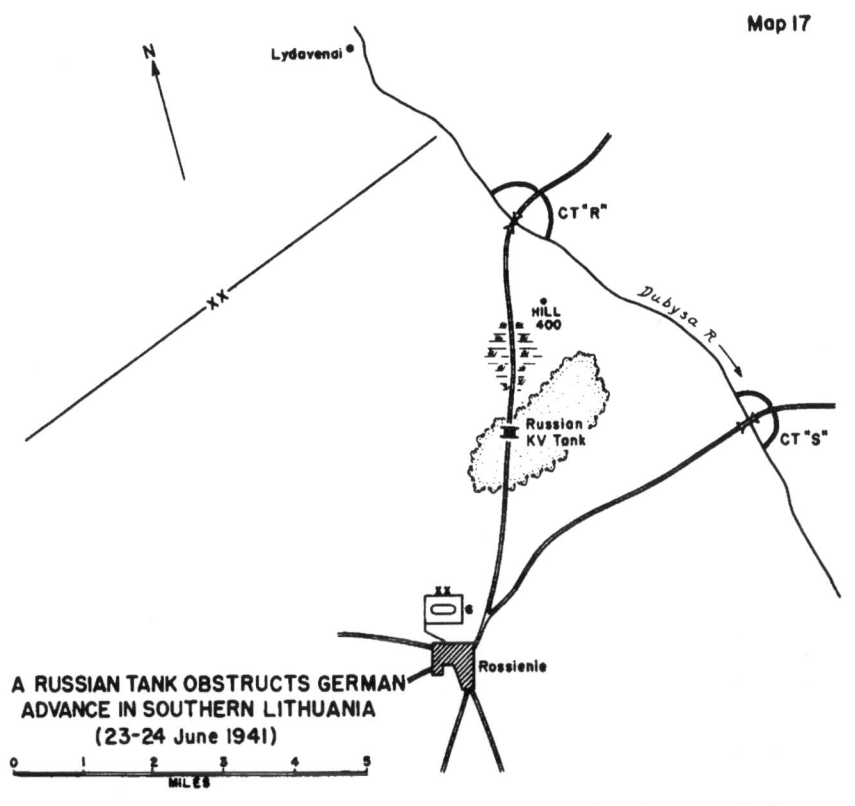

Map 17

A RUSSIAN TANK OBSTRUCTS GERMAN ADVANCE IN SOUTHERN LITHUANIA (23-24 June 1941)

was ordered to occupy the Lithuanian town of Rossienie and thence to seize the two vehicular bridges across the Dubysa River northeast of the town (map 17). After Rossienie was taken the division was split into Combat Teams R and S, which were to establish two bridgeheads, Combat Team R being assigned the bridge nearest Lydavenai, a village situated almost due north of Rossienie. By early afternoon both columns had crossed the river and contact was established between the two bridgeheads.

Mopping-up operations around its bridgehead netted Combat Team R a number of prisoners, about 20 of whom, including a first lieutenant, were loaded onto a truck for evacuation to Rossienie. One German sergeant was placed in charge of the group.

About half-way to Rossienie the truck driver suddenly noticed a Russian tank astride the road. As the truck slowed to a halt, the prisoners pounced upon the driver and the sergeant, and the Russian lieutenant lunged for the sergeant's machine pistol. In the struggle that ensued, the powerful German sergeant freed his right arm and struck the lieutenant such a hard blow that he and several other Russians were knocked down by the impact. Before the prisoners could close in again, the sergeant freed his other arm and fired the machine pistol into the midst of the group. The effect of the fire was devastating. Only the lieutenant and a few others escaped; the rest were killed.

The sergeant and the driver returned to the bridgehead with the empty truck and informed their commanding officer that the only supply route to the bridgehead was blocked by a heavy tank of the KV type. The Russian tank crew had meanwhile severed telephone communication between the bridgehead and the division command post.

The Russian plan was not clear. In estimating the situation, the bridgehead commander felt that because of the encounter with the tank an attack against the rear of the bridgehead was to be expected; accordingly, he organized his force immediately for all-around defense. An antitank battery was moved to high ground near the command post, one of the howitzer batteries reversed its field of fire so as to face southwestward, and the engineer company prepared to mine the road and the area in front of the defense position. The tank battalion, which was deployed in a forest southeast of the bridgehead, prepared for a counterattack.

During the rest of the day the tank did not move. The next morning, 24 June, the division tried to send 12 supply trucks from Rossienie to the bridgehead. All 12 were destroyed by the Russian tank. A German reconnaissance patrol sent out around noon could find no evidence that a general Russian attack was impending.

The Germans could not evacuate their wounded from the bridgehead. Every attempt to bypass the tank failed because any vehicle that drove off the road got stuck in the mud and fell prey to Russians hiding in the surrounding forest.

On the same day, an antitank battery with 50-mm. guns was ordered to work its way forward and destroy the tank. The battery confidently accepted this mission. As the first guns approached to within 1,000 yards of the KV, it remained in place, apparently unaware of the German movement. Within the next 30 minutes the entire battery, well camouflaged, had worked its way to within firing range.

Still the tank did not move. It was such a perfect target that the battery commander felt that it must have been damaged and abandoned, but he nevertheless decided to fire. The first round, from about 600 yards, was a direct hit. A second and a third round followed. The troops assembled on the hill near the combat team's command post cheered like spectators at a shooting match. Still the tank did not move.

GERMAN 50-mm. antitank gun in position.

By the time that the eighth hit was scored, the Russian tank crew had discovered the position of the firing battery. Taking careful aim, they silenced the entire battery with a few 76-mm. shells, which destroyed two guns and damaged the others. Having suffered heavy casualties, the gun crews were withdrawn to avoid further losses. Not until after dark could the damaged guns be recovered.

Since the 50-mm. antitank guns had failed to pierce the 3-inch armor, it was decided that only the 88-mm. flak gun with its armor-piercing shells would be effective. That same afternoon an 88-mm. flak gun was pulled out of its position near Rossienie and cautiously moved up in the direction of the tank, which was then facing the bridgehead. Well camouflaged with branches and concealed by the burned-out German trucks lining the road, the gun safely reached the edge of the forest and stopped 900 yards from the tank.

Just as the German crew was maneuvering the gun into position, the tank swung its turret and fired, blasting the flak gun into a ditch. Every round scored a direct hit, and the gun crew suffered heavy casualties. Machinegun fire from the tank made it impossible to retrieve the gun or the bodies of the German dead. The Russians had allowed the gun to approach undisturbed, knowing that it was no threat while in motion and that the nearer it came the more certain was its destruction.

Meanwhile, the bridgehead's supplies were running so low that the troops had to eat their canned emergency rations. A staff meeting was therefore called to discuss further ways and means of dealing with the tank. It was decided that an engineer detachment should attempt to blow it up in a night operation.

When the engineer company commander asked for 12 volunteers, the men were so anxious to succeed where others had failed that the entire company of 120 volunteered. He ordered the company to count off and chose every tenth man. The detachment was told about its mission, given detailed instructions, and issued explosives and other essential equipment.

Under cover of darkness the detachment moved out, led by the company commander. The route followed was a little-used sandy path which led past Hill 400 and into the woods that surrounded the location of the tank. As the engineers approached the tank, they could distinguish its contours in the pale starlight. After removing their boots, they crawled to the edge of the road to observe the tank more closely and to decide how to approach their task.

Suddenly there was a noise from the opposite side of the road, and the movement of several dark figures could be discerned. The Germans thought that the tank crew had dismounted. A moment later, however, the sound of tapping against the side of the tank was heard and the turret was slowly raised. The figures handed something to the tank crew, and the sound of clinking dishes could be heard. The Germans concluded that these were partisans bringing food to the tank crew. The temptation to overpower them was great, and it probably would have been a simple matter. Such an action, however, would have alerted the tank crew and perhaps have wrecked the entire scheme. After about an hour the partisans withdrew, and the tank turret was closed.

It was about 0100 before the engineers could finally get to work. They attached one explosive charge to the track and the side of the tank and withdrew after lighting the fuse. A violent explosion ripped the air. The last echoes of the roar had hardly faded away when the tank's machineguns began to sweep the area with fire. The tank did not move. Its tracks appeared to be damaged, but no close examination could be made in the face of the intense machinegun fire. Doubtful of success, the engineer detachment returned to the bridgehead and made its report. One of the twelve men was listed as missing.

Shortly before daylight a second explosion was heard from the vicinity of the tank, again followed by the sound of machinegun fire; then, after some time had passed, silence reigned once more.

Later that same morning, as the personnel around the command post of Combat Team R were resuming their normal duties, they noticed a barefoot soldier with a pair of boots under his arm crossing the bivouac area. When the commanding officer halted the lone wanderer, all eyes turned to watch. The colonel was heard asking the soldier for an explanation of his unmilitary appearance. Soon the sound of their voices became inaudible as the two principals in this little drama engaged in earnest conversation.

As they talked, the colonel's face brightened, and after a few minutes he offered the soldier a cigarette, which the latter accepted, visibly embarrasssed. Finally, the colonel patted the soldier on the back, shook his hand, and the two parted, the soldier still carrying his boots. The curiosity of the onlookers was not satisfied until the order of the day was published, together with the following extract from the barefoot soldier's report:

> I was detailed as an observer for the detachment that was sent to blow up the Russian tank. After all preparations had been made, the company commander and I attached a charge of about double the normal size to the tank track, and I returned to the ditch which was my observation post. The ditch was deep enough to offer

protection against splinters, and I waited there to observe the effect of the explosion. The tank, however, covered the area with sporadic machinegun fire following the explosion. After about an hour, when everything had quieted down, I crept to the tank and examined the place where I had attached the charge. Hardly half of the track was destroyed, and I could find no other damage to the tank. I returned to the assembly point only to find that the detachment had departed. While looking for my boots I found that another demolition charge had been left behind. I took it, returned to the tank, climbed onto it, and fastened the charge to the gun barrel in the hope of destroying at least that part of the tank, the charge not being large enough to do any greater damage. I crept under the tank and detonated the charge. The tank immediately covered the edge of the forest with machinegun fire which did not cease until dawn, when I was finally able to crawl out from under the tank. When I inspected the effect of the demolition, I saw, to my regret, that the charge I had used was too weak. The gun was only slightly damaged. Upon returning to the assembly point, I found a pair of boots, which I tried to put on, but they were too small. Someone had apparently taken my boots by mistake. That is why I returned barefoot and late to my company.

Here was the explanation of the missing man, the morning explosion, and the second burst of machinegun fire.

Three German attempts had failed. The tank still blocked the road and could fire at will. Plan 4, calling for an attack on the tank by dive bombers, had to be canceled when it was learned that no such aircraft could be made available. Whether the dive bombers could have succeeded in scoring a direct hit on the tank is questionable, but it is certain that anything short of that would not have eliminated it.

Plan 5 involved a calculated risk and called for deceiving the tank crew. It was hoped that in this way German losses would be kept to a minimum. A feint frontal attack was to be executed by a tank formation approaching from various points in the forest east of the road while another 88-mm. gun was to be brought up from Rossienie to destroy the tank. The terrain was quite suitable for this operation; the forest was lightly wooded and presented no obstacle to tank maneuver.

The German armor deployed and attacked the Russian tank from three sides. The Russian crew, clearly excited, swung the gun turret around and around in an effort to hit the German tanks which kept up a continuous fire from the woods.

SMALL UNIT ACTIONS

RUSSIAN KV TANK demolished by the Germans, July 1941

Meanwhile, the 88-mm. gun took up a position to the rear of the tank. The very first round was a direct hit and, as the crew tried to turn the gun to the rear, a second and a third shell struck home. Mortally wounded, the tank remained motionless, but did not burn. Four more 88-mm. armor-piercing shells hit their mark. Then, following the last hit, the tank gun rose straight up as if, even now, to defy its attackers.

The Germans closest to the tank dismounted and moved in on their victim. To their great surprise they found that but two of the 88-mm. shells had pierced the tank armor, the five others having made only deep dents. Eight blue marks, made by direct hits of the 50-mm. antitank guns, were found. The results of the engineer attack had amounted to only a damaged track and a slight dent in the gun barrel. No trace of the fire from the German tanks could be found.

Map 18

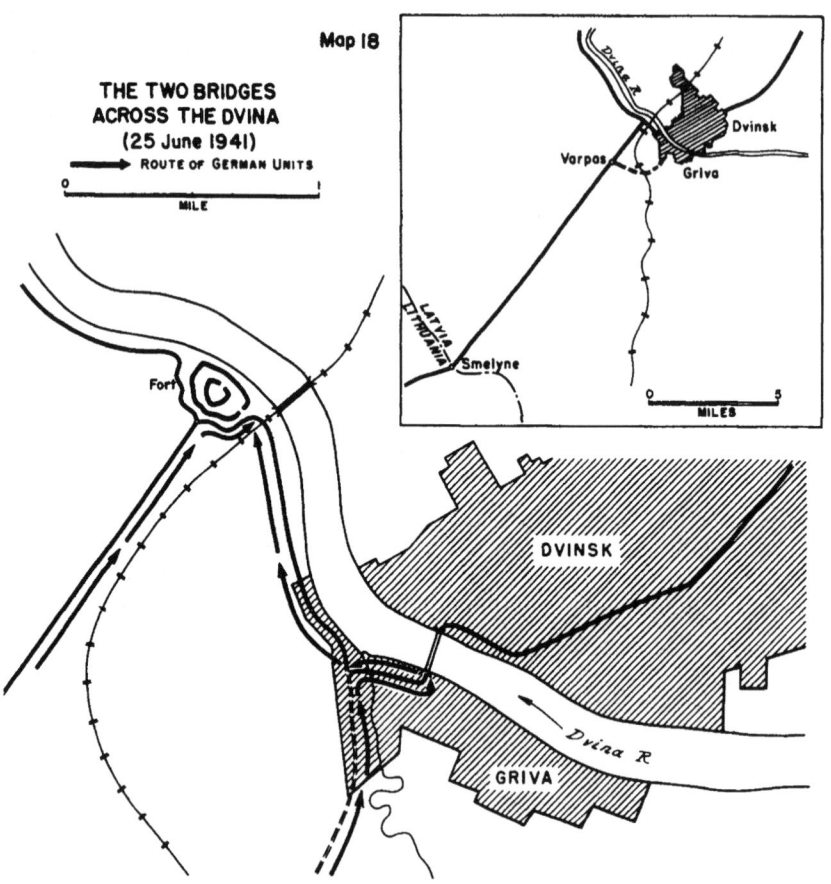

THE TWO BRIDGES ACROSS THE DVINA (25 June 1941)

Driven by curiosity, the Germans climbed onto the tank and tried to open the turret, but to no avail. Suddenly, the gun barrel started to move again and most of the Germans scattered. Quickly, two engineers dropped hand grenades through the hole made by the hit on the lower part of the turret. A dull explosion followed, and the turret cover blew off. Inside were the mutilated bodies of the crew.

The Germans had come off poorly in their first encounter with a KV at this point of the front, one single tank having succeeded in blocking the supply route of a strong German force for 48 hours.

III. German Armored Engineers Capture Two Bridges (June 1941)

While elements of the 6th Panzer Division were thus momentarily delayed, the 8th Panzer Division, which was also part of Army Group North, spearheaded the German attack farther south, taking the Russians completely by surprise. The 8th Panzer Division sped northeastward in the face of sporadic and constantly diminishing enemy resistance, leaving Russian units at its flanks and rear to be mopped up later by the German infantry. On the evening of 24 June the division reached Smelyne, a village on the Lithuanian-Latvian border, 12 miles southwest of Dvinsk. It had advanced over an excellent highway through open and gently rolling terrain.

Late on 24 June the division commander made an estimate of this situation. The division's immediate objective was the city of Dvinsk, situated on the north bank of the Dvina (map 18). However, in order to capture the city the division first had to seize the 2 bridges spanning the river, which was approximately 250 yards wide in this area. While the highway bridge was needed for the division's advance, the other, a railroad bridge situated about a mile downstream, was to be used as an alternate should the Russians succeed in demolishing the highway bridge. German air reconnaissance had indicated that the Russians intended to defend Dvinsk and that the two bridges across the Dvina had been prepared for demolition. The destruction of these bridges, however, would delay the division's advance and thus upset the Army Group's timetable. Consequently, the two bridges had to be seized in a surprise raid before the Russians could destroy them.

The division commander decided to act without delay and ordered the commander of the division's advance guard and Lieutenant Schneider, CO of Company C, 59th Armored Engineer Battalion, to report to his CP immediately. After the two officers arrived there, he briefly outlined the general situation and then issued the following verbal orders :

One platoon of Company C, divided into four assault detachments, will launch a surprise attack against the two bridges at Dvinsk. The detachments will jump off at 0130 on 25 June and head for the bridges in the four Russian trucks that the division captured earlier today. The Russians must be led to believe that the trucks are friendly, so that the assault detachments can get within striking distance of the bridges without being challenged.

Once the detachments have reached the bridges, they will immediately cut all cables leading to the bridges from both banks to prevent the enemy from setting off the demolition charges electrically, cut all detonating cords leading to the charges, and defend the bridges against Russian counterattacks.

The main body of Company C will also jump off at 0130, but will proceed somewhat more slowly so as to arrive at the bridges about 15 minutes after the assault detachments, which it will relieve. Company C will be followed by the division's advance guard, which will arrive at the highway bridge at 0305. Since the highway bridge should be firmly in German hands by this time, the advance guard, consisting of one armored infantry battalion and one tank battalion, will cross over into Dvinsk and spearhead the division's northeastward advance.

Gentlemen, I have confidence in your ability to execute this difficult mission successfully and wish you luck. If there are no questions, that is all.

Preparations for the impending mission were quickly made. Schneider organized the 4th Platoon of his company into four assault detachments, each consisting of 10 men equipped with machineguns, submachine guns, hand grenades, and wire cutters.

The main body of Company C was to march in the following order:

1st and 2d Platoons, each equipped with five special engineer tanks. These vehicles were Mark II tanks, each armed with a 20-mm gun and a machinegun. At the back of each tank a special boom had been mounted for the purpose of depositing demolition charges and removing obstacles.

The seven half-tracks of the 4th Platoon, equipped with frame-type rocket projectors, were to follow the first two platoons. On the march the half-tracks were to be occupied only by the drivers, since the other men of the 4th Platoon were to form the assault detachments.

The 5th Platoon, composed of combat engineers equipped with demolition charges, was to follow in trucks.

Company C's 3d Platoon was engaged in bridge construction elsewhere and was not available for the operation.

Company C moved out of its bivouac near Smelyne at 0130. With their headlights on, the trucks carrying the assault detachments sped northeastward at 40 m. p. h. over the hard-surfaced road in the direction of Dvinsk. The company's tanks and half-tracks followed the trucks at a lower rate of speed. Initially, everything proceeded according to plan. The assault detachments did not encounter any Russians and continued toward the bridges at unabated speed.

At Varpas, 2 miles from the river, the first three trucks turned east and continued toward the highway bridge, while the fourth truck headed straight for the railroad bridge. The detachments passed several Russian infantrymen, but the latter apparently assumed that the trucks were friendly and did not challenge them.

a. The Struggle for the Highway Bridge. After turning east at Varpas, the three trucks continued on at full speed, reaching Griva on the south bank of the Dvina at 0215. The southwestern outskirts of Griva were occupied by a Russian rear guard of about 50 men, who

SMALL UNIT ACTIONS

let the trucks pass through. Only a short distance separated the assault detachments from the bridge, and the men became tense. At the approach to the bridge Russian sentries blocked the road and challenged the first truck, which then slowed down. It seemed to the detachment commander that his luck had finally run out. Since deception was no longer possible, only quick action could save the day. The driver of the first truck pulled up close to the Russian sentries as if to stop. Then, at the last moment, he stepped on the gas, and the truck lurched forward with a roar and headed across the bridge, followed by a second truck. A few of the Russians standing in the path of the trucks managed to jump out of the way. Others, less fortunate, were run over. Those that were able to do so, leaped to the aid of their injured comrades. In the confusion, little attention was paid to the third truck, which had halted at the approach to the bridge. At a given signal, its occupants suddenly jumped the dazed Russians with knives and bayonets, killing them all. Four of the men then rushed to the bridge and cut all the wires they could locate. The first truck meanwhile succeeded in crossing the bridge without being attacked; the second, however, which had stopped briefly at the middle of the bridge to drop off a wire-cutting detail, received small-arms fire from the north bank and quickly moved on to the far end of the bridge where it joined the first. The wire-cutting detail had barely completed its work when enemy machineguns and antitank guns on the north bank of the Dvina opened fire, pinning the men down. The two detachments at the north end of the bridge also drew fire and suffered their first casualties. At 0230 the Russians launched a strong counterattack in an attempt to drive the two detachments from the north end of the bridge. In the ensuing close combat both sides suffered heavy losses. Ten minutes after the trucks had first rolled onto the bridge the Russian rear guard arrived from Griva and attacked the detachment at the south end. However, despite their numerical superiority, the Russians were unable to dislodge the three assault detachments from the bridge, although they did prevent the German engineers from conducting a systematic search for the demolition charges. Even though the Germans had cut all cables on the bridge, making it impossible for the Russians to set off the charges electrically, there was still the danger that they would set them off by means of detonating cords if they succeeded in getting onto the bridge.

At 0240, just as the assault detachments began to run short of ammunition and hand grenades, they were relieved by the main body of the company. During the 20 minutes of fighting the three assault detachments, which altogether numbered 30 men at the outset, had suffered heavy casualties. One officer, one NCO, and three privates were killed, and four men were wounded.

With the arrival of the main body of the company, tanks of the 1st and 2d Platoons went into position on the south bank and began to fire at Russian troops in Dvinsk. Ten minutes later the half-tracks of the 4th Platoon joined the special engineer tanks and fired rockets into Dvinsk. Large fires soon broke out in the city.

After a brief struggle the remnants of the Russian rear guard on the south bank surrendered. A strong Russian force, which had assembled north of the bridge for a counterattack, was caught in the German barrage and dispersed before the attack could get under way.

By 0255, when the division's advance guard arrived, Company C had accomplished its mission of seizing the highway bridge intact. At 0305 the division's advance guard began to cross the bridge and push on into Dvinsk against fierce Russian resistance.

There remained only one more task to be carried out by Company C: the removal of the demolition charges on the bridge. A hasty check indicated that the Russians had prepared each of the three spans for demolition. However, the check did not reveal any charges at the piers.

While a detail was preparing to remove the charges, one of the men suddenly noticed a puff of smoke nearby and discovered that a Russian had crawled onto the bridge, apparently unnoticed, and had lighted a detonating cord. Jumping forward, the engineer wrenched the cord from the charge only 10 seconds before the explosion would have taken place. At almost the same time a similar incident occurred near the north end of the bridge. Here the detonation was also prevented just in time.

With the company's mission at the highway bridge accomplished, Lieutenant Schneider was able to turn his attention to the railroad bridge, where the noise of battle was audible, indicating that the 4th Assault Detachment had run into trouble. Schneider dispatched Company C's 2d and 5th Platoons to that bridge by way of the road which ran parallel to the river.

b. The Struggle for the Railroad Bridge. When the first three assault detachments, en route to the highway bridge, turned east at Varpas shortly after 0200, the other truck continued north on the main highway, which led directly to the railroad bridge. Several hundred yards short of the bridge, at the intersection with the road that parallels the river, there was an old fort whose outer wall the truck had to pass. As the vehicle turned right onto the river road it received small-arms fire from the fort. In a matter of seconds the truck caught fire and was hastily abandoned. The detachment then attempted to fight its way toward the bridge on foot, a distance of some 500 yards. However, the men were soon pinned down by the Russian fire, despite which they slowly and laboriously crawled toward the bridge. Just as the detachment had inched close enough to rush the bridge, there was a terrific explosion. Apparently aware of German intentions, the Russians had detonated charges attached to the steel piers. As the smoke cleared, it became evident that the demolition had not been very effective. The bridge was still intact. The wood planking and the rail ties had, however, caught fire, and there was danger that the fire might set off additional charges, which would normally be placed beneath certain girders of the truss sections. Quick action on the part of the assault detachment was therefore necessary if the fire was to be extinguished and the bridge saved.

At 0330 the 2d and 5th Platoons of Company C arrived at the east entrance to the fort, which was blocked by a heavy steel gate. Since the fire at the railroad bridge was still unchecked and fire-fighting equipment could not be brought up as long as the Russians kept the bridge under fire, the two platoons were ordered to take the fort by direct assault.

The men of the 5th Platoon, who had dismounted and tried to place a demolition charge next to the gate, drew heavy Russian small arms fire. An estimate of the situation indicated that it would be inadvisable to approach the gate without the protection of armor. Accordingly, one of the 2d Platoon's special engineer tanks was ordered to back up to the gate and lower a 110-pound HE charge from its boom. As soon as the charge had been deposited and the tank had moved to a safe distance, the charge was set off. The terrific explosion destroyed the gate and stunned the Russians in the immediate vicinity. However, as the German tanks advanced through the breach, they again drew fire. Their progress was further impeded by a second wall, whose gate, also of steel, was on the side facing the river. Again a special engineer tank had to be brought up with a 110-pound HE charge, which was set off with the same results as the first. At this point a few Russians surrendered. The remainder of the garrison, about 20 in number, continued to resist from the CP, which was located in a structure at the very center of the fort. While the Russians in the fort were trying desperately to repulse the German attack, Company C's fire-fighting equipment proceeded to the railroad bridge and quickly extinguished the blaze. Using shaped charges and hand grenades the 5th Platoon finally succeeded in driving the Russians from their last foothold within the fort. At 0400 the fight for the fort came to an end. Of the company of Russians that had held the fort, 70 had been killed or wounded and 30 taken prisoner.

The entire action had been carried out with great speed, only half an hour having elapsed between the initial assault on the fort and its capture. When interrogated, Russians captured at the fort stated that they had been ordered to hold out as long as possible, even if the bridge were demolished. They were to keep the Germans from moving up bridge equipment over the highway and to delay the German advance as long as possible.

With both bridges firmly in German hands, Company C's mission was accomplished. In the fierce fighting which continued until evening the 8th Panzer Division captured Dvinsk and continued its northeastward advance toward Leningrad.

The preceding example illustrates to what extent the commitment of armor in situations where speed is imperative can result in major successes. The seizure of the two bridges at Dvinsk was possible mainly because the four captured Russian trucks were sent ahead of the main body of Company C, thus taking the Russians by surprise and preventing them from demolishing the bridges before the Germans could reach them.

The selection of Company C for this mission was justified because its special engineer tanks and half-tracks had sufficient fire power to

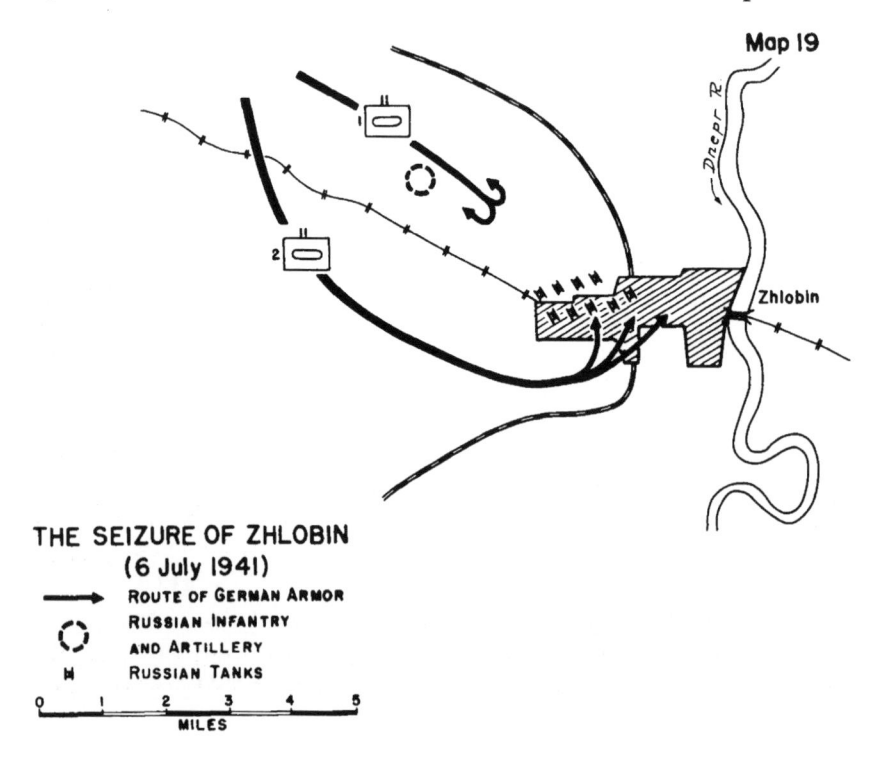

THE SEIZURE OF ZHLOBIN (6 July 1941)

pin the Russians down north of the highway bridge and pave the way for the division's advance into Dvinsk. During the fighting for the fort, the special engineer tanks once more proved invaluable in destroying the two gates. Only armor could get close enough to the gates to place the demolition charges in the face of the heavy Russian small-arms fire.

IV. Russian Tank Trap (July 1941)

By the beginning of July 1941 the 3d Panzer Division, which was part of Army Group Center, had reached the Dnepr River north of Zhlobin and was preparing to attack across the river. On 6 July the division's tank regiment, then in reserve, was ordered to relieve an infantry division which had encountered strong Russian resistance while attacking Zhlobin from the southwest. The infantry attack had bogged down about 2½ miles southwest of the town (map 19).

The terrain around Zhlobin was gently rolling grassland alternating with swampy ground. The weather was warm and sunny.

The tank regiment commander decided to employ 2 battalions, each with about 40 tanks. According to his plan the 1st Battalion was to advance straight toward Zhlobin. The 2d Battalion was to follow the 1st up to a point approximately 1 mile from the Russian MLR northwest of Zhlobin, turn southward, cross the railroad tracks, and drive southeastward to smash the Russian forces which—so he presumed—were holding positions immediately south of the town. This two-pronged thrust would put him in possession of Zhlobin and simultaneously relieve the German infantry.

The march column advanced according to plan. About 2½ miles northwest of Zhlobin the 1st Battalion penetrated the Russian MLR against weak resistance, overran some Russian infantry elements, and then bypassed an artillery battery. Suddenly, when the lead tanks were only a mile from the outskirts of the town, they received devastating fire from Russian tanks which had been cleverly concealed among houses, farmyards, and barns at the edge of the town. The Russian tanks, lying in ambush, had held their fire until the last moment. When the 1st Battalion tanks veered to escape the onslaught, they received point-blank fire from the artillery battery they had bypassed. The Russian artillerymen had turned their pieces on the German battalion. In all the Germans lost 22 tanks as a result of this ambush.

The 2d Battalion had meanwhile received desperate calls for assistance over the radio, but could not come to the rescue because the high railroad embankment obstructed its path. The battalion commander therefore decided to bring relief by a direct thrust on Zhlobin. Upon finding the Russian left flank open, the battalion entered the town from the south and destroyed 25 of the 30 Russian tanks without suffering any losses. The Russians had not expected a thrust from this direction and had devoted all their attention to fighting the 1st Battalion.

The failure of the 1st Battalion's frontal attack must be ascribed to its laxity in reconnaissance before attempting to relieve the infantry division. Moreover, tanks on an independent mission should be accompanied by armored infantry. In this instance armored infantry might have been able to capture the Russian artillery battery.

Had the 2d Battalion followed the 1st, the artillery battery could have been neutralized and immediate assistance given to the 1st Battalion. In obscure situations it is better to advance in depth in order to meet possible surprise with unfettered forces than to advance on a relatively wide front where contact may be lost and separate elements of one's forces may be pinned down. In the ambush of the 1st Battalion the discipline of the Russians, combined with their characteristic craftiness, more than compensated for their inferiority in training and equipment. An ambush is indeed an economical operation against a careless foe.

V. German Armored Engineers on the Road to Leningrad (August 1941)

During the last days of August 1941 Army Group North forces drove toward Leningrad from Kingisepp and from Luga. In an effort to keep open the route of withdrawal of their forces that had been defeated at Luga, the Russians put up strong resistance to the German armor thrusting eastward from Kingisepp. Continuing their relentless drive, the German panzer divisions broke through the Russian front southwest of Leningrad at several points. By that time the Russian top-level command seemed to have lost overall control of the forces employed in the vicinity of Leningrad, but individual units—probably driven by their commissars—continued to fight stubbornly.

On 28 August the 8th Panzer Division, which was assembled approximately 30 miles southeast of Kingisepp, received orders to spearhead the thrust from the southwest on the following day. By advancing via Moloskovitsy and Volosovo the division was to reach the Luga-Leningrad highway at a point south of Gatchina (map 20). Upon arriving at the highway the division was to turn southeastward and thus, by attacking the withdrawing Russian forces from the rear, facilitate the advance of those German infantry divisions that were fighting their way northward. Meanwhile, other German armored forces were to capture Gatchina and various objectives farther to the north on the road to Leningrad.

The terrain through which the German armor was to advance was swampy forest land. A few minor elevations afforded a good view of the surrounding countryside. At this time of the summer all highways and roads, with the exception of those leading through extremely swampy terrain, were passable for vehicular traffic. The sun rose at 0300.

The 8th Panzer Division moved out at 0400 on 29 August and entered Moloskovitsy during the early morning hours. Weak Russian forces entrenched at the railroad station were quickly dispersed, and the advance guard continued its march toward Volosovo. Isolated nests of resistance failed to delay the Germans.

Company C of the 59th Armored Engineer Battalion, marching at the head of the first divisional column, arrived in Volosovo at 1230 and halted for a short break. A liaison officer and motorcycle messengers maintained contact with the advance guard which, according to the latest report, had reached Kikerino at 1215.

At 1235 Lieutenant Schneider, the commander of Company C, heard machinegun and antitank gun fire from the northeast. Just as he was stepping into his vehicle with the intention of investigating the situation, a supply truck of the advance guard drove up and stopped. The driver reported that his truck column had been ambushed about 1½ miles east of Volosovo. While the other truck drivers had tried to escape by accelerating their vehicles, he had turned around and headed back to notify the march column commander.

On the basis of this information Schneider ordered the 1st and 2d (Tank) Platoons [*Ed:* For organization of Company C, see page 86] to move to the road fork at Lagonovo and the 4th Platoon, consisting of rocket projectors mounted on half-tracks, to a point immediately south of that road fork. The 5th Platoon, composed of combat engineers, was to take up positions on the northeast outskirts of Volosovo. Schneider got into his vehicle and drove off in the direction of Kikerino. About 1 mile east of the Lagonovo road fork he stopped at the top of a low ridge from which he was able to observe approximately 300 Russian riflemen emerging from the west side of the woods south of Gubanitsy at a point about half a mile north of the highway (Point B). They were heading for the ridge just a few hundred yards west of the woods. Schneider also noticed that one Russian machinegun and one antitank gun were emplaced at the southwest edge of the forest. He felt certain that these must have been the weapons that had ambushed the truck column. Two burning trucks lay in the ditch along the highway about 500 yards east of his observation point. Small arms ammunition was exploding in one of the trucks.

Schneider arrived at the conclusion that the Russians were attempting to cut off the advance guard and recapture Volosovo. Quick action seemed imperative if the Russians were to be prevented from delaying the division's advance toward the Luga-Leningrad highway.

Upon his return to the Lagonovo road fork at 1305 Schneider met the march column commander who approved his plan to eliminate the Russian threat. Schneider thereupon called his platoon leaders and issued the following verbal orders:

    1. Company C will immediately attack the Russian companies approaching the ridge, disperse them, and prevent any additional Russian forces from emerging from the forest.

    2. The 1st Tank Platoon will deploy immediately along the Lagonovo-Gubanitsy road midway between the two villages, lay down a smoke screen when the rocket projectors fire their salvo, and drive to Point A, which is shown on your map, at the forest's edge. The platoon will protect its own left flank.

    3. The 2d Tank Platoon will assemble east of the road fork and jump off simultaneously with the 1st, directing its thrust toward point B.

    4. The 4th Platoon will take up positions outside of Lagonovo and fire a salvo of 24 rockets at the two aforementioned points. It will then close up to the 2d Platoon and annihilate the Russian forces caught between the ridge and the edge of the forest. The 1st Squad of the 4th Platoon will remain in its firing position as company reserve.

    5. The 5th Platoon will proceed along the highway, detruck at a point about 1,000 yards east of the road fork, occupy that stretch of the road which crosses the ridge, and form the right wing of the attack force. This platoon will also clear the southwest edge of the forest and secure the portion of the highway that borders on the forest.

    6. I shall be with the 4th Platoon.

At 1330 the four platoons were assembling for the attack and Schneider was driving toward Gubanitsy. On his way he saw the first Russians coming down the west side of the ridge. They advanced in extended formation with scouts moving about 20 yards ahead of the main body. He also observed some Russians pulling antitank guns from the forest toward the ridge. Two more Russian infantry companies were just emerging from the woods at Points A and B. This second wave followed in the steps of the first.

Five minutes later the 4th Platoon fired its salvo of rockets, which landed in the center of the deploying second wave. The smoke screen laid down by the two tank platoons hid the advancing vehicles from view of the Russians who began to fire from the ridge. The tanks retaliated and the fire fight grew more intense as Company C's counterattack gained momentum.

When the smoke began to lift several minutes later, Schneider saw that the tanks had reached the crest of the ridge and that their fire was pinning down the Russian infantry, whose ranks were beginning to break. In a vain attempt to escape annihilation, individual riflemen bunched together, but were mowed down by machinegun fire from the tanks. The Russian antitank guns stood in the middle of the field, abandoned by their crews. Isolated nests of resistance continued to fire, but their small arms were ineffective against the German tanks, which drove straight toward their designated objectives. The 5th Platoon mopped up behind the tanks, rounding up the prisoners. Remnants of the second wave that had escaped the rocket salvo tried to make their way to the woods.

By 1400 the four platoons had accomplished their missions, and the fighting was all but over when the 1st Platoon's left flank suddenly came under heavy weapons fire from the north. The platoon leader radioed that enemy infantry was attacking in company strength. Schneider immediately committed the reserve squad of the 4th Platoon plus one tank of the headquarters section and ordered that 12 rockets be fired at the Russian attack force. By 1420 the flank attack had been beaten off, and 10 minutes later Schneider informed the march column that traffic on the highway to Kikerino could be resumed. The entire operation had taken less than 2 hours. The Russian forces in the forest had suffered such heavy losses that no further attacks on German march columns were expected at that point.

In its further advance toward the Luga-Leningrad highway the 8th Panzer Division encountered little resistance. On the other hand, the German infantry divisions moving north from Luga made little progress. They were opposed by Russian forces that had not disintegrated and were therefore able to offer sustained resistance. On the evening of the same day the Luga-Leningrad highway was cut when leading elements of the 8th Panzer Division reached Sivoritsy, a village situated about 10 miles south of Gatchina.

Plans for the following day called for the division to split into two task forces. One column was to advance southward along the highway toward Luga, while the other was to drive southeastward toward Staro-Siverskaya. During the night of 29–30 August Schneider and his men were to drive via Kobrino to Kurovitsy and occupy the latter. The division commander considered Kurovitsy an important junction through which the Russians might channel reinforcements or withdraw their troops toward Vyritsa. In any event, possession of the town was important for the successful accomplishment of the division's mission to assist the advance of the infantry divisions.

With the 1st and 5th Platoons in the lead, the company drove through Kobrino without stopping and reached Kurovitsy at 2145. Here it again made contact with Russian troops when its lead tanks suddenly observed 10 trucks loaded with Russian infantry just about to pull out in the direction of Vyritsa. The German tanks immediately opened fire, but one truck escaped in the direction of Vyritsa and two more along the road leading to Staro-Siverskaya. The remaining trucks were immobilized, but most of their occupants escaped into the night, which was so dark that the Germans refrained from pursuit.

Schneider decided to organize the defense of Kurovitsy for the

GERMAN TANK attacks with mounted infantry, 1942.

remainder of the night. At the southern outskirts the 1st Platoon and one squad from the 5th were to mine and block the two roads to Staro-Siverskaya. The 2d Platoon less one tank was to obstruct the road to Vyritsa at the eastern outskirts. Another squad of the 5th Platoon was to take up positions at the forest's edge about a mile down the same road and mine the roadbed at that point. The 5th Platoon, less the two above-mentioned squads, was to move to the forest's edge northeast of the village and establish an outpost line. The remaining combat forces were to form the company's reserves and assemble in the northern and northwestern parts of the village. The service vehicles had stayed behind in Kobrino. Schneider felt that these measures would provide adequate security against a sudden attack which, despite the prevailing quiet, was expected at any time.

At 0015 the 2d Platoon reported hearing the noise of tracked vehicles approaching from the direction of Vyritsa. Forty-five minutes later a Russian truck proceeding north from Staro-Siverskaya hit a mine. One wounded Russian officer was captured and two men were killed; the rest escaped.

At 0230 the 2d Platoon sent another message indicating that the noise of tracked vehicles could be heard, this time nearer than before. Shortly thereafter the noise stopped and quiet reigned until 0400, when the 2d Platoon reported that its platoon leader had just been shot from ambush. Half an hour later the 1st Platoon sent a message stating that five trucks were approaching from Staro-Siverskaya and soon afterward Schneider, at his CP just northwest of the village, heard the noice of fighting, which seemed to be coming from the southern outskirts. He soon found out that the trucks had been immobilized after hitting the German mines. While German machineguns fired at them from pointblank range, about thirty Russians had jumped off the trucks and sought cover on both sides of the road. Two of the German tanks finally dispersed them, and the few Russians who managed to escape withdrew to the nearby woods.

A few minutes later isolated small-arms fire coming from within the village could be heard. A messenger arrived on foot at Schneider's CP to report that he had been attacked two blocks down the main street and forced to abandon his damaged motorcycle. The noise of battle gradually came closer, when the 2d Platoon radioed that it was receiving fire from houses on the eastern outskirts. Schneider realized that immediate countermeasures had to be taken and ordered the 5th Platoon to assemble all of its squads on the northern outskirts and to comb out the village from north to south.

At 0510 the 5th Platoon, supported by two tanks, began to advance southward astride the main street. Bitter house-to-house fighting developed. The approaching Germans were met by sniper fire from houses, hedges, and hay stacks. The armored engineers used concentrated charges, hand grenades, and machinegun and tank-gun fire to clear one house after another. Some of the Russian soldiers feigned death only to resume fighting as soon as the Germans had passed.

The struggle within Kurovitsy reached its climax at 0520. Twenty minutes later the eastern section had been combed out and 10 prisoners were brought in. To clean out the western part, however, Schneider had to employ all his reserves. Each hay and straw stack had to be sprayed with bullets. Every Russian had to be ferreted out if he was not to resume the fight by sniping at the Germans. Those Russians who surrendered did so only because there was no other way out. By 0600 Russian resistance within Kurovitsy had collapsed.

Even though the town was now firmly in German hands, Schneider felt that further attacks from the direction of Staro-Siverskaya were possible and he therefore strengthened the 1st Platoon. At 0750, while Schneider was inspecting the defenses at the southern outskirts, the 2d Platoon reported the noise of tanks approaching from Vyritsa. Shortly thereafter the first shells landed in the center of Kurovitsy. Just as Schneider was about to leave for the new danger area on the eastern outskirts, Russian infantry, emerging in company strength from the woods southwest of Kurovitsy, closed in on the positions of the 1st Platoon. At the same time a German observer perched on a high roof reported suspicious movements at the forest's edge due west of the village.

Schneider hardly knew where to turn first. When he arrived at the 2d Platoon's CP, he was informed that a KV tank stood just beyond the mine obstacle on the Vyritsa road and was lobbing shells into Kurovitsy. No other tanks, however, had been observed. Schneider ordered the rocket projectors of the 4th Platoon to assemble at the northern outskirts and prepare to fire in the direction of both the tank and the western approaches to the village.

At 0815 the 5th Platoon took up positions on the western outskirts to defend the village against an attack from that direction. The men arrived in time to see a Russian infantry company moving straight toward them. The Germans opened fire at a range of about 1,000 yards and a lively fight developed. The 1st Platoon was still engaged in warding off the Russian attack from the south when a heavy explosion was heard from the direction of the Vyritsa road. The

KV had touched off a mine. Through his glasses Schneider could see the crew climb out of the tank, inspect the damage, and remount. Shortly afterward the KV's gun resumed fire, but the shells went over the roof tops and landed outside the western outskirts of the village.

By 0850 the defense of Kurovitsy had reached a critical stage. The Russian attack from the west was making slow but steady headway against the stubborn resistance of the 5th Platoon. Simultaneously, the fighting in the southern part grew more lively as additional Russian infantry forces came up from the south. The fire from the tank gun became more accurate. During the entire action Schneider's repeated radio messages requesting assistance from the task force commander brought no response.

Schneider thereupon decided to try to reduce the enemy pressure by first silencing the tank gun and then launching a counterattack on the west side. He ordered the rocket projectors to fire a salvo at the tank. Several direct hits were scored, knocking out the tank. However, before the half-tracks had time to turn around and prepare another salvo against the Russian infantry advancing from the west, the range had grown too short for firing rockets. Schneider quickly assembled all the available tanks and half-tracks, led the column 500 yards up the road toward Kobrino, turned off to the left, and drove with all guns ablaze into the flank and rear of the Russian infantry company, which by that time was only some 250 yards from the western outskirts of the town. This thrust caught the Russians by surprise. Most of them were overrun by the tanks, the rest ran for cover or surrendered. The appearance of the German tanks on the west side of the village led the Russian forces attacking from the south to withdraw to the woods north of Staro-Siverskaya. By 0915 the fighting was over and 15 minutes later the advance guard of the 8th Panzer Division's task force entered Kurovitsy from Kobrino.

The task force commander explained to Schneider that his advance had been delayed by a Russian attack from Gatchina during the early morning hours. His force had to assist in the capture of Gatchina before it could jump off on its southward drive. Schneider and his men were ordered to take a well-deserved rest.

During the aforementioned actions the armored engineer company proved effective as an independent combat unit. Excellent teamwork between the tank, rocket projector, and combat engineer platoons made this small unit a formidable fighting force.

The preceding examples are isolated instances in which the Russians were able to delay the German advance during the first months after the invasion of their country. In general, however, the attackers were able to push back the defenders, most of whose armor was destroyed by the combined effort of German antitank guns, artillery, air attacks, and panzer units. The German Army advanced relentlessly to within a short distance of Leningrad and Moscow, forcing the Russians to leave behind even slightly damaged equipment that could have been recovered and repaired. By the winter of 1941–42 the Russians had relatively few tanks to commit. Even so, they never missed an opportunity to counterattack.

VI. The Struggle for Shelter (December 1941)

The winter of 1941–42 was particularly severe and the fighting on many sectors of the front centered around inhabited localities that could offer shelter from the cold. In mid-December a German patrol captured an operations order that revealed that the Russians planned to attack southwestward along a road leading from the direction of Lisichansk, on the Donets, with the intention of disrupting the German lines of communication. On 18 December the 203d Infantry Regiment moved into a new battle position in and around Berestovaya, a village situated along the expected Russian axis of advance. The regiment organized its center of resistance around the stone buildings in the center of the village (map 21).

The 203d had been engaged in heavy defensive fighting for several weeks, and its combat efficiency had dropped sharply. The average strength of the infantry companies had been reduced to approximately 50 riflemen, and the regiment had lost about one-third of its heavy weapons.

Sprawling villages and a few trees were predominant features of the rolling landscape around Berestovaya, whose stone houses—rare in this part of Russia—provided ample shelter against December temperatures, which averaged about 15° F. The snow cover varied from 4 inches to several feet in depth.

From 18 through 22 December the Russians deployed their forces and pushed back one German outpost after another, an indication that a major attack was imminent. On the evening of 22 December the 2d Battalion was hit by a Russian infantry force of regimental strength. German defensive fire succeeded in stopping the Russian advance on both sides of the Lisichansk-Belogorovka road; however, a German strong point on F Company's left flank was overrun and Russian elements penetrated Berestovaya as far as the 2d Battalion command post. The battalion commander then committed his reserves and restored the situation.

On 23 December the Russians made unsuccessful piecemeal attacks in company to battalion strength against the 2d Battalion sector astride the Lisichansk-Belogorovka road. After darkness had fallen, the Russians fired a brief artillery concentration against the forward positions of G company in the area east of the road; then they attacked the company with 2 battalions of infantry supported by 10 tanks and broke through near Hill 676. German artillery was then brought to bear on the Russian armor, forcing it to withdraw, and the infantry, deprived of tank support, was unable to advance. The Germans thereupon committed Companies I and K of the reserve battalion and sealed off the Russian penetration.

On the 24th the Russians, using only infantry, attacked along the road and, for the first time, against the left flank of the adjacent 1st Battalion.

On Christmas morning the Russians attacked along the road and eastward with two battalions of infantry, but were stopped by artillery fire. Shortly afterward, two Russian assault groups, each consisting of one to two companies supported by mortar fire, debouched from draws northwest of Berestovaya and attacked A and C Companies. Despite their numerical inferiority, the Germans managed to repulse these attacks.

About 1400, in the face of a sharp east wind, 12 Russian tanks suddenly emerged from the same draws and made a surprise attack toward Berestovaya from the west. Accompanied by infantry, the tanks advanced slowly and brought the German strong points under fire. Within an hour the tanks had broken through Company A's position, where 40 men were trying to hold a 1,000-yard-wide sector. A few of the tanks broke off from their accompanying infantry and moved southward toward the railroad embankment, but withdrew after two tanks had been lost to antitank fire.

Company K counterattacked from the south and cleared the village of those elements that had broken through its defenses. Headquarters Company of the 3d Battalion and I Company were moved up from Belogorovka and committed; by 2100 the German MLR was restored.

The heavy casualties that had been suffered in the action up to that point forced the 203d Infantry Regiment to reorganize the three battalions being assigned adjoining sectors, with the 3d Battalion in the center, flanked by the 1st and 2d on the left and right, respectively. Each battalion held one company in reserve.

At dawn on the 26th the Russians began heavy attacks in the area between Berestovaya and that portion of the rail line due west of the village. Seventeen Russian tanks, accompanied by infantry, moved against the right wing of the 1st Battalion, smashing B Company's position. As the Russians reached the railroad embankment they were halted by German artillery fire. Some of the Russian tanks moved on southeastward toward Hill 728, a conspicuous plateau in the otherwise rolling terrain. The hill offered no cover to the Germans who could not hold it against the Russian tank fire and therefore withdrew southward to the railroad. In order to strengthen the regiment's defenses, division moved one infantry battalion and a squadron of dismounted bicycle infantry to Belogorovka.

German ground-support aircraft were committed during the early morning hours with but little success—the situation on the ground was so confused that accurate bombing and strafing was impossible. At 0930 the Russians penetrated Berestovaya from the west and at noon the regimetal commander gave the 2d Battalion permission to withdraw from the village. However, with the arrival shortly thereafter of reinforcements and five assault guns, the battalion was able to withstand Russian pressure until 1600, when Russian infantry, together with a few tanks, made a fresh attack along the road. The Germans lost two strong points near Hill 676 as the Russians broke through. With the aid of the reserve battalion and the assault guns, the 2d Battalion was able to throw the Russians back. By midnight the 2d Battalion's MLR was restored, but contact had been lost between the 3d and 1st Battalions, the latter having taken up a new defensive position close to the railroad embankment.

At dawn on the 27th the Russians launched an attack fully as powerful as that of the preceding day. Striking from the gap between the 1st and 3d Battalions, a strong infantry force supported by at least 20 tanks attacked the 1st Battalion's positions along the railroad embankment. The battalion's eight 37-mm. antitank guns on the embankment were ineffectual against the Russian T34 tanks and were soon knocked out, whereupon the Germans were forced to give up the embankment.

Toward 1100, after a strong artillery preparation, Russian infantry with tank support attacked from the area just west and northwest of Berestovaya and succeeded in reaching the center of the village. The Germans then counterattacked and recaptured it, following which another Russian force enveloped it by sweeping around the south side.

At 1400, a Russian infantry force, accompanied by several tanks, broke into Berestovaya from the west. Shortly afterward a tank-infantry force attacked along the Lisichansk-Belogorovka road and entered the village from the east. The commander of the 2d Battalion then ordered the evacuation of Berestovaya during the night.

The night withdrawal was carried out without interference. The Russians, who had suffered heavy losses, continued to attack the next

FIGHTING WEST OF KURSK (January 1942)

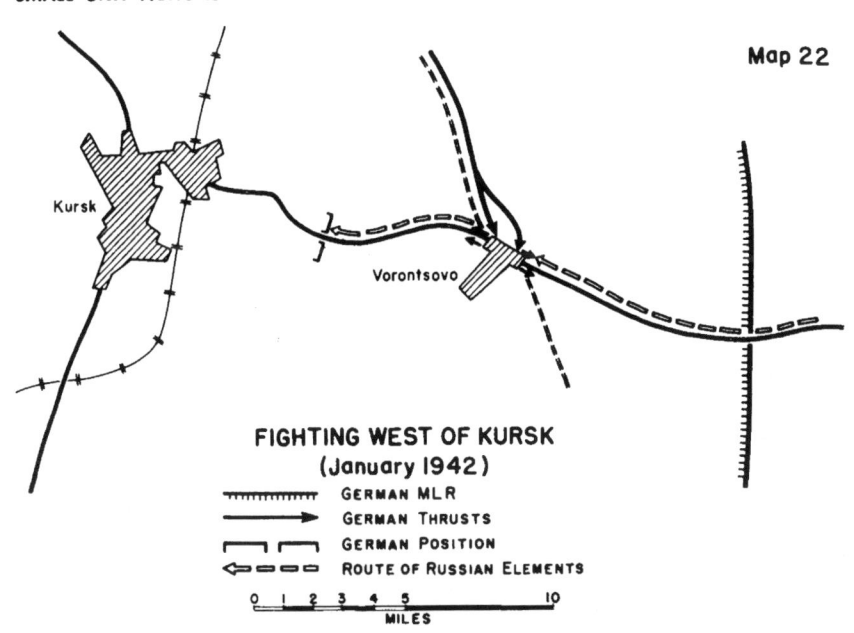

day, but were so weak that the Germans had no difficulty in stopping any attempt to advance.

This action exemplifies the tenacity with which both parties fought for villages or other permanent-type shelter during the bitter winter of 1941–42. The German defense of Berestovaya was facilitated by the existence of stone houses, which were not as easily destroyed as the usual Russian structures of wood, clay, or straw.

Throughout the course of their repeated attacks the Russians dissipated their offensive strength without forming points of main effort. Tanks were employed exclusively in support of infantry, a characteristic often evident during the first few months of the war. The Russians could have seized Berestovaya with much less effort if they had tried to envelop it from the beginning. An early Russian thrust to the dominating terrain of Hill 728 would have isolated the German forces in and around Berestovaya and made a prolonged defense impossible.

VII. Seesaw Battle in Subzero Temperatures (January 1942)

The beginning ascendancy of Russian armor over its German counterpart is exemplified in the following action, during which the Russian tank units showed themselves more aggressive than usual. In January 1942 the German front near Kursk ran north and south about 20 miles east of the city (map 22). Because of heavy snowfall cross-country movements was hampered by deep drifts, and temperatures dropped to −30° F. as sharp winds swept across the rolling countryside.

Since there were no woods in the area, visibility was good, except in low places. The monotony of the landscape was relieved only by a number of villages and towns.

Exposed for the first time to the rigors of a Russian winter, the Germans struggled desperately against the elements, as their tanks, trucks, and automatic weapons broke down in the bitter cold. Timber for the improvement of the positions was scarce; accordingly the exhausted German infantry units, then employed along broad sectors, concentrated their defense in village strong points.

The Russians, taking advantage of their numerical superiority and greater experience under winter conditions, sought to undermine the German defense by a series of local, limited-objective attacks.

In the sector of the German 16th Motorized Infantry Division, Russian reconnaissance patrols had skillfully identified a weak spot at the boundary between two regiments. A combined arms team of Russian armor and infantry succeeded in breaking through the German MLR where it crossed the east-west road leading to Kursk, through which a railway and highway vital to German supply movements ran parallel to the front.

Exploiting the breakthrough, a force of about 25 T34 tanks with infantry mounted on them drove on toward Kursk and easily captured the communities in its path which were held solely by German service units. The Russian thrust continued into the next day, when it was stopped about 5 miles from Kursk by a hastily assembled German force. Several attempts to close the gap in the MLR with weak local reserves failed, and the Russians were able to follow up their tank force with two or three battalions of infantry, including some mounted in trucks.

The town of Vorontsovo, situated on the road leading to Kursk, was occupied by a weak Russian force. A German tank battalion, whose tank strength had fallen to 22, was released from another sector and sent in from the north against the right flank of the breakthrough force. The battalion took Vorontsovo by a *coup de main*, whereupon the Russians had to discontinue their westward advance.

After receiving meager reinforcements in the form of one 88-mm. antiaircraft gun and a battalion of infantry replacements that had just arrived from the zone of interior, the Germans conducted harassing raids in the areas east and west of Vorontsovo, effectively interfering with the supply of those Russian troops that had been cutoff

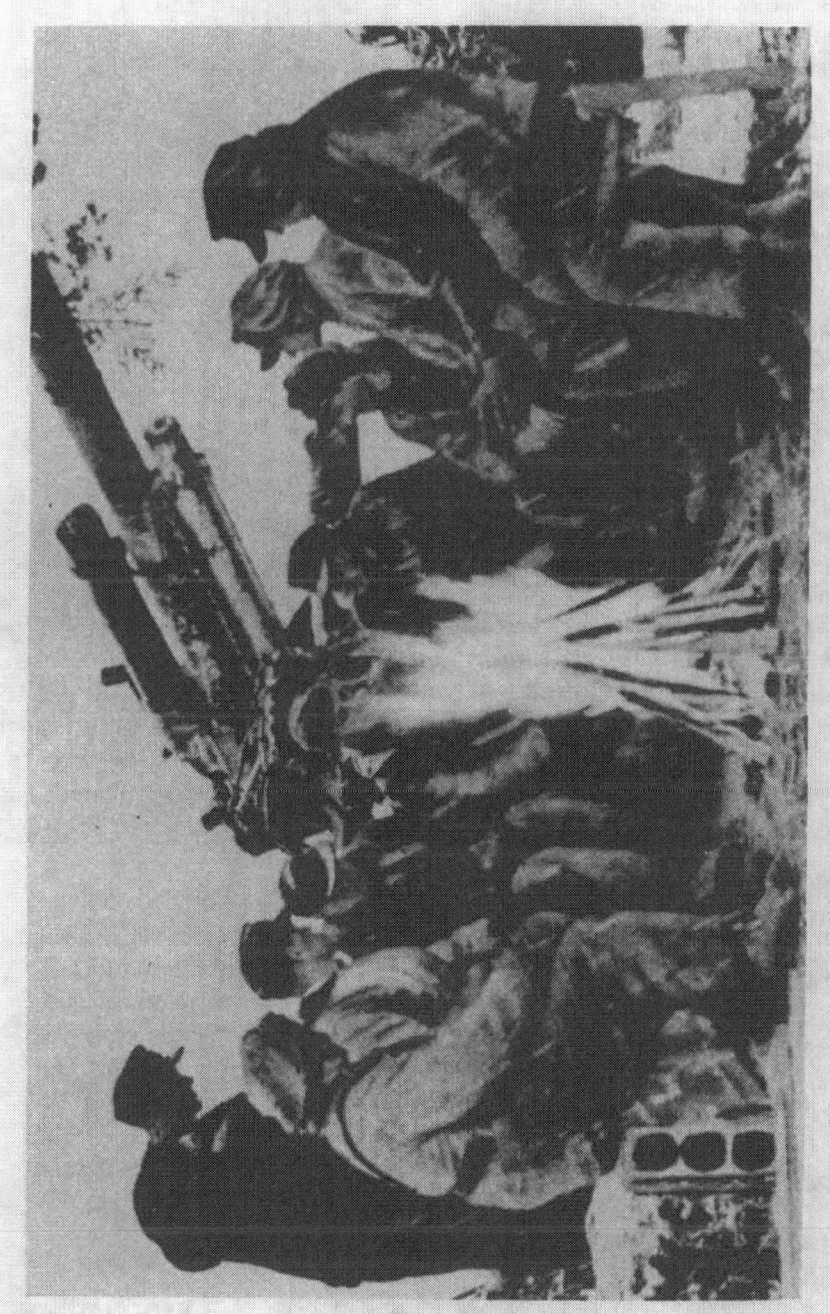

GERMAN 88-mm. gun crew keeping warm, Winter 1942.

west of the town. On the third day of the action these isolated Russian forces attacked with infantry and tanks but were repulsed.

On the following day, during a driving snowstorm, the Russians attacked Vorontsovo from both the east and west, the thrust from the west being supported by tanks. Taking advantage of their greater ground clearance and lower ground pressure, the Russian tanks swept across terrain that the Germans had considered impassable for armor.

The young German infantry replacements, untested in battle, lacked experience in hand-to-hand fighting in villages and towns. They had not yet learned to fight in conjunction with tanks and were quickly overcome. Inferior in fire power and mobility to their Russian opposites, the German tanks were almost completely wiped out, and Vorontsovo was once again in Russian hands.

The Russian attack on this key town from two opposite directions was perfectly coordinated. The Germans never found out whether the two Russian forces had established radio contact or whether, perhaps, they were assisted by civilians who had remained in the town. Executed in a driving snowstorm, the Russian attack achieved surprise because the German precautions were inadequate. Extensive reconnaissance and security measures are elementary precautions that must be taken, regardless of the weather. To be derelict in these essentials is to risk lives.

The German counterattack was inadequately supported and led, and the inexperienced infantry were more a hindrance than a help in the operation. An armored unit on an independent mission must be accompanied by seasoned troops equipped with the necessary supporting weapons.

VIII. The Fedorenko Order (June 1942)

The Russians realized the superiority of the T34 tank early in the war and converted their plant facilities to the sole production of this one model. During their first winter in Russia the Germans encountered enemy tanks either singly or in small groups. This scarcity of armor came about because the production of new tanks was low and because many of those which did become available were used far behind the front to train crews on the latest tactical doctrine. With the improvement in optical and radio equipment, the Russian command was finally able to organize large armored formations and employ them in far-reaching operations.

Although the Russian military had reason to be satisfied with the local successes achieved during the winter of 1941–42, it was nevertheless fully aware of the deficiencies still inherent in the tactics of large armored formations. It thus felt obliged to intervene in armored affairs at the end of June 1942, and did so by issuing a new directive, which was particularly important because its author, Fedorenko (Chief Marshal of Tanks and Mechanized Forces and Deputy Commander of Defense), drew the right inference from previous mistakes. That these conclusions were correct was proved by subsequent developments. It is to be assumed that the basic principles expressed in this order continue to govern the employment of Russian armor to this very day. The following is a translation of the Fedorenko Order:

SUBJECT: Employment of Armored Formations
TO: All Armored Forces Commanders at Front Headquarters and Army Headquarters, and Commanding Generals of Armored Armies and Corps

An analysis of the combat operations of several armored corps in May 1942 indicates that commanders of armored forces at front headquarters [*Ed*: Russian equivalent of an army group, subsequently referred to as such] and at army headquarters lack comprehension of the basic principles governing the employment of major armored formations in modern warfare. The XII Armored Corps, for instance, committed on the right of a force attacking in the direction of Kharkov, was split up into single brigades and employed piecemeal, with the result that the commander of armored forces at the superior army group headquarters was unable to conduct the operations of the corps. The XXI and XXII Armored Corps on the left of the attack force were identified by the enemy long before their commitment in battle. Once again, the commander of armored forces at army group headquarters had no control whatsoever over his subordinate corps.

Until the official regulations for the employment of armored troops are approved and issued by the People's Commissar for Defense, the following orders will be observed:

1. The armored corps is a basic unit and will be reserved for the execution of strategic missions.
2. The armored corps is subordinate to the army group headquarters and will be committed for the execution of strategic missions in conjunction with other troop formations of the army group.
3. It is forbidden to place armored corps under the command of armies and to split them up for the purpose of reinforcing the infantry. An armored corps committed within the area of an army will operate in conjunction with that army for the duration of a designated operation, while simultaneously maintaining contact with army group headquarters.

4. In an offensive operation conducted by an army group, an armored corps has the mission of massing its forces for a deep thrust, enveloping the enemy's main forces, encircling them, and destroying them in co-operation with the air force and with other ground units.

5. In order to preserve the striking power of an armored corps for a strategic envelopment and the ensuing struggle deep in the enemy's rear, it is forbidden to employ armored corps for breaking through fortified positions. However, when reinforced by artillery, tactical air force, infantry, and engineers, an armored corps may be committed for a frontal breakthrough attempt against prepared enemy positions.

6. An armored corps may drive ahead of the other friendly forces and penetrate the enemy sector to a depth of 25 to 30 miles, provided that a second wave is sent through the gap. The situation will often require that, immediately after a breakthrough of the hostile positions, the enemy's main forces—located 10 to 15 miles behind the MLR—are enveloped, encircled, and annihilated with the assistance of other formations.

7. The armored corps is considered to be capable of 72–96 hours of uninterrupted commitment.

8. The accomplishment of an armored corps' mission depends essentially upon the training and *esprit de corps* of its personnel, on air support, and on proper coordination with the artillery, tactical air force units, engineers, and other arms and services.

9. Once it has achieved a strategic envelopment, an armored corps will establish contact with airlanded troops and partisan units.

10. During defensive operations an armored corps will be committed in counterattacks against any enemy forces that have broken through the friendly MLR or have enveloped the flanks, especially if these forces consist of armored and motorized units. In such instances the counterthrust will not be executed as a frontal maneuver, but will be delivered against the enemy's flank or rear.

11. In any event, surprise is of the essence in committing an armored corps. For this reason the assembly or regrouping of forces will always be carried out by night. Should a regrouping during the day become inevitable, it will be carried out in groups of no more than three to five tanks.

12. Terrain factors must be given foremost consideration in select-

ing the direction for an armored corps attack. They must be favorable for the mass commitment of armor.
13. If intact rail facilities are available, the cross-country movement of tanks over distances exceeding 30 miles is forbidden.
14. In planning the commitment of an armored corps, especially in a strategic envelopment, adequate supplies of fuel, ammunition, rations, and spare parts must be prepared for the entire duration of the operation, and the tank recovery service must be appropriately organized. The following quantities of supply will normally be carried by the combat trains:

Fuel—Equivalent of three times the vehicle's capacity.
Ammunition—Two to three basic issues.
Rations—Five daily.

The tank crews will carry the following additional rations: two to three tins of canned meat or hard sausage, canned ham, soup concentrates in cubes, bread, zwieback, sugar, and tea or water in vacuum bottles.
15. The armored corps commanders and the armored forces commanders, as well as the military council of the army group, will be held responsible for the proper employment of the armored corps in combat as well as for their logistical and technical support.

The effect of the Fedorenko Order was not immediately noticeable. In the summer of 1942 the Germans once more seized the initiative on most sectors of the Russian front. The Russians, still handicapped by a shortage of up-to-date tanks, were forced to use their slower and less maneuverable heavies in conjunction with the T34's. They resorted to a number of ruses and ambushes in an effort to gain a maximum of time at the loss of a minimum of space. Backed by a steadily mounting tank production, they made every effort to ward off the German onslaught by skillful defensive maneuvers.

IX. Feint, Ambush, and Strike (July 1942)

The following actions took place in July 1942 on the central front during an attack by two panzer divisions supported by two infantry divisions. The Russians held well-fortified positions protected by extensive mine fields. At some points the Russian defensive system reached a depth of 3 miles. The German objective was to thrust toward the Resseta River, in the vicinity of which additional Russian fortifications were under construction. Aerial photographs taken before the attack was launched did not reveal the presence of any Russian tanks.

GERMAN ADVANCE TO THE RESSETA RIVER (July 1942)

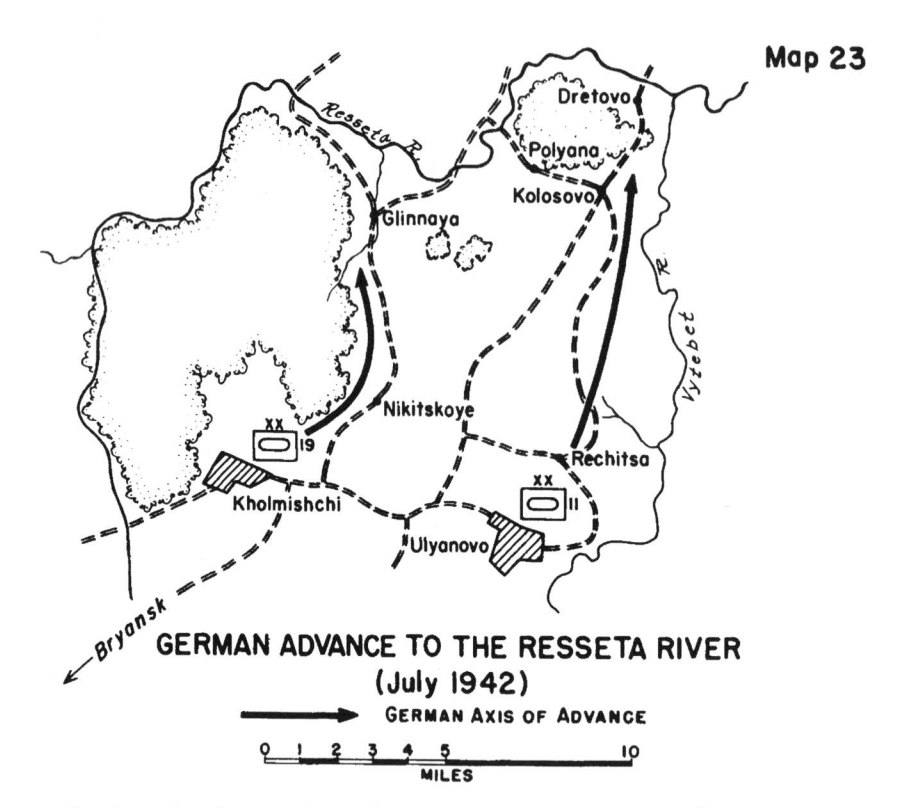

During the first 2 days the attack proceeded according to plan. The two infantry divisions crossed the mine belt and fought their way through the Russian positions. On the third day the two panzer divisions were moved up and committed in the direction of the Resseta. The 11th Panzer Division was at full strength, whereas the 19th had only 60 percent of its prescribed T/O & E. Only about half the armored infantry units were motorized, the others had to march on foot. The Russians, meanwhile, had moved up reinforcements, including tanks. Their air forces, particularly the fighter-bomber squadrons, were quite active.

The fighting took place in or near very dense forests, where visibility was poor. The watercourses could be forded at several points. The weather was warm and sunny.

When the 19th Panzer Division attacked northeastward from Kholmishchi, the forward armored elements ran into strong Russian antitank defenses south of Nikitskoye (map 23). In devising their defense system, the Russians had taken full advantage of the concealment offered by the terrain and vegetation. One German armored

SMALL UNIT ACTIONS

column drove straight into an antitank gun front disposed on a semicircle facing south. The Russian guns, emplaced in pairs for mutual support, were dug in so that the muzzles were just above the surface of the ground. Between each pair of guns was an additional antitank gun mounted on a two-wheeled farm cart. The cart-mounted guns were camouflaged, but no effort had been made to conceal them.

As the German tanks advanced, the dug-in guns fired a volley, then ceased. Seeking the source of the fire, the Germans noticed the guns mounted on carts, and moved toward the newly discovered targets. As soon as a German tank turned to bring the cart-mounted guns under fire, it was hit from the side by Russian antitank fire from the concealed positions. The cart-mounted guns were dummies. Several of the tanks were lost in the action before the Germans succeeded in knocking out all the real antitank guns. In emplacing the dummy guns, the Russians were careful to leave just enough of the gun visible to make it an attractive target. Taken in by this ruse, the Germans turned their tanks to face the decoys, thereby exposing tracks and lateral armor, the most vulnerable parts.

After elements of the 19th Panzer Division had pushed through Nikitskoye they ran into trouble north of the town, where they were repeatedly attacked by groups of five to seven Russian tanks emerg-

GERMAN TANKS attack with Luftwaffe support, 1942.

ing from the large forest adjacent to the division's left flank. After allowing the German armored point to pass, the Russian tanks pounced upon the wheeled vehicles which followed. Whenever the Germans counterattacked, the Russian tanks immediately withdrew into the forest, only to emerge at another point. The tanks used in this operation were of an older type, no match for their German counterparts in open terrain. Hence the Russians used them—and with telling effect—only for hit-and-run operations. These Russian tactics cost the Germans a large number of casualties and caused considerable delay.

The German division commander thereupon ordered one tank battalion to cover the left flank of the advancing column. Echeloned in depth and supported by armored engineers, the tanks proceeded to comb the edge of the forest. In this manner the column was protected against any further surprise attacks.

When committing tanks in densely wooded areas, the Germans found it expedient to have them accompanied by infantry or engineers because the tank crews were unable to see or hear enough to proceed safely on their own.

Meanwhile, the 11th Panzer Division, driving toward the Resseta on the right of the 19th, attacked northeastward from Ulyanovo according to plan. As the leading tanks approached the village of Rechitsa, several T34's suddenly debouched from deep gullies and attacked the German armor from the left flank. After a stiff fight the T34's disappeared into the gullies only to renew their attacks at another point farther north.

The German medium tanks sent in pursuit were suddenly hit by flanking fire delivered from nearby gullies. In seeking the source of this fire the Germans observed that the Russians had dug in heavy tanks in such a way that only the turrets and guns were visible. The Russian heavies held their fire until the German tanks were within range or, when bypassed by the Germans, rolled backward out of the gullies and raced northward.

Although the Russian tanks were outnumbered, their tactics, well suited to the terrain, took a heavy toll of German armor. The Russians skillfully exploited the superior fire power of their heavy tanks and the maneuverability of their T34's in a way that compensated for the slowness of the former and the shortage of the latter.

At first the 11th Panzer Division commander tried to cope with these unusual tactics by committing artillery and antitank guns. When these proved ineffective, he asked for air support. Reconnaissance planes, protected by fighters, hovered over the area, maintaining con-

SMALL UNIT ACTIONS

stant radio contact with division headquarters. At least one reconnaissance plane circled at all times above the division's axis of advance and reported the hideouts of the Russian tanks by radio or flares. This information was relayed to the German tank commanders. As a result of good air-ground teamwork, the Russian armor was driven back after suffering heavy losses.

Despite the initial setback, this armored action was brought to a rapid and successful conclusion. Once the reconnaissance planes had established the presence of Russian armor, they kept the hostile tanks under observation until the latter were annihilated by their German counterparts or were withdrawn toward the north.

But the 11th Panzer Division had not seen the last of the elusive T34's. As the division attacked Kolosovo, its last objective before reaching the Resseta, the Russians dispatched twenty T34's from the direction of Dretovo, less than a mile from the river.

As soon as they established contact with the advancing elements of the German armor just north of Kolosovo, the T34's began to withdraw, fighting a delaying action. After the German tank formations had all passed through Kolosovo, they were brought under heavy antitank fire from the woods north of the town. Most of the German armor then swung to the left, toward the forest, while the remainder held to the main axis of advance. As the German tanks that had veered off were approaching the immediate vicinity of the forest, an entire brigade of T34's broke out of Polyana, west of Kolosovo, and hit the German tanks from the flank and rear, forcing them to withdraw to Kolosovo, which changed hands several times during the bitter tank battle that ensued. Only after the German division commander had thrown in all his artillery and antitank guns were the Germans able to obtain a firm hold on the town.

The advance and subsequent withdrawal of the twenty T34's slowed the German northward advance, setting up a perfect target for the antitank guns north of Kolosovo. This antitank-gun ambush, insufficient in itself to hurt the German division seriously, diverted the attention of the Germans while the Russian tank brigade struck a punishing blow against the German flank and rear. The three phases of the Russian tactical plan—the feint, the ambush, and the strike of the tank brigade—were perfectly coordinated. On the other hand, if the German air and ground reconnaissance had operated effectively, the panzer division commander would have been warned of the Russian intentions in time.

During the actions which took place south of the Resseta River, the Russians revealed their skill in adapting armored tactics to different types of terrain. Despite numerical inferiority they were able to inflict severe losses and delay the German advance.

In contrast to the engagements that were fought during the winter of 1941–42, Russian tanks appeared in brigade formation in the early months of 1942. The majority of these newly formed units were composed of T34's, occasionally interspersed with a few light tanks and some 52-ton KV's. The armored brigades had no organic infantry, artillery, or antitank units. In most instances they were employed to penetrate the German MLR, to widen the gap, and to achieve a breakthrough in depth. Rifle brigades or divisions were usually coupled with the armored brigades, either during the first phase of the attack—when the infantrymen rode into battle mounted on tanks—or after a penetration had been achieved to widen the gap and secure the flanks. For the latter purpose the Russians employed both foot and motorized infantry. Even on foot Russian infantrymen often kept pace with the advancing armor and proved capable of consolidating and holding the territory gained by the tanks.

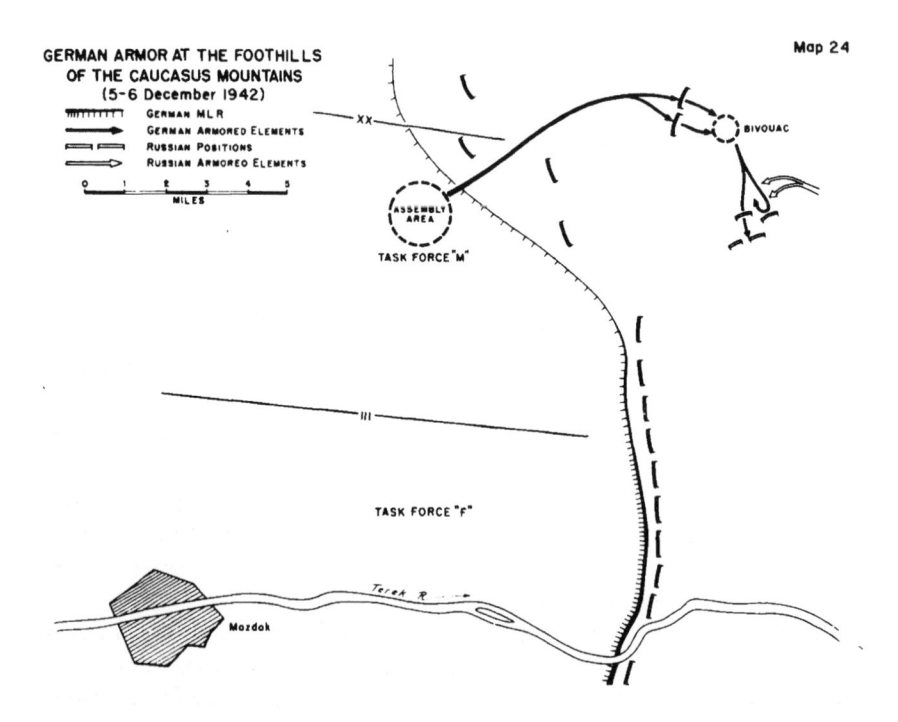

Map 24. German Armor at the Foothills of the Caucasus Mountains (5–6 December 1942)

SMALL UNIT ACTIONS

X. Ambush Without Followup (December 1942)

In December 1942, when the Germans were putting up a desperate struggle in the Stalingrad pocket, their drive into the Caucasus had been stopped about 300 miles from the Baku oil fields. The German 3d Panzer Division was in the area northeast of Mozdok covering the left flank of the First Panzer Army, which had gone over to the defensive. In front of the division's right wing a continuous line of defense had been formed which dwindled to a mere security line as it ran northward toward the division boundary (map 24). The Russian forces north of the Terek River were steadily receiving reinforcements and their reconnaissance patrols constantly probed the weaker sectors of the division front. Between the division and Stalingrad, 250 miles to the north, there was only a German armored infantry division and "Group Velmy," a motley unit composed of non-German volunteers.

The steppe in this area was devoid of vegetation and habitation, the monotony of the desertlike terrain being relieved only by small hills.

At noon on 4 December the division was ordered to attack the Russian forces to its left while continuing to provide flank protection for the army's left. The attack was set for the next day.

Carrying out simultaneous holding and attack operations presented a serious problem, in that the division was understrength and had sufficient gasoline for an operational radius of only 100 miles.

The division commander divided his forces into two groups: Task Force M was to mount the attack and Task Force F was to hold. The attack force, under one of the regimental commanders, comprised two tank companies, one infantry company mounted in armored personnel carriers, two armored reconnaissance platoons, and one battery of self-propelled 105–mm. howitzers.

On 5 December Task Force M moved out. After a slow march of about 7 miles over difficult terrain, it encountered stiff resistance from dug-in Russian infantry. About 3 hours later the Russian defenses were finally overcome, but further movement that day was rendered impractical by the approach of darkness. Just before nightfall German air reconnaissance reported Russians in unknown strength about 3 miles southeast of the site selected for the bivouac. To the east and northeast, however, no enemy forces were reported.

Early on the morning of the 6th the task force fanned out in two columns toward the reported enemy concentration. The tank companies formed the left column; the armored infantry company, somewhat weakened by the previous day's engagement, the right. Some

Map 25

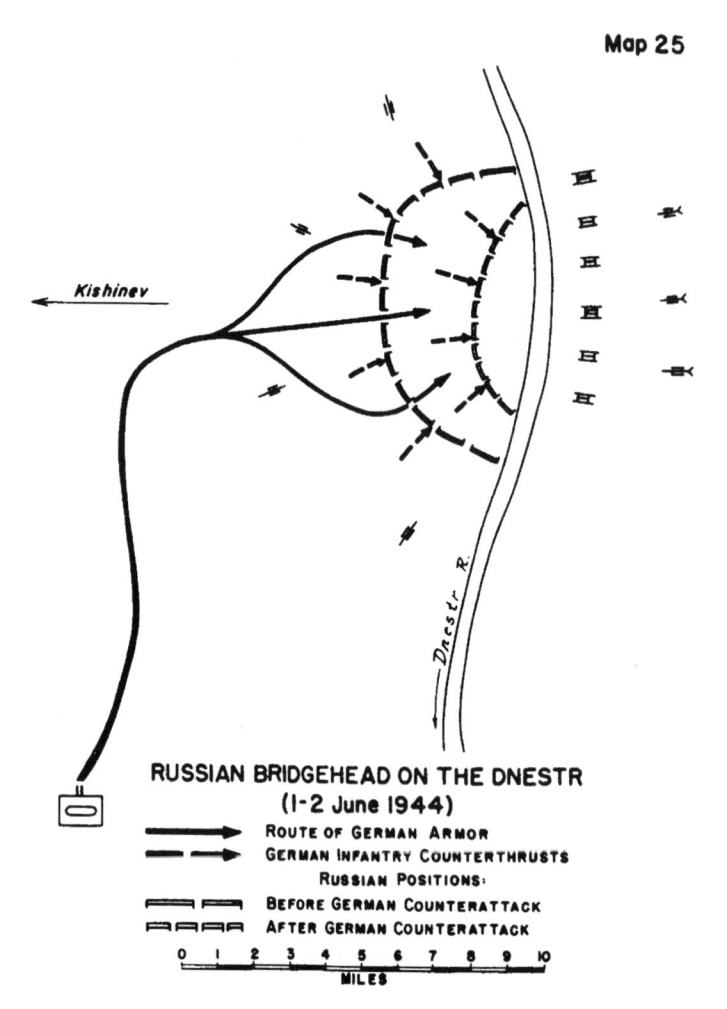

**RUSSIAN BRIDGEHEAD ON THE DNESTR
(1-2 June 1944)**

→ ROUTE OF GERMAN ARMOR
⇢ GERMAN INFANTRY COUNTERTHRUSTS
RUSSIAN POSITIONS:
▭▭▭ BEFORE GERMAN COUNTERATTACK
▭▭▭ AFTER GERMAN COUNTERATTACK

0 1 2 3 4 5 6 7 8 9 10
MILES

infantrymen were assigned to protect the artillery battery that covered the advance.

After an advance of about 1 mile the German columns ran into Russian infantry, which was well supported by mortars and antitank guns. As the Russian infantry engaged the task force frontally, 15 Russian tanks suddenly emerged from a hollow and fired point blank on the flank of the German left column. One of the two German tank company commanders was killed and two tanks were knocked out. It was only by virtue of the fact that the Russians did not attempt to pursue their advantage that the task force was able to disengage.

Here was an instance where the Russians skillfully withheld their tanks until the German armor was pinned down by frontal fire. The task force was not strong enough to be deployed in depth. Had it been, an attack could have been mounted against the Russian flank.

The Germans failed to perform ground reconnaissance and to secure their flanks during the advance.

XI. Tanks Fail to Eliminate a Bridgehead (June 1944)

This action, which occurred in 1944, shows that the principles laid down by Fedorenko had taken root and were being put into practice. It was symptomatic of the progressive improvement in Russian methods of employing armor.

At the end of May 1944, following a series of retrograde movements, the German front in the Kishinev area ran along the west bank of the Dnestr River. The characteristic terrain features in that area are the low hills and patches of forest. The east bank of the Dnestr overlooked German defenses (map 25).

Anticipating an early resumption of the Russian offensive, the German corps commander organized a task force of 40 tanks and armored infantry with personnel carriers and held it in reserve at a centrally located point about 10 miles from the river. Assembly areas for a counterattack and approach routes to the river line were carefully reconnoitered and extra fuel was loaded onto all vehicles.

At 2200 on 1 June the Russians attacked in force across the river and quickly established a bridgehead 3 to 5 miles deep and about 7 miles wide. The German task force was immediately alerted to counterattack at dawn in conjunction with the infantry that had been pushed back from the river line.

The German counterblow began with an artillery preparation. At first the tanks encountered heavy fire from Russian antitank guns, but, once these were neutralized, the German counterattack made good progress, and the Russian infantry was routed from its unfinished field fortifications along the bridgehead perimeter.

The task force did not encounter any tanks within the bridgehead because the Russians had not had opportunity to put them across the river. However, as soon as the Russian tank commander was informed of the German counterattack, he moved his armor out of the staging area where it had been awaiting the signal to cross. The tanks then drove onto the higher ground overlooking the river and supported the Russian artillery that was deployed along the bank. While the artillery fired on the advancing German infantry, the tanks were employed as roving antitank guns in the absence of tank destroyers.

Without the protection of a dense smoke screen and strong artillery and fighter-bomber support, the German task force was unable to eliminate the bridgehead. No chemical ammunition was available, and the ground-support aircraft, even though it did knock out a few Russian tanks at the beginning of the engagement, had to withdraw soon afterward when Russian antiaircraft fire over the bridgehead area grew more intensive. The German counterattack finally bogged down about 2,500 yards short of the river bank, having reduced but not eliminated the Russian bridgehead.

Had the counterattack taken place before daylight, the German task force might have reached its objective. This could only have been achieved by launching a night attack immediately after the first enemy crossings, while most of the Russian forces were still astride the river. Although the task force was assembled only 10 miles from the river, it had to drive 19 miles over winding roads to reach the crossing site. In an ideal situation the task force would have been just far enough from the river to be out of effective artillery range, and yet near enough to be within immediate striking distance of any potential landing site. It should be pointed out, however, that by 1944 tanks were so scarce in the German Army that relatively small armored units had to act as reserves along overextended frontages. In this instance shortages forced the Germans to abandon established tactical principles and, as a result, they suffered the consequences.

XII. An Armored Task Force Seizes Two Vital Bridges (August 1944)

In those isolated instances in which German armored units were at full strength, they were still able to attain local successes, even in the summer of 1944. During the nights of 13 and 14 August 1944 the 3d Panzer Division detrained at Kielce in southern Poland. The division's mission was to stop the advance of Russian forces that had broken through the German lines during the collapse of Army Group Center and to assist the withdrawing German formations in building up a new defense line near the upper Vistula.

In order to allow all units of his division the time needed to prepare for their next commitment and at the same time secure his route of advance, the division commander decided to form an armored task force from the units that had detrained first. The force was to be led by the commander of the 2d Tank Battalion and was to consist of Tank Companies E and F, equipped with Panther tanks, one armored infantry company mounted in armored personnel carriers, and one battery equipped with self-propelled 105-mm. howitzers. The task force was to launch a surprise attack on Village Z,

SMALL UNIT ACTIONS

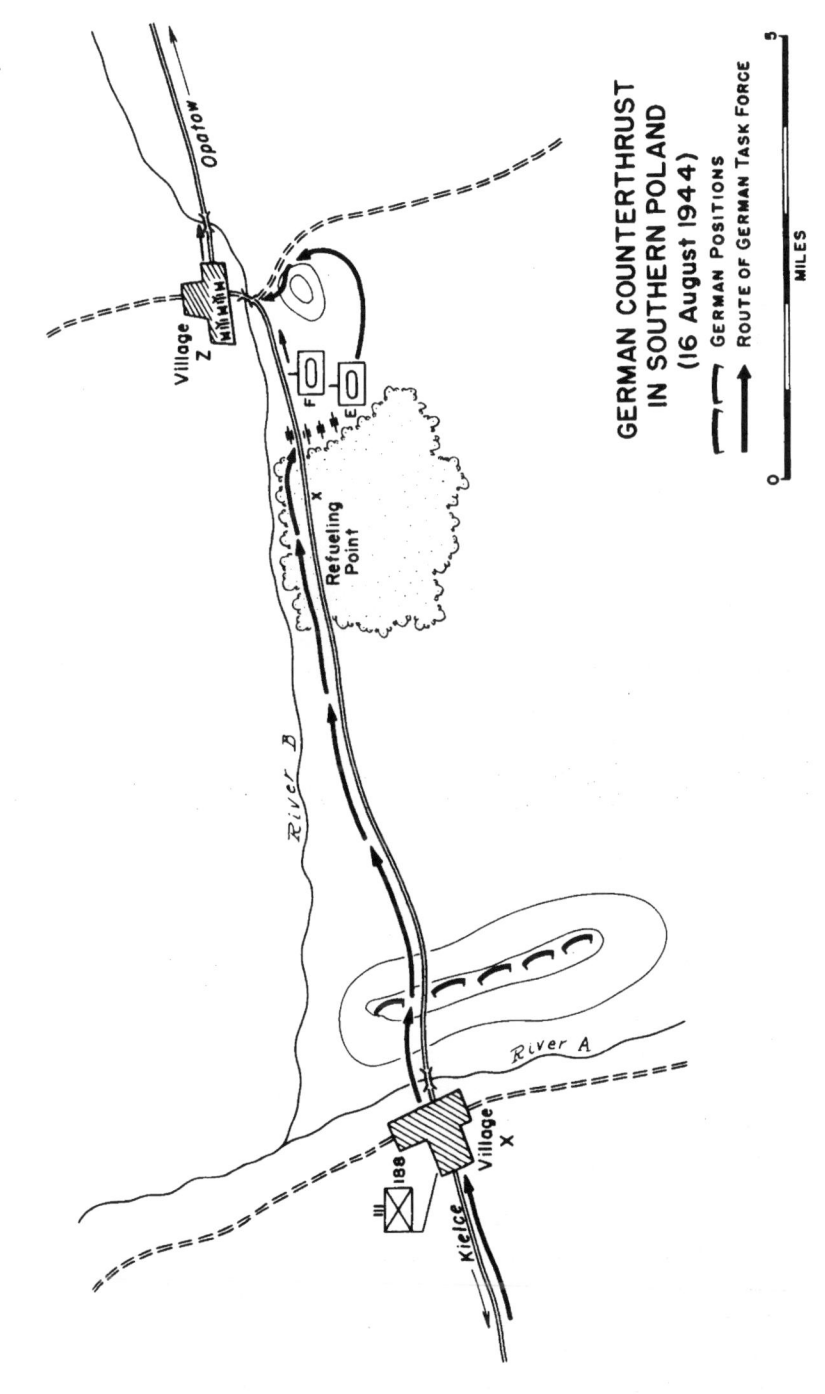

Map 26

GERMAN COUNTERTHRUST
IN SOUTHERN POLAND
(16 August 1944)

⌒⌒⌒ GERMAN POSITIONS
➔ ROUTE OF GERMAN TASK FORCE

0 ————— 5 MILES

situated approximately 30 miles east of Kielce, and seize the bridges south and east of the village in order to permit the main body of the division to advance along the Kielce-Opatow road toward the Vistula (map 26).

The attack was to be launched at dawn on 16 August. According to air reconnaissance information obtained at 1800 on 15 August, Village Z was held by relatively weak Russian forces and no major troop movements were observed in the area. The only German unit stationed in the area between Kielce and Village Z was the 188th Infantry Regiment, which occupied the high ground east of River A and whose command post was in Village X.

The terrain was hilly. Fields planted with grain, potatoes, and beets were interspersed with patches of forest. The weather was sunny and dry, with high daytime temperatures and cool moonlit nights. The hours of sunrise and sunset were 0445 and 1930, respectively.

The task force commander received his orders at 2000 on 15 August and immediately began to study the plan of attack. Since the units that were to participate in the operation had not yet been alerted, the entire task force could not possibly be ready to move out before 2300. The maximum speed at which his force could drive over a dusty dirt road without headlights was 6 miles an hour. The approach march to Village Z would therefore require a minimum of 5 hours. Taking into account the time needed for refueling and deploying his units, the commander arrived at the conclusion that the attack could not be launched before dawn. Since the operation might thus be deprived of the element of surprise, he decided to employ an advance guard that was to move out one hour earlier than the bulk of his force, reach Village X by 0200 at the latest, and cover the remaining 9 miles in 1½ hours. After a short halt the advance guard could launch the attack on Village Z just before dawn.

At 2020 the task force commander assembled the commanders of the participating units at his CP and issued the following verbal orders:

> Company F, 6th Tank Regiment, reinforced by one platoon of armored infantry, will form an advance guard that will be ready to move out at 2200 in order to seize Village Z and the two bridges across River B by a *coup de main*. A reconnaissance detachment will guide the advance guard to Village X. Two trucks loaded with gasoline will be taken along for refueling, which is scheduled to take place in the woods two miles west of Village Z.
>
> The main body of the task force will follow the advance guard at 2300 and form a march column in the following order: 2d Tank

Battalion Headquarters, Company E of the 6th Tank Regiment, Battery A of the 75th Artillery Regiment, and Company A of the 3d Armored Infantry Regiment (less one platoon). After crossing River A, the tank company will take the lead, followed by battalion headquarters, the armored infantry company, and the artillery battery in that order.

The task force will halt and refuel in the woods 2 miles west of Village Z. Radio silence will be lifted after River A has been crossed.

The commander of Company F will leave at 2100 and accompany me to the CP of the 188th Infantry Regiment and establish contact with that unit. Company E's commander will take charge of the march column from Kielce to Village X.

Upon receiving these instructions the commander of Company F, Lieutenant Zobel, returned to his unit, assembled the platoon leaders, the first sergeant, and the maintenance section chief and briefed them. He indicated the march route, which they entered on their maps. For the march from Kielce to Village X, the headquarters section was to drive at the head of the column, followed by the four tank platoons, the armored infantry platoon, the gasoline trucks, and the mess and maintenance sections. The ranking platoon leader was to be in charge of the column until Zobel joined it in Village X. Hot coffee was to be served half an hour before the time of departure, which was scheduled for 2200. The reconnaissance detachment was to move out at 2130 and post guides along the road to Village X.

After issuing these instructions to his subordinates, Zobel rejoined the task force commander, with whom he drove to Village X. When they arrived at the CP of the 188th Infantry Regiment, they were given detailed information on the situation. They learned that, after heavy fighting in the Opatow region, the regiment had withdrawn to its present positions during the night of 14–15 August. Attempts to establish a continuous line in conjunction with other units withdrawing westward from the upper Vistula were under way. The Russians had so far not advanced beyond Village Z. Two Polish civilians who had been seized in the woods west of the village had stated that no Russians were to be seen in that forest.

The task force commander thereupon ordered Zobel to carry out the plan of attack as instructed. Zobel awaited the arrival of the advance guard at the western outskirts of Village X. When the column pulled in at 0145, Zobel assumed command and re-formed the march column with the 1st Tank Platoon in the lead, followed by the headquarters section, the 2d and 3d Tank Platoons, the armored infantry platoon, the wheeled elements, and the 4th Tank Platoon.

A guide from the 188th Infantry Regiment rode on the lead tank of the 1st Platoon until it reached the outpost area beyond River A. The column arrived at the German outpost at 0230. The sentry reported that he had not observed any Russian movements during the night. Zobel radioed the task force commander that he was going into action.

To permit better observation the tanks drove with open hatches. The tank commanders stood erect with their heads emerging from the cupolas, listening with a headset. The other apertures of the tanks were buttoned up. Gunners and loaders stood by to open fire at a moment's notice. In anticipation of an encounter with Russian tanks the guns were loaded with armor-piercing shells.

At 0345 the advance guard reached the wooded area in which it was to halt and refuel. The tanks formed two rows, one on each side of the road, while armored infantrymen provided security to the east and west of the halted column. Sentries were posted at 50-yard intervals in the forest north and south of the road. Trucks loaded with gasoline cans drove along the road between the two rows of tanks, stopping at each pair of tanks to unload the full cans and picking up the empties on their return trip. The loaders helped the drivers to refuel and check their vehicles. The gunners checked their weapons, while each radio operator drew coffee for his tank crew. Zobel gave the platoon leaders and tank commanders a last briefing and asked one of the returning truck drivers to hand-carry a message on the progress of the operation to the task force commander in Village X.

According to Zobel's plan of assault, the advance guard was to emerge from the woods in two columns. The one on the left was to comprise the 1st Tank Platoon, headquarters section, and the 4th Tank Platoon, whereas the right column was to be composed of the 2d and 3d Tank Platoons and the armored infantry platoon. The 1st Platoon was to take up positions opposite the southern edge of Village Z, the 2d at the foot of the hill to the south of it. Under the protection of these two platoons the 3d and 4th Platoons were to seize the south bridge in conjunction with the armored infantry platoon, drive through the village, and capture the second bridge located about half a mile east of the village. The 2d Platoon was to follow across the south bridge, drive through the village, and block the road leading northward. The 1st Platoon was to follow and secure the south bridge. The tanks were not to open fire until they encountered enemy resistance.

Zobel did not send out any reconnaissance detachments because he did not want to attract the attention of the Russians. In drawing up his plan Zobel kept in mind that the success of the operation would depend on proper timing and on the skill and resourcefulness of his platoon commanders. Because of the swiftness with which the raid was to take place, he would have little opportunity to influence the course of events once the attack was under way.

At 0430, when the first tanks moved out of the woods, it was almost daylight and the visibility was approximately 1,000 yards. As the 1st and 2d Platoons were driving down the road toward Village Z, they were suddenly taken under flanking fire by Russian tanks and antitank guns. Three German tanks were immediately disabled, one of them catching fire. Zobel ordered the two platoons to withdraw.

Since the element of surprise no longer existed and the advance guard had lost three of its tanks, Zobel abandoned his plan of attack and decided to await the arrival of the main body of the task force. He reported the failure of the operation by radio, and at 0515 his units were joined by the main force. After Zobel had made a report in person, the task force commander decided to attack Village Z before the Russian garrison could receive reinforcements. This time the attack was to be launched from the south under the protection of artillery fire.

The plan called for Zobel's company to conduct a feint attack along the same route it had previously taken and to fire on targets of opportunity across the river. Meanwhile Company E and the armored infantry company were to drive southward, skirt the hill, and approach Village Z from the south. While the 3d and 4th Platoons of Company E, the armored infantry company, and Company F were to concentrate their fire on the southern edge of the village, the 1st and 2d Platoons of Company E were to thrust across the south bridge, drive into the village, turn east at the market square, and capture the east bridge. As soon as the first two platoons had driven across the bridge, the other tanks of Company E were to close up and push on to the northern edge of the village. The armored infantry vehicles were to follow across the south bridge and support the 1st and 2d Platoons in their efforts to seize the east bridge. Company F was to annihilate any Russian forces that might continue to offer resistance at the southern edge of the village. The artillery battery was to go into position at the edge of the woods and support the tanks.

No more than two tank platoons could be employed for the initial thrust because the south bridge could support only one tank at a time. All the remaining fire power of the task force would be needed to lay down a curtain of fire along the entire southern edge of the village. This was the most effective means of neutralizing the enemy defense during the critical period when the two tank platoons were driving toward the bridge. To facilitate the approach of the tanks to the bridge, the artillery battery was to lay down a smoke screen south of the village along the river line. Having once entered the village, the two lead platoons were not to let themselves be diverted from their objective, the east bridge. The elimination of enemy resistance was to be left to the follow-up elements. The attack was to start at 0600.

The tanks of Company E refueled quickly in the woods, and the battery went into position. The task force was ready for action.

Company F jumped off at 0600. The task force commander and an artillery observer were with the company. The battery gave fire support against pinpoint targets. At 0610 the tanks of Company E emerged from the woods in columns of two, formed a wedge, turned southward, and made a wide circle around the hill. The vehicles of the armored infantry company followed at close distance. As the tanks and armored personnel carriers approached the hill from the south, they were suddenly taken under Russian machinegun and antitank rifle fire from the top of the hill. The commander of Company E slowed down and asked for instructions. The task force commander radioed instructions to engage only those Russians on the hill who obstructed the continuation of the attack. The tanks of Company E thereupon deployed and advanced on a broad front, thus offering protection to the personnel carriers which were vulnerable to antitank grenades. Soon afterward Company E reported that it had neutralized the Russian infantry on the hill and was ready to launch the assault. The task force commander thereupon gave the signal for firing the artillery concentration on the southern edge of the village. Three minutes later the 1st and 2d Platoons drove toward the bridge and crossed it in single file, while Company F's tanks approached the crossing site from the west.

As soon as the last tank of the 1st and 2d Platoons had crossed the bridge, the other two platoons of Company E and the armored personnel carriers closed up at top speed. The two lead platoons drove through the village and captured the east bridge without encountering any resistance. The 3d and 4th Platoons overran the Russian infantry troops trying to escape northward and knocked out two retreating Russian tanks at the northern edge of the village. Soon afterward all units reported that they had accomplished their missions.

The task force commander then organized the defense of Village Z, which he was to hold until the arrival of the main body of the 3d Panzer Division. Two tank platoons blocked the road leading northward, two protected the east bridge, two armored infantry platoons set up outposts in the forest east of River B, and the remaining units constituted a reserve force within the village. The artillery battery took up positions on the south bank of the river close to the south bridge. Its guns were zeroed in on the northern and eastern approach roads to the village.

In this action the task force commander made the mistake of ordering Zobel's advance guard to halt and refuel in the woods 2 miles west of Village Z. In issuing this order he applied the principle that tanks going into combat must carry sufficient fuel to assure their mobility throughout a day's fighting. Although this principle is valid in general, it should have been disregarded in this particular instance. Since the element of surprise was of decisive importance for the success of the operation, everything should have been subordinated to catching the Russians unprepared. If necessary, the advance guard should have refueled as far as back as Village X or shortly after crossing River A. Since the woods actually used for the refueling halt was only 2 miles from Village Z, the German commander should have foreseen that the noise of starting the tank engines would warn the Russian outposts who happened to be on the hill south of the village. A surprise attack must be planned so carefully that no such risk of premature discovery is taken.

Moreover, the task force commander should not have stayed behind in Village X, but should have led the advance guard in person. By staying up with the lead elements, he would have been able to exercise better control over both the advance guard and the main body of his force.

The attack by the fully assembled task force was properly planned and its execution met with the expected quick success.

XIII. Tank Battle Near the Berlin Highway (March 1945)

By the beginning of 1945 Russian tactics governing major armored formations had improved considerably; however, even in the last few months of the war the general standard of training was only mediocre. This was hardly surprising considering the heavy losses suffered during the preceding years. Some individual units did, however, give superior performances. In this connection it may be well to remember that the sweeping successes achieved by the Russians during the later stages of the campaign gave their troops so much added impetus that the still-existing training deficiencies had little effect on the net result. An equally important factor was the steady decline of German combat efficiency.

In March 1945 the Russians concentrated strong forces on both sides of the Oder River north and south of Kuestrin, which was still in German hands. From Kuestrin the main highway leads west to

TWO GERMAN TIGER TANKS meet near a forest, 1944.

SMALL UNIT ACTIONS

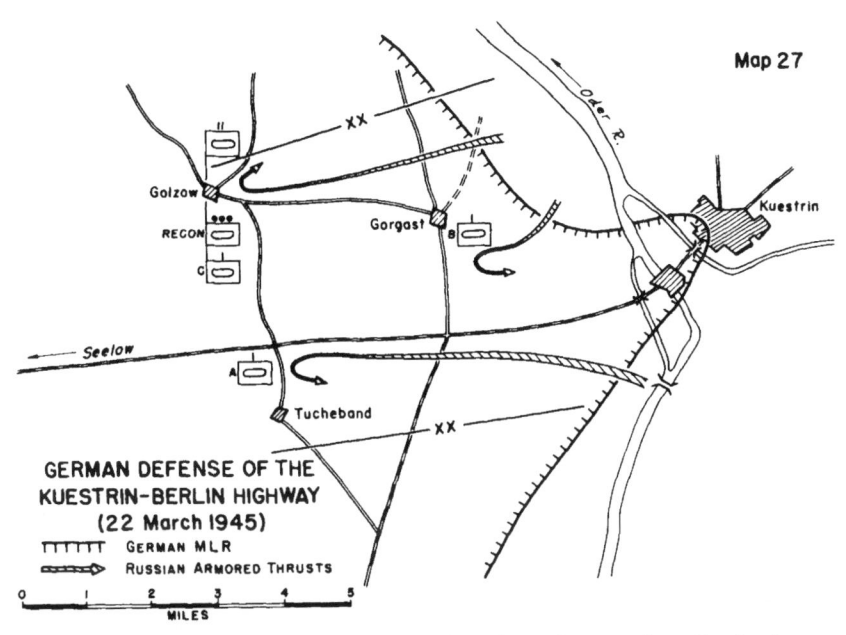

GERMAN DEFENSE OF THE KUESTRIN-BERLIN HIGHWAY (22 March 1945)

TTTTT GERMAN MLR
⇨ RUSSIAN ARMORED THRUSTS

0 1 2 3 4 5 MILES

Map 27

Berlin via Seelow. To prevent the Russians from using the highway as an axis of advance toward their capital, the Germans brought up an improvised panzer division and placed it astride the traffic artery. The total number of tanks then possessed by this formation was 55, a figure far below the tank strength of a regular panzer division.

The division's only tank battalion was held in reserve behind the MLR to counter any enemy armored thrust. This battalion comprised battalion headquarters, the reconnaissance platoon of which had 5 Panther tanks; Company A, which had 22 Panthers; and Companies B and C, which had 14 Tiger tanks each.

The level terrain in the division's sector presented no obstacle to tank movement. Company A, on the battalion's right wing, blocked the Kuestrin-Seelow highway near Tucheband; Company B was in the center southeast of Gorgast; and Company C, together with the reconnaissance platoon and the battalion staff, was in Golzow (map 27).

At 0600 on 22 March, Russian tanks and infantry attacked the division front under the cover of a 90-minute barrage. The Russian infantry was pinned down by the German defensive fire, but the tanks broke through the German positions and drove toward the highway from three directions. The main attack force, consisting of approximately 50 Russian tanks, advanced south of the Berlin highway and ran head-on into Company A's tanks, which were deployed north of Tucheband. After a short, but costly engagement the Russian tanks were forced to withdraw. The second attack force, of almost equal strength, jumped off from the bridgehead west of Kuestrin and started to bypass Gorgast to the south. Just before the lead tanks reached the road connecting Gorgast with the Berlin highway, they were intercepted by Company B. The German tanks launched a flank attack which disorganized the Russian force and compelled it to pull back after heavy losses.

The northern prong of the Russian drive was meanwhile advancing straight across the fields toward Golzow, where the German battalion had its CP and which was held by Company C and the reconnaissance platoon. Although he had been informed of the Russian attack, the battalion commander stayed in Golzow instead of dispersing his forces in the immediate vicinity. This mistake was to lead to a critical situation.

Heavy Russian artillery fire prevented the German tanks from assembling in Golzow before pulling out. The general confusion among the Germans grew even worse when the Russian artillery laid a dense smoke screen across the eastern edge of the village. When the German battalion commander finally succeeded in assembling most of his tanks, he suddenly found himself face to face with a column of Russian tanks emerging from the smoke. In the ensuing battle the Germans were able to extricate themselves and stop the Russian advance, but solely because of the better maneuverability of their tanks and their superiority in close-range tank combat.

The Russians finally broke off the engagement and withdrew, leaving 60 tanks on the field of battle. Their failure to achieve a breakthrough in any of the three thrusts may be attributed to the infantry's inability to follow up and support the advance of the armor. In any event, the right-wing attack force should have bypassed Golzow and turned south in the direction of the Berlin highway instead of entering the smoke-filled town.

The German battalion commander had disposed his relatively weak armored forces as well as the situation and open terrain would permit. Anticipating correctly the direction eventually taken by the Russian left and center attack forces, he employed two companies to block their route of advance and deny them access to the Berlin highway. He kept the third company in reserve, ready to lend assistance to Companies A and B and to seal off an enemy penetration. His only mistake was in permitting his reserve force to stay in Golzow, instead of deploying it outside the village, as were the other two companies.

Chapter 3

Engineers

I. General

Engineer units are organized and trained for specific technical combat missions that fall primarily under the headings of construction, obstruction, and destruction. To commit engineer troops as infantry is usually a mistake because they will thus be engaged in tasks for which they are not intended and will not be available for the specialized duties for which they have been trained. The highly specialized training given engineers justifies their conservation for those missions which are within the scope of their functional duty.

The Germans failed to observe this principle in many instances. Particularly at the beginning of the Russian campaign, there were frequent minor infractions of standing operating procedures. Hitler and his military advisers had estimated that the campaign could be concluded in a short time; hence, delays had to be avoided at all costs. This may explain why one corps commander sent an engineer battalion ahead of his infantry and armored units and assigned it the mission of constructing a bridge at a certain point before the far bank of the river had been secured. The dangers inherent in such an improvisation are illustrated by the following example.

II. A River Crossing That Almost Failed (July 1941)

On 6 July 1941—15 days after the start of the invasion—the Fourth Panzer Group (later redesignated Fourth Panzer Army) was moving eastward along the south bank of the upper Dvina River, before launching an enveloping attack on Vitebsk. In this attack, army formed the northern wing of the forces fighting for the so-called Gateway of Smolensk—the vital land corridor that is the divide between the upper Dvina and Dnepr Rivers and that leads straight to Moscow. Constituting part of the army's northern wing, the LVII Panzer Corps was to cross the Dvina at Ulla, midway between Polotsk and Vitebsk, and capture Gorodok, north of Vitebsk (map 28).

After their defeats at Bialystok and Minsk, where they had suffered exceptionally heavy losses in manpower and materiel, the Russians streamed eastward, conducting delaying actions in the course of which they carried out demolitions of every description. Almost all of the bridges in the wake of their withdrawal were blown. That the Russian movements in this area resembled a rout was substantiated by statements of prisoners, the discovery of huge quantities of abandoned materiel, and such desperate measures as the burning of villages that were still far out of German reach. The movements of the advancing Germans were substantially impeded by local counterattacks from ambush, which usually took place at night.

German air reconnaissance failed to spot any organized movements of large Russian units in the path of the LVII Panzer Corps. The aerial observers, however, did report that the vital bridges that had spanned the Dvina at Ulla, Beshenkovichi, and Vitebsk had been destroyed. Aerial photographs did not disclose the existence of any field fortifications along the Ulla or the Dvina.

The Russian Air Force limited its activities to isolated bombing attacks, which rarely penetrated more than 25 miles beyond the German forward elements.

Northeast of the mountain range that stretches across the Vilna-Minsk area, the terrain on the banks of both the Berezina and the Dvina was very marshy and intersticed by lakes and brooks. In general the terrain was open and afforded an extensive view even from slight elevations. Patches of birch and alder trees stood so densely along the brooks and streams, however, that they formed veritable screens. Grain and other crops stood high and were ready for harvesting. Typical midsummer weather with its characteristically short nights prevailed.

Many Russian stragglers had discarded their uniforms and put on civilian clothes. Under local leadership they formed the nucleus of the partisan bands that later were to appear everywhere. Even at this early stage, they made their presence felt by terrorizing the populace, disrupting German supply lines, and transmitting information concerning German troop movements.

The road net was in poor condition and at many points proved incapable of sustaining the heavy traffic load of the LVII Panzer Corps in its march toward the Dvina. Parts of the road from Lepel to Ulla via Bocheykovo were paved and had only recently undergone extensive repairs but, because of the narrow and unpaved secondary roads that connected the limited number of improved sections of the road, the columns of the 7th Panzer and 22d Motorized Infantry Divisions were strung out far beyond their normal march length and, in many instances, became badly entangled. Many of the vehicles were subjected to severe strain. The division commanders therefore welcomed the enforced delay while a bridge was being constructed

GERMAN ADVANCE through Ukrainian wheat field during attack on Stalin Line, July 1941.

across the Dvina since the respite would enable them to close up, reorganize their march columns, and overhaul the vehicles.

The panzer corps commander decided to assign the 1st Engineer School Battalion to the task of constructing the bridge across the Dvina, an operation which appeared to be a simple matter technically. The organic engineer battalions could thus remain with their divisions and prepare for the resumption of the advance by reorganizing their elements and replenishing their supplies.

The 1st Engineer School Battalion was composed of a motorized signal platoon, three motorized engineer companies, and one motorized light equipment column. Ever since the start of the Russian campaign one motorized engineer assault boat company with 35 assault boats and their operating crews had been attached to the battalion. The bridging equipment available to the corps consisted of a ponton trestle bridge, composed of six bridge columns, which was the standard type used by the German Army. The bridge columns were GHQ units that the corps commander could concentrate at points of main effort.

When Lieutenant Colonel Graf, the battalion commander, reported to corps headquarters at 0900 on 7 July, he was handed orders defining his mission that read as follows:

Elements of the 1st Engineer School Battalion will cross the river during the afternoon of 7 July. On the basis of information obtained by daytime reconnaissance, the battalion will throw a bridge across the Dvina at Ulla the following night and cover the operation with its own security forces. For this purpose all of the GHQ bridge columns will be attached to the battalion. Engineer battalion and bridge columns will have traffic priority on the roads leading to Ulla. Reports on the progress of the operation will be sent by motorcycle messenger. In case of emergency, radio may be used until wire lines have been strung as far as Ulla. Bridge construction must be completed by dawn (0300) on 8 July.

These plans and orders had been based on the premise that the German forces were dealing with a weak and utterly disorganized enemy.

In preparing to carry out his mission, Graf was faced with difficult problems from the very outset. First of all, he had to extract his companies from the 7th Panzer Division's march columns and move them to a point about 3 miles south of Ulla. Separate orders had to be issued for the approach march of the bridge columns. Once these movements were in progress, he deputized his executive officer to direct the assembly and concentration of the battalion. Meanwhile Graf, accompanied by another officer and several men, set out in a staff car to reconnoiter the crossing site. Before long the reconnaissance party was aware that the approach route was infested with Russian stragglers. Upon reaching the river, the party was harassed by small-arms fire from every direction, including the far bank of the river. Before noon, nevertheless, Graf was able to survey the Dvina near Ulla from several vantage points and, about half an hour later, transmitted the following report to corps headquarters:

1. Individual stragglers are scattered throughout the swampy terrain in the vicinity of Ulla, which is difficult to penetrate and survey. The far bank of the river also appears to be infested with snipers.

2. The highway bridge across the Dvina—a three-arch span supported by two massive columns—is demolished in such a way that the roughly 150-foot-long center arch has been severed from the southern 15-foot-high support column. This column is intact and can be used to support an emergency bridge. No substantial stores of lumber can be found anywhere.

3. About 500 yards northwest of the bridge is the former ferry site, which has a paved approach road that can accommodate tanks. An exit road of unknown condition was observed on the other shore. Spurs of sand protrude approximately 50 feet from each shore. This site would be ideal for constructing the bridge.

4. Both river banks rise rather sharply some 20 yards from the river line. The bank of departure is 15 to 20 feet high and negotiable only where the approach road terminates. The far bank is considerably higher and covered with vegetation; it offers excellent natural cover and, at the same time, a good observation point. On the near side where there is little vegetation, the buildings in Ulla offer the sole cover for our movements.

5. Roughly estimated, the river is 500 feet wide. The current is slow. In the quite shallow water close to the near bank, water plants grow in abundance.

The contents of this report did not lead to any modification in the river crossing plan, and the suggested bridge site was approved.

As he returned from his reconnaissance mission, Graf encountered Company A, which had posted guards on all sides while halting midway between Bocheykovo and Ulla. The rest of the battalion, including the assault boat company, was still on the other side of Bocheykovo. Graf ordered the assault boat company to move up to Company A bivouac area. Incoming radio messages indicated that the bridge columns were hampered in their march movement, and corps headquarters was therefore requested to take the necessary steps to clear the route of advance, particularly within inhabited localities, by strict enforcement of traffic control regulations. The bridge columns were ordered to expedite their movement to the battalion advance message center, about three miles north of Bocheykovo, and to await further orders there.

At 1430, upon returning to Company A, Graf ordered that unit to clear the approach route and occupy Ulla. An advance party, consisting of two armored cars previously attached to the battalion, led the company into the town. Within an hour Ulla was fully occupied, and the rest of the battalion, with the assault-boat company, had closed up to the outskirts of the town. Russian reconnaissance aircraft were flying over the area at medium altitudes. Whenever German troops became careless, they drew immediate small-arms fire from the far shore. Most of the inhabitants had fled Ulla, and no useful information could be obtained from the few remaining sick and aged people.

When the first two bridge columns were approaching, Graf ordered Company A to cross the river in the assault boats and establish a small bridgehead in order to provide a security screen around the bridge site. The company was to reconnoiter the exit road, mark the approaches, and probe the river's depth near the spur of land.

To provide for all contingencies, the two armored cars, as well as the machine gun and mortar platoons of Companies B and C, were to act as a covering force along the river bank. Company B was to assist in moving up two of the bridge columns with trestle equipment so that the shore connection, which is always the most difficult part of bridge construction, could be built on the bank of departure before nightfall. Company C was to assemble a ponton which, towed by the assault boats, was to ferry the trestle equipment for the far shore connection to Company A. After this was accomplished, Company C was to stand by to assemble additional pontons and float them into place.

In the face of sporadic small arms fire, Company A crossed to the far shore between 1600 and 1630, flushed Russian snipers out of their hideouts, and occupied the high bank.

After making an air reconnaissance earlier in the day, the Russians sent over low-flying planes, singly and in group formation, to attack assembly areas, approach roads, and Ulla. Suddenly fire broke out in the town. This presented a grave danger, since the houses were built mostly of wood, peat, and straw. The destruction of Ulla left the Germans exposed to full observation. Moreover—and this was particularly inconvenient from an engineer's point of view—the only readily available construction lumber had gone up in smoke, and wood would have to be hauled over long distances. During the fire the

German covering forces on the outskirts of the town were threatened and could remain in place only because the northwest wind kept the flames away from the river. However, the town was impassable for several hours, a factor that delayed the arrival of the bridge columns.

Some of the bridge columns were unable to move up past the halted march columns of the panzer corps and, therefore, failed to arrive at the bridge site on schedule. Their presence by late afternoon was essential since, according to the bridging plan, at least four columns were needed and only two had thus far arrived. With darkness setting in and enemy interference becoming more active, the execution of the bridge construction plan would be jeopardized. For this reason Graf took the matter into his own hands and set out to make certain that at least two additional bridge columns were moved forward without delay.

Company B had meanwhile moved some trestle equipment and the trucks loaded with the ponton ferry sections through the town and to the river bank. Company A was carrying out its mission on the far shore when strong Russian infantry forces suddenly launched a surprise attack just as dusk settled over the area. Hard hand-to-hand fighting developed. The courageous Russian unit fought stubbornly, but was not supported by artillery or other arms. The German covering forces were driven back and would have been pushed into the river if reinforcements with flame throwers had not been dispatched across the river at the last moment. While this engagement continued to rage along the far bank, the German covering force on the near side was unable to intervene effectively because the contours of the terrain and the vegetation obstructed its field of fire. The situation became critical when Russian planes resumed their attacks on Ulla and the bridge site.

Only the employment of a special weapon, which had been experimentally introduced in this and other motorized engineer battalions, could finally bring relief to the hard-pressed Germans in the bridgehead. Each engineer battalion was equipped with two trucks, each mounting a simple wooden-frame rocket launcher that fired six 280-mm. HE rockets. A primitive sighting device was used, incorporating the principle of an ordinary carpenter's level. The two rocket-carrying trucks, with a supply of 12 rockets each, were driven through the burning town and quickly placed in position at the river edge, from where the projectiles were fired across the river. The sight and accompanying noise of the rockets in flight produced a telling effect upon the Russian troops. At 2200 the commander of Company A was finally able to report that the situation was well in hand.

CONSTRUCTION of a German ponton bridge, 1941.

After he had succeeded in setting the bridge columns in motion, Graf returned to Ulla about 2000, feeling very doubtful as to whether the mission of his battalion could be accomplished in time. At that early stage it was impossible to determine whether the Russian attack was merely a local action or the beginning of a major counterattack. It was clear, however, that the engineer troops engaged on the far side could not be employed for bridge construction as long as they served as combat forces, especially since no infantry units were immediately available to relieve them. Moreover, the 1⅓ engineer companies remaining on the shore of departure would be unable to complete the bridge construction in the short time allotted by corps.

Since the situation developed as suddenly as it did, there was no time to request infantry forces which could be moved across the river to relieve the engineers. At 2030 Graf described the situation to corps over the newly laid telephone line and requested the early arrival of engineer reinforcements. It was subsequently impossible to determine through what channels this request was passed and why engineer troops from the 22d Motorized Infantry or the 7th Panzer Divisions were not employed. The reason was probably to be found in road congestion and other march difficulties, since another march column, comprising elements of a motorized corps, was also being channeled through the same approach route. On orders from army, Company B of the 43d Motorized Engineer Assault Battalion, which was then approaching Bocheykovo, was detached from its parent unit, sent to Ulla, and ordered to assist in the bridge construction operation. The company arrived in Ulla at 2300, shortly after the situation in the bridgehead had been stabilized.

During all this time the Luftwaffe had failed to intervene or protect the crossing site. Late in the evening several German 20-mm. antiaircraft guns did arrive, but proved ineffective because their range was inadequate and they were not supported by searchlights.

While the engagement on the far shore was still in progress, Graf had already decided that, because of the manpower shortage, it would be most expedient to build the two shore connections first. A temporary shuttle service could then be established to ferry some of the heavy weapons across while the rest of the bridge was being completed. It was planned to have the pontons assembled and floated into place one by one. Technically, the bridge construction procedure was a simple one. However, because the river was so shallow, the pontons could not be set afloat any closer than 30 to 40 yards from the shore. This resulted in delay because every piece of equipment had to be carried into the river before assembly. The operation was rendered all the more difficult since the bridge had to be constructed in the dark and since the river bed contained numerous sudden depressions. The newly arrived company immediately began to assemble the 14 pontons, weighing 16 tons each, that were needed. This was a time-consuming job because only one approach road was available to the ponton-carrying vehicles and because Russian air attacks caused frequent interruptions. Each ponton was floated directly to its anchorage as soon as it was assembled. By 0630 on 8 July all of the pontons were in place, and at 0800 the bridge was opened to traffic, only 5 hours later than was originally planned.

The above action indicates that it is a tactical mistake to assign the mission of bridging a river to an engineer battalion without support of infantry units, no matter how favorable the situation may appear to be. In modern warfare situations change quickly, troops can move with lightning speed, and interference from the air can obstruct ground operations. Engineers who are to fulfill a technical mission cannot be expected to engage in infantry combat at the same time. The engineer troops must be protected by covering forces, including antitank and antiaircraft artillery. Such forces should be moved into position ahead of the engineers, even in situations where no enemy interference is expected.

As to the tactics employed by the bridgehead force, the following observations are appropriate: Contrary to all tactical doctrine, the bridgehead line was not secured by outposts. Reconnaissance and security should have been the immediate concern of the bridgehead commander, if only as elementary precautions. His neglect almost resulted in a serious German reverse.

A commander must control his impulses and conduct operations from a point close to the focus of battle. In this action Lieutenant Colonel Graf should have remained at his command post near Ulla and should have delegated authority to a subordinate who could have expedited the movement of the bridge columns. Thus he would have exercised proper control over his unit.

The difficulties encountered by Graf during his initial trip to Ulla through enemy-infested territory make it obvious that engineer battalions, at least those attached to motorized and armored units, must be provided with armored reconnaissance vehicles. Almost every combat action, especially in mechanized warfare, leads the engineer staff officer far ahead into unknown terrain and obscure situations where he needs the protection afforded by armored vehicles.

The ineffectiveness of the uncoordinated Russian counterattack demonstrated very clearly that nowadays an attack by infantry alone has little chance of success. An infantry attack, no matter how limited its objective may be, has to be supported by heavy weapons. It is hard to understand why the Russians failed to follow through with their counterattack, since they had not suffered serious losses. By exerting constant pressure on the bridgehead force, the Russians could have delayed the German river crossing.

III. The Hidden Bunker in the Stalin Line (July 1941)

In preparing for a river crossing the attacker must destroy all enemy outposts and capture the defender's fortified positions on the friendly bank. During the first month of the Russian campaign the Germans did not always have sufficient time to comb the area contiguous to a river before starting the crossing operation proper. While the advance of the two army groups in the north and center proceeded according to schedule, Army Group South made only slow progress. By mid-July 1941 two German infantry divisions, the 22d and 76th, stood on the west bank of the Dnestr River just below Mogilev Podolski, poised for a drive to the Black Sea. At 0430 on 17 July both divisions leaped to the attack and crossed the river at several places.

The initial assault was a complete success and quickly led to the occupation of the high ground on the east bank (map 29).

However, in their great haste the Germans bypassed some strong Russian fortifications that constituted the southernmost extremities of the so-called Stalin Line. One of these bunkers was located deep in an acacia grove where it nestled snug against a steep bluff within the 76th Infantry Division's attack zone. Neither air nor ground reconnaissance had revealed the existence of this position—its camouflage was excellent. Because of the heavy shroud of smoke that hung over the area, its guns had remained silent during the artillery preparation preceding the German crossings and did not open fire on the assault forces advancing behind a dense smoke screen. Even as the attacking infantry streamed past toward its immediate objectives along the high ground to the rear of the fort, the Russians continued to hold their fire, since the smoke, which had meanwhile settled at tree-top level, completely obstructed their field of fire. It was sheer coincidence that not a single German infantryman stumbled upon the bunker.

Not until 0630, a full 2 hours after the Germans had launched their attacks, did the Russians suddenly open fire from the bypassed fort. From two 76.2-mm. guns on the north side of the bunker, enemy fire was directed at German approach traffic behind the left flank of the 76th Infantry Division, and at the left flank of the 230th Infantry Regiment, which at that moment was warding off concerted Russian counterthrusts from the north. A second pair of 76.2 mm. guns on the east side of the fort shelled the 22d Division's approach roads, bridge site, and crossing traffic. Machinegun fire from the front of the bunker was directed against Company B, 744th Engineer Regiment, which at the time was making preparations to bridge the river behind the 76th Division. At the same time, observers inside the bunker directed the fire from Russian artillery emplaced some distance behind the river on the bridge site, causing heavy losses in men and equipment.

At 0700 the commander of Company B, 744th Engineer Regiment, ordered Lieutenant Sander, the leader of the 1st Platoon, to prepare his unit for an assault on the bunker. Sander immediately alerted his squad leaders. The operation order issued by the company commander read as follows:

1. An enemy bunker is located in the acacia grove on the east bank of the Dnestr. Its fire obstructs the support of our attack forces on the far side of the river and interferes with bridge construction.

2. Company B is charged with reducing this fortified installation before resuming its primary mission of bridge construction.

THE RUSSIAN BUNKER in the Stalin Line (Dnepr bridge in the center).

SMALL UNIT ACTIONS

3. The 1st Platoon will attack the bunker and neutralize it in close combat. Its first objective will be to locate and silence the guns whose fire has been directed against our flanks. Six assault craft will be available to ferry this platoon across the river a short distance upstream from the projected bridge site.

4. Direct fire support during the crossing will be provided by one light howitzer, one 37-mm. antitank gun, and one heavy machinegun emplaced on the shore of departure. For fire support during the assault proper, contact should be established with the antitank guns on the far side, some of which have already exchanged fire with the Russian fortress guns.

5. The company commander will follow up the assault with the 2d Platoon as a reserve force.

To carry out this mission Sander organized his forces as follows:

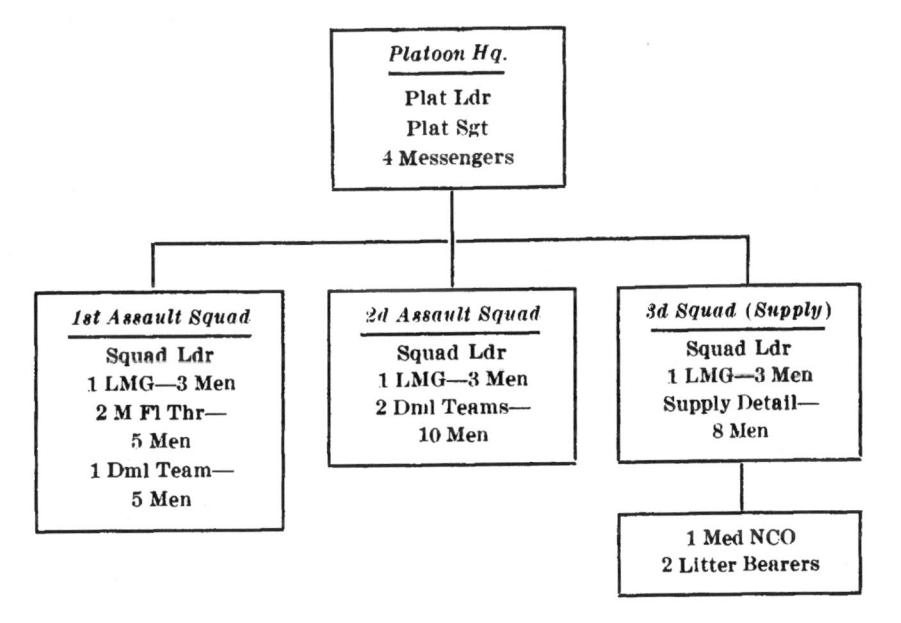

```
                    Platoon Hq.
                    ───────────
                    Plat Ldr
                    Plat Sgt
                    4 Messengers
```

1st Assault Squad	2d Assault Squad	3d Squad (Supply)
Squad Ldr	Squad Ldr	Squad Ldr
1 LMG—3 Men	1 LMG—3 Men	1 LMG—3 Men
2 M Fl Thr—5 Men	2 Dml Teams—10 Men	Supply Detail—8 Men
1 Dml Team—5 Men		

```
                              1 Med NCO
                              2 Litter Bearers
```

Organizational weapons and equipment of the platoon included one extra flame thrower, demolition charges, detonators with time fuzes, friction-type fuze lighters, a tool kit, binding wire, tow ropes, hand grenades, smoke cylinders, machinegun ammunition, and one electric mine detector.

Each individual was issued two smoke cylinders and each demolition team was provided with two regular Bangalore torpedoes for blasting wire and mine obstacles, two short Bangalore torpedoes for use against the bunker guns, and four 13½-pound concentrated charges.

At 0730 Sander gathered his men around him for a final briefing on a scrub-covered hill that afforded concealment and at the same time commanded an excellent view of the enemy position. Each squad was assigned to its respective assault boats, which were to take the platoon across the river shortly before 0800.

The river was crossed without incident. Having reached the east bank the platoon quickly moved into the acacia grove, where it reassembled to await further orders. While waiting, the platoon observed that Russian medium artillery was zeroed in on its support weapons on the opposite bank.

At this point Sander was confronted with the following situation:

The concrete bunker was situated at an elevation of about 250 feet above the river level. Thus far only one firing port had been definitely spotted. It was located in the face of the fort and housed a machinegun that fired almost without letup. The two guns on the north side of the bunker firing in a northerly and northwesterly direction could be roughly identified by their long muzzle flashes, but their embrasures had thus far not been spotted. The two guns on the east side offered no visible clue as to their location. As far as could be determined, there were neither wire obstacles nor field intrenchments around the fort. Entrances to the bunker were not discernible. Whether any enemy riflemen were employed outside the fort was not known; up to then no rifle fire had been encountered.

A survey of the terrain showed that the slope leading to the front and sides of the bunker was intersticed with gullies, depressions, and many other defiladed areas, affording excellent cover to approaching troops. Through gaps between the trees Sander spotted several German riflemen, who apparently belonged to a radio-communication unit, moving unconcernedly on the steep, barren slope directly behind the fort. This was a most opportune discovery, because the fact that they remained unmolested by the Russian garrison indicated that they could not be observed from the rear of the installation. Accordingly, Sander concluded that he would be able to approach the fortress from the rear without arousing enemy suspicion or drawing defensive fire.

From the experience he had gained during the attacks against the French Maginot and the Greek Metaxas Lines, Sander knew well that, should the Russians become aroused and counterattack during the approach of his assault force, the latter would find itself in a most precarious position. Constant alertness and careful observation was therefore of vital importance. During his reconnaissance of the terrain, the lieutenant spotted one of the German 50-mm. antitank guns.

On the basis of his observations and estimates the lieutenant drew up the following plan of action:

The 2d and 3d Squads will approach the fort from both flanks and keep it under close observation. All features discernible from the outside, such as embrasures or other apertures, intrenchments, escape hatches, and entrances will be blocked, and any enemy attempt to escape will be thwarted. At the same time, I and the 1st Squad will approach the bunker from the rear, taking full advantage of the concealment afforded by the terrain. The further course of action will not be determined until the locations of the various gun embrasures are discovered. Despite the short distance to be covered, the approach of the 1st Squad will take considerable time because the men must creep and crawl to avoid detection. During this interlude I will have time to arrange for fire support from the antitank guns.

In accordance with instructions, the 2d Squad dispatched three scouts to the east side of the fort to reconnoiter the area and keep the installation under observation. Two men were to remain near the bunker while the third reported back with any information gathered. Shortly before the lieutenant issued his final orders, one of the scouts returned and reported:

On the east side of the bunker there is a camouflaged entrance some distance below the surface of the ground. The two other scouts are watching it closely. A machinegun port is located high above the entrance, thus creating a dead space of some 60 feet. There is no ditch around the bunker, nor are there any wire entanglements, intrenchments, cupolas, or armored turrets.

Lieutenant Sander then issued the following verbal orders to his squad leaders:

To reduce the bunker, I intend to approach from the rear across the barren slope. I will take the 1st Squad forward through the brush to the slope, then turn right and skirt the steep bank above and behind the objective. We must exercise great care not to be observed by the gun crews and therefore must approach stealthily by creeping and crawling. At this point good concealment will be more essential than speed.

The 2d Squad will move cautiously to its right and cover the east side of the fort as well as the machinegun embrasure in the front of the bunker. The assumed entrance must be blocked by fire or other means; if necessary, even by hand-to-hand combat.

The 3d Squad will move forward to cover the north side of the bunker.

It is imperative that all features of the installation be thoroughly reconnoitered. Do not attack the bunker proper unless its occupants attempt to break out. While the 1st Squad is moving into position, a messenger and I will seek contact with the antitank gun crews off to our left in order to make the necessary arranagements for fire support. If there are no further questions, let's go!

Skillfully exploiting every terrain feature, the 1st Squad succeeded in crossing the zone of fire in front of the two guns on the north side of the fort. Sander meanwhile made contact with the crews of the two 50-mm. antitank guns, outlined his attack plan, and asked that they fire on the gun embrasures only at his signal, explaining that if they should fire too soon the element of surprise would be lost, and further that if they failed to cease fire when given that signal his men would be unable to move in on the enemy guns.

The platoon leader rejoined the 1st Squad just as it reached the jumpoff position directly behind the fort. After briefly orienting himself, he found that there were several factors particularly favorable to the execution of his mission. First, the flanks of the gun embrasures were not protected by apertures designed for close-in support. Second, there were no intrenchments from which hand grenades could be hurled at an attacker, nor was there a continuous trench around the bunker. Third, the steel shutters for the protection of the guns were lying flat on the ground in front of the embrasures. These shutters were rigged to two wires which were threaded through a pair of metal eyelets above the embrasure and thus could be pulled up over the guns from inside. Finally, he noticed that the only features on top of the bunker were several T-shaped exhaust vents. Once the cross piece had been blown off, explosives could be dropped into the bunker through the vents.

Since only the two guns on the east side of the fort were firing at that moment, Sander flashed the signal and the two antitank guns promptly opened fire on the bunker. In the exchange of fire that followed, one of the antitank guns was knocked out. As soon as the two flame throwers opened up on the embrasures from the north, the fire from that side was silenced. Thereupon Sander signaled to the remaining antitank gun to hold its fire. As he raised his head and looked around, he noted that both steel shutters were being pulled up. Without a moment's hesitation the lieutenant, with the demolition team close at his heels, rushed toward the embrasures. Before the shutters could be completely closed, the engineers succeeded in wedging concrete blocks into the openings and then quickly dropped into each embrasure a concentrated charge whose fuze they had shortened to 5 seconds. Having lighted the fuzes the men scurried for cover. Both steel shutters were shattered by the force of the blast and fell to the ground. The team promptly moved in again on the guns that were now exposed to view, inserted short Bangalore torpedoes into each barrel, and ignited the fuzes. While the engineers scrambled for cover, the charges exploded with great force, completely destroying both guns. Flying fragments wounded one of the engineers.

Meanwhile, the leader of the 1st Squad and three of his men had made their way onto the top of the bunker. After blasting open the exhaust vents, they dropped hand grenades and smoke cylinders into the openings. The squad leader then reconnoitered the east side of the fort and reported to Sander that the steel shutters on that side had been closed and that an attempt to break out through the exit on the east side of the fort had been frustrated by the 2d Squad.

At this time light caliber Russian artillery shells began to drop in the immediate vicinity of the bunker killing one and wounding two Germans. By then there could be no doubt that this fire was being directed from within the fort. Sander and his men took cover along the bunker wall from where they could still observe the demolished embrasures. When the company commander joined them, he was briefed and informed that no reinforcements would be needed. After a brief discussion the two officers drew up a plan for further action. The 1st Squad was to force the north entrance and gain access to the bunker. The 2d Squad was to neutralize the two guns on the east side, which for the moment were silent, and to continue its vigil at the exit on that side. In an attempt to confuse the enemy and divert his attention, the 1st Squad was to start its attack shortly before the 2d Squad swung into action. The 3d Squad, meanwhile, was to cover the two destroyed embrasures and silence the machine gun.

Intermittent Russian artillery fire from the rear, and machinegun fire from the fort, still interdicted the bridge site and delayed construction operations. Since the sparseness of the road net precluded the selection of an alternate site, the obstacle presented by the Russian bunker had to be eliminated at any cost and without delay.

The two demolition teams of the 2d Squad took about 90 minutes to draw the necessary supplies and set the stage for the next action. For each of the remaining shutters two charges were tied together with a single detonating cord for simultaneous detonation, the time fuze being adjusted to five seconds. The charges had to be attached to long poles so that they could be lowered from the top of the bunker and hung flush against the shutters. Two Bangolore torpedoes, one for each gun barrel, were prepared and connected for simultaneous detonation with the time fuze cut to three seconds. They were also attached to long poles so that they could be inserted into the tubes from the roof of the fort.

While these preparations were under way the artillery barrage from the main Russian positions gradually died down. Elements of the 3d Squad had meanwhile succeeded in silencing the machinegun on the front of the bunker by using a flame thrower and hand grenades. Russian artillery fire on the bridge site also ceased, but only temporarily. At the very moment the Germans were laying the sill on the east bank of the river, the Russians reopened fire and scored a direct hit.

About 1200 the 1st Squad blasted open the north entrance to the fort and two of the men stepped into the dark corridor that led into the interior. After taking but a few steps they were felled by machinegun bursts. A few minutes later the 2d Squad silenced the two remaining guns on the east side of the bunker by blasting open the steel shutters and inserting the torpedoes in the tubes.

When the company commander realized that the Russians intended to continue resistance inside the bunker, he decided to drop more grenades and smoke cylinders down the ventilation shafts, then seal the openings up tight. In addition, a labor detail was ordered to fill in the blasted gun embrasures with debris, and the 2d Squad was to make another attempt to gain access to the fort through the entrance.

The execution of these orders was again interrupted by Russian artillery fire, which caused some casualties among the attackers. At 1500 the second attack was launched against the north entrance. Flame throwers cleared the way for the demolition team, which placed two charges fastened to long poles inside the entrance. The fumes created by the explosion prevented the engineers from following up immediately.

After about an hour Sander entered the bunker accompanied by the squad leader of the 2d Squad and two men. Approximately 10 paces from the entrances, the corridor made a 45-degree turn to the left from where the steps led down. A few moments after the Germans had entered the corridor they were suddenly met by a hail of machinegun fire from a firing port directly above the stairway. The squad leader was wounded and one of the men killed. Sander promptly hurled several hand grenades at the machinegun and then hurriedly turned back, pulling the two casualties out with him.

At this juncture the corps engineer officer arrived at the scene. After two separate attempts to get inside the bunker had failed, the company commander suggested that the fortification be demolished by heavy charges placed close against the outside walls. In this manner it would be unnecessary to follow up the blast inside the fort and

CLOSEUP view of the Russian bunker.

to get involved in close-in fighting with the defenders, who, while utilizing the interior firing ports, would continue to have the best of it.

The quantity of explosives required to be effective against the 3-foot concrete walls was calculated at 550 pounds. The corps engineer officer suggested that two separate charges be exploded and assured the company commander that the necessary explosives would be made available.

The first demolition had to be delayed until 1800 because Russian artillery once again covered the bunker area and the bridge site with well-directed fire. Approximately 30 minutes after the first charge had been set off, a Russian, on the point of exhaustion, was seen staggering out of the bunker.

Upon interrogation he revealed that the fort had two underground levels. Its complement was purported to be 60 men, amply supplied with ammunition and rations. It was equipped with an elaborate ventilation system, electricity, and running water. According to the prisoner the various explosions had killed or rendered unconscious about half of the garrison. Its commander, a captain, had supposedly wanted to surrender, whereupon he was promptly shot by the commissar. The latter, a true fanatic, insisted on holding out to the last man and continued to direct the Russian artillery fire personally by means of an underground cable connected with the rear area.

Meanwhile, the artillery fire had again resumed with increased intensity, and the German assault forces had to scurry for cover. When at 2200 the barrage let up momentarily, the second blast was quickly set off. After that explosion the Russian artillery fire finally stopped altogether, and the bridge construction operation could proceed without further interruption. The bridge was completed and became trafficable by 0400 on 18 July.

When Sander entered the bunker at dawn he found that the entire complement had either been killed directly by the demolition or had died from suffocation.

The favorable location of the bunker and the stubborn, fanatical resistance of its garrison enabled the Russians to delay the German advance for several hours by virtue of the artillery fire from both the bunker itself and the main Russian positions to the rear. However, the installation had a number of deficiencies. The existence of numerous dead spaces in the terrain within its immediate vicinity permitted an attacker to approach unmolested. All-around wire obstacles on the ground as well as on top of the bunker were conspicuous by their absence. There was no intrenchment or water-filled ditch surrounding the fort. Apertures for close-in support as well as intrenchments from which to hurl grenades at the assault forces were not provided.

There were no close-in defensive features, such as cupolas or armor-plated turrets, atop the bunker. Another shortcoming on the part of the Russians was their failure to post sentries and to commit patrols in the immediate vicinity of the bunker.

IV. The Capture of Balta (August 1941)

Early in August 1941 Eleventh Army, advancing on the right wing of Army Group South in the Ukraine, skirted the Romanian border with the Black Sea port of Odessa as its primary objective. The small town of Balta, located about 120 miles northwest of Odessa, had changed hands several times during recent fighting but at the time of this action was held by the Russians. The Germans concluded that the town was occupied by at least one battalion and that the Russians had prepared defensive positions within the town. The weather was clear, hot, and dry, and a moderate northeast wind was blowing.

On orders from higher headquarters, Balta was to be bypassed. The 239th Infantry Division attacked to the east of the town and the Romanian 6th Infantry Division to the west. The 744th Engineer Regiment, less Company C, was given the mission of seizing Balta singlehanded, preparatory to building a 24-ton highway bridge across the Kodyma River just south of the town. The regiment was to move into its assembly area north of Balta under the protection of Romanian covering parties and was scheduled to launch its attack on Balta at 0600 on 3 August 1941.

At that time Company C, 744th Engineer Regiment, under the command of First Lieutenant Ehrhardt, was temporarily attached to the 239th Division. The company had the mission of supporting the offensive operations of the division by building several footbridges and repairing a vehicular bridge across the Kodyma east of Balta (map 30).

Because of the recent arrival of well-trained replacements, Company C was at full strength. Having participated in the attacks across the Pruth and Dnestr Rivers, the company was experienced in infantry and assault tactics.

The company's headquarters platoon included a wire section with 3 miles of cable. The platoon's organic transportation included a staff car and five motorcycles, two of which had sidecars. Each of the three other platoons was composed of 3 squads of 14 men each. In addition to rifles and submachineguns, each squad had one light machinegun. The company motor section consisted of three trucks, while each platoon had two animal-drawn carts which carried the organizational weapons, equipment, and ammunition.

Jumping off at 0400, the attack elements of the right wing of 239th Infantry Division quickly crossed the Kodyma and continued to advance southward across the railroad. There was little resistance from Russian infantry, but here and there the Germans met heavy enemy artillery fire. However, the river line proper was not under fire.

Having reinforced a slightly damaged wooden bridge and built three footbridges, Company C had completed its mission in support of the infantry division. Shortly before 0600 all but two squads of the company were resting. In the center and on the left wing of the 239th Infantry Division heavy traffic was moving across the Kodyma.

Meanwhile, steadily increasing enemy mortar, machinegun, and rifle fire had been heard from the area north and northwest of Balta since 0500. At the same time, Russian fighters and bombers carried out low-level attacks, but were driven off by effective antiaircraft fire. At approximately 0530, fifteen Russian planes bombed and strafed the area north of Balta, striking primarily at the assembly areas of the 744th Engineer Regiment.

The wire section of a German artillery battery, passing through the Company C area from northeast of Balta, reported that about 0500, while winding their cable, they had heard firing from the wooded hills facing the northern outskirts of Balta and had seen Romanian infantry running northward. The signal men added that they, too, had drawn fire from one or two riflemen hidden somewhere in a sunflower field east of Balta.

Relieved of his original mission, Ehrhardt wanted to take an active part in the capture of Balta. He presumed that the attack by his regiment would be delayed because of the covering parties' hasty retreat and of the impact of the Russian air attacks. The Russians in Balta constituted a danger to the exposed flank of the advancing 239th Division. At the moment nothing prevented them from launching an attack toward the east, if only with the limited objective of capturing the wooden bridge. Moreover, he knew that a 24-ton bridge had to be constructed without delay so that the main highway through Balta could be opened to traffic as soon as the town was cleared.

In considering his next move, Ehrhardt felt that to dig in and remain on the defensive could offer no protection to the exposed flank of the division. To await new orders, or even only to take the time to ask for instructions from the 239th Engineer Regiment, would have meant the loss of valuable minutes. He therefore decided to attack

RUSSIAN POSITION in the Ukraine, August 1941.

Balta from the east in an effort to support the main attack on the town that his own regiment was to launch from the north.

Having reached his decision, Ehrhardt gathered his platoon and reconnaissance patrol leaders around him and issued the following verbal orders:

    1. A change in the enemy situation seems to have delayed the attack of our regiment on Balta from the north. I have, therefore, decided to attack the town from the east. Our initial objective is

to seize the southern edge of the town including the all-important bridge site.

2. Combat reconnaissance will be carried out by all three platoons. The 1st Platoon, under Lieutenant Kuehne, and the 3d Platoon will employ their regular reconnaissance patrols, while the 2d Platoon will designate a special three-man patrol.

3. The 3d Platoon will reconnoiter the sunflower field north of the road leading into Balta; the 1st, the area between that road and the river; and the 2d will cover the south side of the river as far as a point opposite the southeast corner of the town.

4. Determine what enemy troop dispositions are in the sunflower field and in the depressions along both sides of the river. Find out also the enemy's troop strength and disposition of weapons and obstacles along the eastern outskirts of Balta. Note particularly whether he has tanks and antitank guns. I want an estimate of enemy capabilities together with a report on the terrain, on the basis of which the attack can be planned and executed. For example, would it be better to enter Balta from the east through the sunflower field or from the south? Finally, I need an estimate of the enemy garrison holding the railroad station located on the highway about three-quarters of a mile south of the town.

5. The patrols will hold whatever points they are able to take and will act as covering parties during the approach of the company. Report your findings to me at my command post. Patrols will move out as soon as practicable.

6. For the time being, one squad of the 3d Platoon will occupy the area near the small woods and guard the road leading to Balta. The 1st Squad of the 2d Platoon will be left behind to guard the Kodyma crossings so that there will be no interruption in the flow of traffic.

7. The platoon leaders will report to me when ready to move out.

Ehrhardt then prepared the following two messages for transmittal by motorcycle messenger:

Message No. 1

Company C, 744th Engineer Regiment

¼ mile north of Kodyma bridge
1½ miles east of Balta
3 August 1941, 0620 hours

To: CO, 239th Engineer Regiment

1. A 4-ton wooden bridge and three footbridges have been in use by the 346th Infantry Regiment since 0530.

SMALL UNIT ACTIONS

2. Because of enemy bombing and strafing attacks on its concentration areas at 0530, the 744th Engineer Regiment's frontal assault on Balta from the north has probably been delayed.

3. Company C will attack Balta from the east leaving one squad to guard the bridges. The attack will be launched in about one hour.

4. Company command post will remain here for the time being.

EHRHARDT
First Lieutenant
Company Commander

Message No. 2

Company C, 744th Engineer Regiment

¼ mile north of Kodyma bridge
1½ miles east of Balta
3 August 1941, 0630 hours

To: CO, 744th Engineer Regiment

1. Company C will attack Balta from the east in about 1 hour in an effort to capture the southern edge of the town, including the highway bridge site.

2. The following signal flares will be used:

White—We are here;
Green—We are attacking in a northerly direction; and
Red—Help needed.

3. Company command post will remain here for the time being.

EHRHARDT
First Lieutenant
Company Commander

At 0635, while the company was preparing for the attack, two Russian light tanks moved eastward from Balta along the road adjacent to the sunflower field and came to a halt in front of the mine obstacle that the 3d Platoon squad had laid across the road. Both tanks opened fire, but this was ineffectual because the sunflower field and the brushwood obstructed their field of fire. When the 3d Platoon squad set up a smokescreen and attacked the lead tank with frangible grenades, it caught fire and its guns were silenced; the second one, however, continued to fire. While moving into position near the wooden bridge, a horse-drawn light howitzer battery (Battery B, 239th Artillery Regiment) suffered losses in men and horses as it came under the tank's fire. Thereupon one of the howitzers was hurriedly unlimbered, and its second round finished off the burning tank. The second tank quickly turned around and fled through the field, shielded by a small patch of trees.

At 0650 Ehrhardt briefed the commanding officer of the artillery battery as to the situation and his intentions, requesting that one field howitzer be temporarily attached to the company to support its attack on Balta. After this request was granted, Ehrhardt issued the following orders to the section chief of the howitzer crew:

1. I intend to commit my company in an attack on **Balta**. Whether we will advance on the right, on the left, or on both sides of the road leading to that town has not been decided.

2. Establish your firing position near the patch of woods north of that road. Your mission is to provide antitank protection and to pave the way for the attack forces by fire on point targets in Balta. You will open fire at a signal from me. The company wire section, with 2 miles of cable, will be at your disposal and will report shortly.

Toward 0700 lively artillery and machinegun fire was heard from the area north of Balta, a probable indication that the 744th Engineer Regiment was preparing for the subsequent assault on the town. Twenty minutes later a messenger from Lieutenant Kuehne's patrol arrived at the company CP with a Russian prisoner. The messenger told the following story:

While probing westward through the area just north of the river, our patrol surprised and overpowered an enemy outpost. The prisoner I brought back was one of the sentries. Moving on, we reached a farmhouse with a large garden near the southeast corner of Balta, but made no further contact with enemy forces. After digging in, we spotted the 2d Platoon patrol on the opposite side of the stream near an unguarded enemy footbridge.

We observed Russians moving between Balta and the railroad station. It is possible to approach the objective through a depression near the river where dense brushwood affords concealment from observers in the town and at the railroad station. The terrain appears unfavorable for tanks because of the many pools and swampy ground.

About a quarter of a mile east of the destroyed bridge there is a ford. On the north bank near that ford we saw about 10 Russians building a corduroy road. We held our fire so as to remain undetected. Two of our men are still watching the area from well-concealed points in the underbrush.

We noticed that the reconnaissance squad of the 3d Platoon in the sunflower field was under fire and saw one tank withdrawing to

Balta. We have thus far been unable to observe the disposition of the enemy troops and weapons at the outskirts of the town, but a reconnaissance of this area is now under way.

Lieutenant Kuehne asked me to emphasize that the depression near the river would be an ideal route of advance for the company, and that a surprise attack launched from the farmhouse our reconnaissance patrol is occupying at the corner of Balta seems entirely feasible.

On the basis of the above report and his own estimates of the enemy capabilities and terrain, Ehrhardt drew up his plan of attack. At 0730 he issued the following verbal orders to his platoon leaders and to the chief of the attached howitzer section:

1. Company C will move to the outskirts of Balta where it will occupy jump-off positions. During the first phase of the attack we shall seize the southern edge of the town, including the bridge site. After this has been accomplished we shall establish a defense line facing north in an effort to cut off any enemy forces that might attempt to withdraw to the south once our regiment begins its attack.

2. Missions:

    a. The 1st Platoon, with the 2d following at a distance of about 200 yards, will advance to within about 100 yards of Balta. Thereupon both platoon leaders and the squad leaders of the 1st Platoon will report to Lieutenant Kuehne's CP, where I will issue further orders.

    b. The 3d Platoon will approach Balta through the sunflower field and close up to within 100 yards of the objective. This platoon is to divert the enemy's attention from the movements of the 1st and 2d Platoons.

    c. The howitzer crew has already been instructed. If practicable, direct fire should be placed on the houses at the outskirts of the town. White tracers may also be used for target designation. The howitzer fire will be directed and observed by the section chief from my command post.

3. The following signal flares are to be used:

White—We are here;

Green—We are attacking in a northerly direction; and

Red—Help needed.

4. I will move with company headquarters, the howitzer section chief, and the 2d Platoon leader to the farmhouse occupied by Lieutenant Kuehne. If there are no further questions, platoon leaders will prepare to move out.

By 0740 all movements had been initiated. Thirty minutes later Ehrhardt and the advance party arrived at the farmhouse. By then the telephone line to the howitzer was already in operation. Kuehne briefed Ehrhardt on the latest development:

A Russian heavy machinegun has been set up in a house at the edge of town on the north side of the main street leading into town from the east and had fired several bursts into the sunflower field. In the yard of another house the Russians have moved two mortars into position and are unloading ammunition from a *Panje* cart. Russian soldiers were seen double timing northward along a side street. A 76.2-mm. field gun is emplaced on the main street behind a barricade built some 250 yards inside the eastern edge of town.

At 0830 the 1st and 2d Platoons arrived at their destinations, and the platoon leaders reported to Ehrhardt. Since the targets within Balta had been pinpointed, the howitzer section chief was ordered to zero in on the 76.2-mm. gun and the heavy machinegun. Within 10 minutes the gun crew reported that it was ready to fire for effect.

Thereupon, the 1st Platoon was ordered to attack and seize the field gun in the street and the houses where the heavy machinegun and mortars were emplaced. While securing its right flank, the platoon was to continue to advance westward along the main street. The 2d Platoon was to seize the Russian-held ford, and then have one man report back for further orders. The firing of the howitzer was to be the signal to start these attacks.

As the 1st Platoon crossed the garden and the 2d Platoon approached the thicket northeast of the ford, Russian riflemen suddenly approached the farmhouse, apparently unaware that it was occupied. The detachment was met by a hail of fire and completely wiped out. After this unexpected interlude, Ehrhardt ordered the howitzer to open fire, first on the Russian field gun and then on the heavy machinegun. The Russian gun answered the howitzer's fire until it was silenced by the latter's fourth round, which scored a direct hit. Thereupon, the fire quickly switched to the house where the heavy machinegun was emplaced; the target was hit and destroyed by delayed-action shells. Led by Ehrhardt, the 1st Platoon rushed its objectives on the main street and seized them after brief hand-to-hand fighting. A few of the Russians succeeded in withdrawing to the northern section of the town. Meanwhile, the 2d Platoon had reached the thicket near the ford and, using automatic weapons, attacked the Russians guarding it.

Acting on its own initiative, the 3d Platoon also entered Balta from the east and, using a flame thrower and demolition charges, took a house where a light machinegun had been in action. The platoon continued to move westward one block north of the main street, took one intersection and successfully repelled the Russians' counterattacks. The two squads that were fighting for a stubbornly defended house at the next intersection found they could not approach the front side of the house. The platoon leader thereupon decided to set off a demolition charge in the adjoining house in order to gain access through the breach. While two German engineers were engaged in setting the explosive charge, the Russians detonated a charge from within their stronghold, collapsing the very same wall and burying the two Germans under the debris. During the confusion that ensued some of the Russians succeeded in getting away.

While Ehrhardt was issuing orders for the resumption of the attack along the main street, the sound of heavy gun fire and exploding hand grenades and demolition charges could be heard from the direction of the 2d Platoon's zone of attack. Noticing that red signal flares were being fired over that area, Ehrhardt rushed from his position with the 1st Platoon to the edge of town, where he observed that two to three Russian infantry platoons were simultaneously attacking the front and left flank of the 2d Platoon. Some of the enemy had already penetrated the thicket. However, Ehrhardt felt reassured when he noticed several flamethrower bursts and heard the detonation of explosive charges; the platoon was holding its own. Just then the German howitzer opened fire on the Russian attack forces and pinned them down.

Nevertheless, Ehrhardt realized that immediate assistance would have to be provided. Not only was the 2d Platoon threatened with annihilation, but the entire attack plan was jeopardized. Rushing back to the 1st Platoon, he ordered one squad to establish security posts at the nearest street intersection and the rest of the platoon to follow him in a flanking thrust against the Russian infantry platoons. Effectively supported by two light machineguns, the platoon hurled itself against the enemy force, which was totally unprepared to meet an attack from this direction. Ehrhardt and his men inflicted heavy casualties and took many prisoners, thus bringing the Russian attack to an early collapse. Thirty minutes after the German counterattack had begun, the beaten Russian remnants made their way southward across the ford where they came under the fire of the 2d Platoon's reconnaissance squad.

At 0945 Ehrhardt conferred with his platoon leaders and the howitzer section chief. After reviewing the situation, he issued the following orders:

1. To exploit our initial success it will be necessary to occupy the main street up to the highway intersection, thereby cutting the Russians' routes of withdrawal to the south. The 1st Platoon will push on through the main street and occupy the intersections up to the highway. I will follow behind the 1st Platoon.

2. The 2d Platoon will secure the north bank of the Kodyma between the footbridge and the highway bridge site in order to prevent Russian forces south of the river from entering the town.

3. The 3d Platoon will strengthen its positions inside the town and send out a combat patrol to probe northward and seek early contact with our regiment.

4. The howitzer will zero in on the ford, the bridge site, and the highway intersection.

Although the 1st Platoon did succeed in taking the next intersection (one block from the highway) and in repelling a counterthrust from the north, it was unable to prevent the enemy from withdrawing southwestward. While these enemy elements were making their way across the marshes toward the Kodyma, they were caught by fire from the 2d Platoon and forced to turn west and head toward the bridge site. When Ehrhardt became aware of this enemy movement, he ordered the howitzer crew to fire on the retreating enemy forces.

The intersection of the main street and highway as well as the one just above it were seized by elements of the 1st Platoon. Although the Russians' counterattacks were blocked at the latter intersection, they were able to retreat through the western section of the town.

Shortly after 1000, small enemy detachments of from three to six men with heavy machineguns and mortars were seen west of the causeway heading in the direction of the bridge site. Two 2d Platoon scouts opened fire with their rifles and signaled a light machinegun to move up and join the fray. Meanwhile, the howitzer also brought its fire to bear on the bridge site, where the Russians had built an emergency footbridge over the wreckage of the highway span. To cover their withdrawal, the Russians had brought up a heavy machinegun which fired at the Germans on the causeway.

During this exchange of fire at short range, the German light machinegun was knocked out by a direct hit, but the riflemen, especially the one who was now perched atop a tree, scored many a bull's eye. Soon the enemy gave up the struggle and, abandoning the heavy machinegun, disappeared ilnto the brushwood southwest of the bridge site. Later examination of the area revealed that one heavy machinegun, one mortar and several Russians had fallen victim to the precision fire of the Germans.

SMALL UNIT ACTIONS

At 1040 two Russian light tanks appeared on the south bank at the ford. While one provided cover, the other tank crossed the stream. The Germans on the opposite bank hurled smoke grenades, which, aided by a favorable northeast wind, enshrouded both tanks in such dense smoke that their machinegun and cannon fire overshot their mark.

The tank that had crossed the river started off toward Balta, but soon thereafter was destroyed by a concentrated demolition charge hurled against its side by the leader of the machinegun squad. Thereupon, the second tank quickly headed west toward the bridge site and then south toward the railroad station, which was already ablaze and from the direction of which the din of hand-to-hand fighting could be heard.

By 1100 Company C held the entire southern half of Balta, thus blocking any major breakout attempt by the enemy. However, the company was unable to prevent small groups and individual riflemen from infiltrating its lines and escaping southward.

Meanwhile, the noises accompanying the 744th Engineer Regiment's attack from the north had come considerably closer. A squad from Company A broke through the remaining Russian forces and effected

GERMAN PONTON BRIDGE, 1941

the initial link-up with Company C's 1st Platoon in the western part of Balta.

Ehrhardt thereupon ordered the 2d Platoon and the surveying section of the headquarters platoon to proceed to the bridge site and make the necessary preparations for the construction of a 24-ton ponton-trestle bridge as soon as the bridging equipment arrived. Two mine detectors were dispatched to the bridge site by motorcycle messenger.

Since the howitzer was no longer needed, Ehrhardt released the gun crew and ordered it to return to its battery.

At the bridge site the 2d Platoon began to carry out its orders by surveying the area, drawing up plans, and removing the wreckage. While awaiting the arrival of the mine detectors, some of the men probed for mines along the causeway leading into the town, using their bayonets. Others disposed of felled trees and similar obstacles. Toward 1145 medium caliber artillery shells suddenly began to drop near the crossing site but caused no losses. The Russians were apparently adjusting their fire on the bridge site. This was at first puzzling because, being situated in a deep depression, the bridge site could not be seen from the railroad station or even from the high ground south of the station. Moreover, since German planes controlled the air in this region, Russian aerial observation was out of the question. The platoon leader therefore concluded that a Russian artillery observer was probably concealed in the sunflower field between the bridge site and the railroad station.

Realizing that bridge construction would be seriously impeded once the Russians began to fire for effect, the platoon leader left the mine detecting detail and surveying section to their tasks at the bridge site and took the rest of the platoon to comb out the sunflower fields along both sides of the highway. His efforts were soon crowned with success when his men discovered and took prisoner a Russian artillery observer equipped with a portable radio set sitting in a foxhole in the sunflower field about 400 yards south of the bridge site. Then the platoon leader dispatched a two-man reconnaissance patrol to the station, while the rest of the men returned to the bridge site and resumed their work without further interference from enemy artillery.

Meanwhile, the electric mine detectors had arrived and four metallic mines had already been uncovered. Six wooden box mines were detected by men using bayonets and mine-probing rods. The platoon leader ordered his men to take cover while one metallic and one wooden mine were being removed with lengths of wire manipulated from a safe distance. In the process, one of the mines exploded

SMALL UNIT ACTIONS

since it had been rigged to a pull igniter in anticipation of such removal. The men thereupon continued probing but desisted from further removals until the necessary explosives arrived.

About 1300 Ehrhardt, who was driving south along the causeway in his staff car, came to a halt in front of a barrier which the mine-detecting detail had erected to fence off the uncleared portion of the roadway. He informed the platoon leader that Balta was now firmly in German hands and that thus far 300 prisoners had been taken. Ehrhardt then had the men get explosives and igniters from his car and detonate the remaining mines as rapidly as possible. Finally, he told the platoon leader that the field kitchen was to arrive in half an hour and that the company had reverted to battalion control. With the platoon leader he then went over the plans for the bridge construction so as to be able to make a report to the battalion commander, whose arrival was expected momentarily.

The decision to attack Balta made by Ehrhardt on his own initiative and based on a timely and appropriate estimate of the situation was undoubtedly correct. To have waited for explicit orders would have led to a needless loss of time. Not only would the 744th Engineer Regiment have encountered much greater resistance in its attack but also Balta and the vital bridge site could not have been captured so quickly. Had the enemy force within Balta been eliminated with less dispatch, much greater losses would surely have been sustained along the interior flanks of the advancing infantry divisions.

Ehrhardt's preparatory measures left nothing to chance. He issued his verbal and written orders rapidly, succinctly, and in proper sequence. Having outlined his assault mission clearly, he gave his company sufficient time to switch from routine construction jobs to preparation for the projected attack mission. The interim period gave the patrols time to carry out field reconnaissance, without which the company could not have been effectively employed.

In his estimates Ehrhardt considered the attack zone of the 1st Platoon as the most important one. It was for this reason that the reconnaissance patrol sent out by this platoon was led by the platoon leader in person. Thus, Lieutenant Kuehne was at the jumpoff point before his platoon arrived and had an opportunity to look over the terrain and organize his unit accordingly. Also noteworthy is the fact that the company commander issued his initial orders in the presence of the platoon and reconnaissance patrol leaders. To have given his reconnaissance instructions to the platoon leaders, so that they, in turn, could pass them on to the patrols, would not only have taken more time but might also have led to distortions.

Before the platoons moved out to their jumpoff positions, Ehrhardt briefed them thoroughly. Whether he could have given such a detailed briefing at the outskirts of Balta is doubtful. His officers and noncommissioned officers had to be completely informed of his intentions so that they could act independently but still in accordance with the overall plan.

Ehrhardt's request for the temporary attachment of a light field howitzer to his unit was a timely measure. Normally, however, the supporting arms are not favorably disposed to the idea of detaching separate elements, such as a single gun, and rightly so. In this case, support by a howitzer platoon—two guns—would have been even more advantageous, particularly for reasons of fire direction.

Sound tactical planning and clear, mission-type orders permitted the execution of the operation under the direction of the platoon leaders, acting independently of company headquarters. The 3d Platoon, for example, was on its own during the entire action. The decision to commit this platoon in a frontal attack through the sunflower fields against the eastern outskirts of Balta was a sound one, since the pinning down of enemy forces in that sector facilitated the operations of the 1st Platoon attacking from the south.

The 2d Platoon's determination in repelling Russian counterthrusts with only two of its squads was noteworthy. During this close-in fighting, the engineers used concentrated demolition charges as hand grenades. Ehrhardt showed excellent judgment when he diverted elements of the 1st Platoon for a counterthrust to relieve the hard-pressed 2d Platoon.

At the time of this action, the German Army's close-in antitank weapons included only smoke pots, concentrated charges, and frangible grenades—the latter, Russian booty—all of which the engineers were well-trained to handle. The shaped charge and recoilless grenade launcher were not developed until later in the war.

The Russians had turned their attention to the Romanian covering forces north of Balta, neglecting to keep an eye on the German forces to the east. The weakness of the Russian security forces along the river, where observation was difficult, also contributed to the rapid seizure of Balta by the Germans, who were able to overpower the sentries without attracting attention. Had the Russians not left the farmhouse and garden near the southeast corner of the town unoccupied, the German attack on Balta would have been rendered more difficult and costly.

SMALL UNIT ACTIONS

V. Russian Mine-Clearing Methods (July 1942)

In mid-July 1942 three Russian battalions faced one German battalion in a sector of the Voronezh salient on the central front. The distance between the opposing lines varied between 1,500 and 2,000 yards. Each Russian battalion was composed of one mortar and three rifle companies, one howitzer platoon, and an undetermined number of engineer troops. The German positions were protected by wire entanglements and a mine field, the latter consisting of antipersonnel mines operated by direct pressure. By sending out numerous patrols, some of which suffered casualties from mine explosions, the Russians were soon able to determine the approximate boundaries of the mine field (map 31).

One night, when there was no moon, a Russian engineer detachment numbering 15 men moved close to the forward limit of the mine field and dug in. They worked throughout the night in relays, carrying the excavated dirt to the rear and bringing up boards with which they covered the foxholes and dugouts and on which they spread top soil. A wire line was laid on the ground to connect this forward position with the Russian MLR. So skillfully was this accomplished that no change in the terrain was noticeable to the Germans the following morning. Even aerial photographs taken later that day showed nothing that aroused the faintest suspicion. Although the entire area was under constant observation throughout the day, no movement betrayed the presence of the Russian detachment.

During the second night a four-man mine-clearing detail emerging from the forward position inched its way up to the mine field and examined every foot of the ground. Since the four men were familiar with the mechanism of the German mines, they had no difficulty in neutralizing and disarming them in the dark. By proceeding methodically they succeeded in clearing a 25-foot long lane during the course of the night. Russian artillery laid down harrassing fire along the entire German sector to mask the noise that accidental detonation of a mine would cause. Four other mine-clearing technicians stood by to replace any possible casualties. Although it was a starlit night, a German patrol that passed within less than 30 paces of the Russian engineer detachment during a reconnaissance through no man's land failed to notice anything unusual.

The following day the Russian detachment stayed under cover and again remained unnoticed. With the advent of darkness, the artillery fire was resumed, and the mine-clearing detail went back to work and cleared another 60 feet. Toward 0400 one of the men accidentally set off a mine and lost his left arm. The explosion, though heard and promptly reported by the nearest German sentry, was believed to have been caused by a Russian shell that had fallen short. The wounded Russian was quietly evacuated.

On the fourth night a new mine-clearing detail was sent up. The men succeeded in reaching the wire entanglements after about an hour's work. After probing the ground beneath the entanglements, they found that it was not mined and reported back to the detachment commander in the forward position, who withdrew the engineer detail and ordered one commissioned and one noncommissioned officer to crawl through the mine lane. They watched the relief of the German sentry, whose post was some 20 yards beyond the point where they had emerged from the entanglement, and carefully noted that it was then 0130. Russian artillery continued its barrage throughout the night.

On the fifth night a Russian reconnaissance detachment, numbering 55 men equipped with automatic weapons and hand grenades, moved up into the forward position. Its mission was to break into the German positions, demolish the dugouts, and return with some prisoners. The commanding officer and three of the men spoke some German and had practiced a few simple phrases until they could repeat them without noticeable accent. The original plan called for an immediate followup by a reinforced rifle company that was to widen the gap and exploit the situation.

Led by the engineer detail and the observers of the previous night, the detachment reached the wire entanglements and quickly cut its way through. The detachment commander sent a small advance detail ahead at 0145, having allowed time for the relief of the German sentry at the nearby outpost to be completed. After the sentry was overpowered, gagged, and bound, a group of 12 was dispatched to the left to block access to the outpost from that side. The main body of the detachment slowly made its way forward along the trench in the opposite direction. The latter force had gone some 60 yards when it was confronted by a German patrol coming toward it. The Russians were ordered to halt within five paces of the patrol and give the password. In his well-rehearsed German the Russian officer replied, "Shut up, don't make any noise!" The German patrol leader then shouted, "Password or I fire!" To this the Russian answered, "Keep the noise down!" When the two officers had closed to within two paces of each other, one of the Germans suddenly opened fire and felled the Russian officer. A second German was unable to fire his rifle because the trench was too narrow. As the Russian soldiers jumped the first German, the second one made a run for it, firing wildly into the air and shouting for help. Soon another German sentry came to his assistance, whereupon both turned and opened fire on the oncoming Russians.

Leaving a blocking force about 40 yards beyond the spot where the German patrol had been contacted, the Russians leaped out of the trench and raced for the connecting trench some 60 yards ahead and off to their left. Here they suddenly faced a German platoon leader and three men. As the Russians stormed forward they were met with machinegun fire and hand grenades. Meanwhile, the German company commander responsible for the defense of this particular sector had alerted his men for a counterattack that was carried out from three directions. Within 2 hours the entire Russian detachment was wiped out.

This action shows how much time and what painstaking efforts the Russians were willing to expend in the preparation of a mere patrol action. For 4 days and nights a Russian engineer detachment remained in close proximity to the German positions, clearing a lane through a mine field during the hours of darkness. The Russians demonstrated great skill in their use of concealment and in disarming the German mines at night. Their discipline was exemplary.

When it became apparent that the reconnaissance detachment could not attain its objective, no attempt was made to effect a timely withdrawal. As an explanation of why the promised followup by the rifle company did not materialize, it is not unreasonable to conjecture that the responsible Russian commander had no intention of sending additional forces, having promised their commitment merely to bolster the morale of the engineer and reconnaissance forces. Whatever the reasons for this inaction may have been, this was not an isolated incident. On frequent occasions, after painstaking preparations by Russian engineer troops, reconnaissance patrols were able to enter deep into German-held territory during the hours of darkness. However, when they failed to return, no attempt was made to rescue them.

VI. Russian Excavation Methods (September 1943)

In another instance, which occurred in the Army Group North area more than a year later, Russian engineers outwitted their opponents by digging a tunnel directly under a German strong point. They were able to conceal their excavation work even though several weeks were needed for its completion and they had to work right under the noses of the Germans.

In late August 1943 the 2d Battalion of the German 474th Infantry Regiment moved into the area south of Gaytolovo, located about 10 miles south of Lake Ladoga. The terrain around Gaytolovo is broken by many minor elevations and ridges which readily lend themselves to underground excavations. In this sector the Germans occupied a number of Russian bunkers and dugouts. One of the latter, referred to as Strong Point Olga, was situated on a little ridge about 20 feet above the level of a swamp in which the Russians had established their positions. The ridge sloped down so steeply toward the Russian lines that its base could not be observed by the troops occupying the strong point. The German and Russian positions were about 55 yards apart at this point. The intermediate terrain contained a number of trenches, which the Russians had vacated. Company E, which occupied Strong Point Olga, had frequently reconnoitered the intermediate terrain, but nothing unusual was ever noticed.

At 0515 on 15 September 1943 the Russians directed heavy artillery fire on the strong point. The intermediate terrain was not visible to Company E because of a heavy ground fog which the Russians had supplemented by a smoke screen. At 0520 Russian infantry moved out from their jumpoff positions and stealthily crossed the intermediate terrain. The artillery fire continued until 0525. Then, just as the advancing Russian infantry was about to storm Strong Point Olga, a terrific explosion suddenly rocked the German troops in the area, pulverized Strong Point Olga, and all but wiped out Company E, leaving only 13 stunned and bleeding survivors. More than 100 Russians who had ventured too close to the German position before the explosion were buried under the debris.

The commander of the adjoining sector quickly assembled his men and rushed toward the site of the former strong point, just as another wave of Russian infantry came over the top. In the ensuing fighting the Germans successfully repulsed three Russian attacks. The Russians, who had not expected such determined resistance after the blast, suffered heavy losses and were forced to withdraw to their jumpoff positions.

The blasting of Strong Point Olga took the Germans by complete surprise. Russian engineers had dug a tunnel under no man's land until they had reached a point almost directly below Olga. Instead of placing explosives at the end of this tunnel, they continued their excavation work on both sides and constructed two 15-yard extensions parallel to the strong point and placed three tons of explosives at equal distances along this tunnel (map 32). The explosion that followed caused the entire front wall of the position to cave in and buried most of Company E's personnel under tons of debris.

While the tunnel was under construction the Russians were extremely careful in disposing of the excavated earth. For a period of several weeks they carried away the dirt in bags and dumped it into

SMALL UNIT ACTIONS

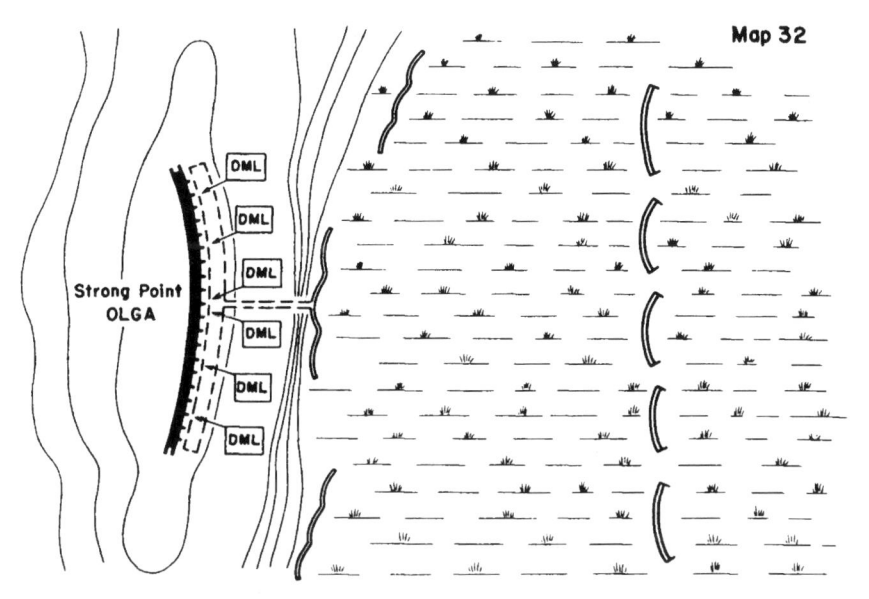

Map 32

RUSSIAN TUNNELS DUG SOUTH OF LAKE LADOGA
(15-30 September 1943)

== == == Tunnel
⌒ ⌒ Russian Positions
⌢ Unoccupied Trenches

0 10 20 30 40 50
YARDS
Form Line Interval 5 Feet

distant swamps. They skillfully concealed the tunnel entrance which was located in one of the former Russian trenches.

The Russians' plan might have worked to perfection had their infantry not begun to rush the strong point just before the blast. As a result of this poor timing, more Russians than Germans were killed by the explosion.

The successful excavation of the tunnel induced the Russian engineers to dig another tunnel in the same area. This time, however, the German defenders were on their guard. Anticipating other excavations along this vulnerable front, the German sector commander set up listening posts manned by engineers who kept night-and-day watch with special sound detectors. They had to report three times a day on any enemy movement or discoloration of the soil that they might observe in and around the Russian positions.

As early as 19 September the German engineers were able to report the first suspicious movements. At 1245 several observers noticed a Russian labor detail carrying cables and heavy tools. The column disappeared into the so-called Commissar Bunker, followed by five officers. Ten minutes later another detail carried heavy crates into another nearby bunker.

Soon afterward, the men at the listening posts reported that their detectors registered the sounds of excavation work. During the following days these observations were confirmed in detail. Another tunnel was being dug in the direction of Company C's command post. The entrance to the tunnel was believed to be in the immediate vicinity of the Commissar Bunker. A German combat patrol penetrated to the enemy position in front of the bunker, but was driven back before it could reach the entrance to the tunnel. Thereupon, the howitzer battery was ordered to direct harassing fire on the presumed location of the entrance as well as on the Commissar Bunker.

Since these attempts at interference did not seem to interrupt the Russian construction effort, the German regimental commander decided to dig a vertical shaft toward the Russian tunnel and to evacuate from the danger area all personnel whose presence was not absolutely essential. Only an outpost line was to be left to protect the German engineers during the construction of the shaft. The excavating work was rendered more difficult by the fact that the engineers hit a layer of quicksand which delayed their progress. Finally, on 30 September, upon reaching a depth of 56 feet, the German engineers suddenly entered the enemy tunnel without being noticed by the Russians. While a German patrol overpowered the Russians in the tunnel and blocked the entrance near the Commissar Bunker, the engineers cut the firing wire and recovered 20 tons of explosives.

VII. The Recapture of Goldap (November 1944)

During the last year of the war German engineers were frequently employed as infantry, particularly to launch counterattacks against heavily mined enemy positions. At that time the manpower problem was growing more and more acute in the German Army, and many field commanders were compelled to sacrifice their specialized troops in order to comply with direct orders from Hitler.

During the autumn of 1944 the German Fourth Army was engaged in defensive fighting around Gumbinnen in East Prussia. After the Russian 88th Guards Division had succeeded in occupying the town of Goldap on 21 October, the Russian front line formed a salient skirting Goldap. This salient led from the northern tip of Lake Goldap past the western limits of the town and then continued in a straight line southeastward, parallel to the Goldap-Treuburg highway. Approximately 2 miles south of Goldap the Russians had occupied an advance position on Mount Goldap, whose 1,014-foot

SMALL UNIT ACTIONS

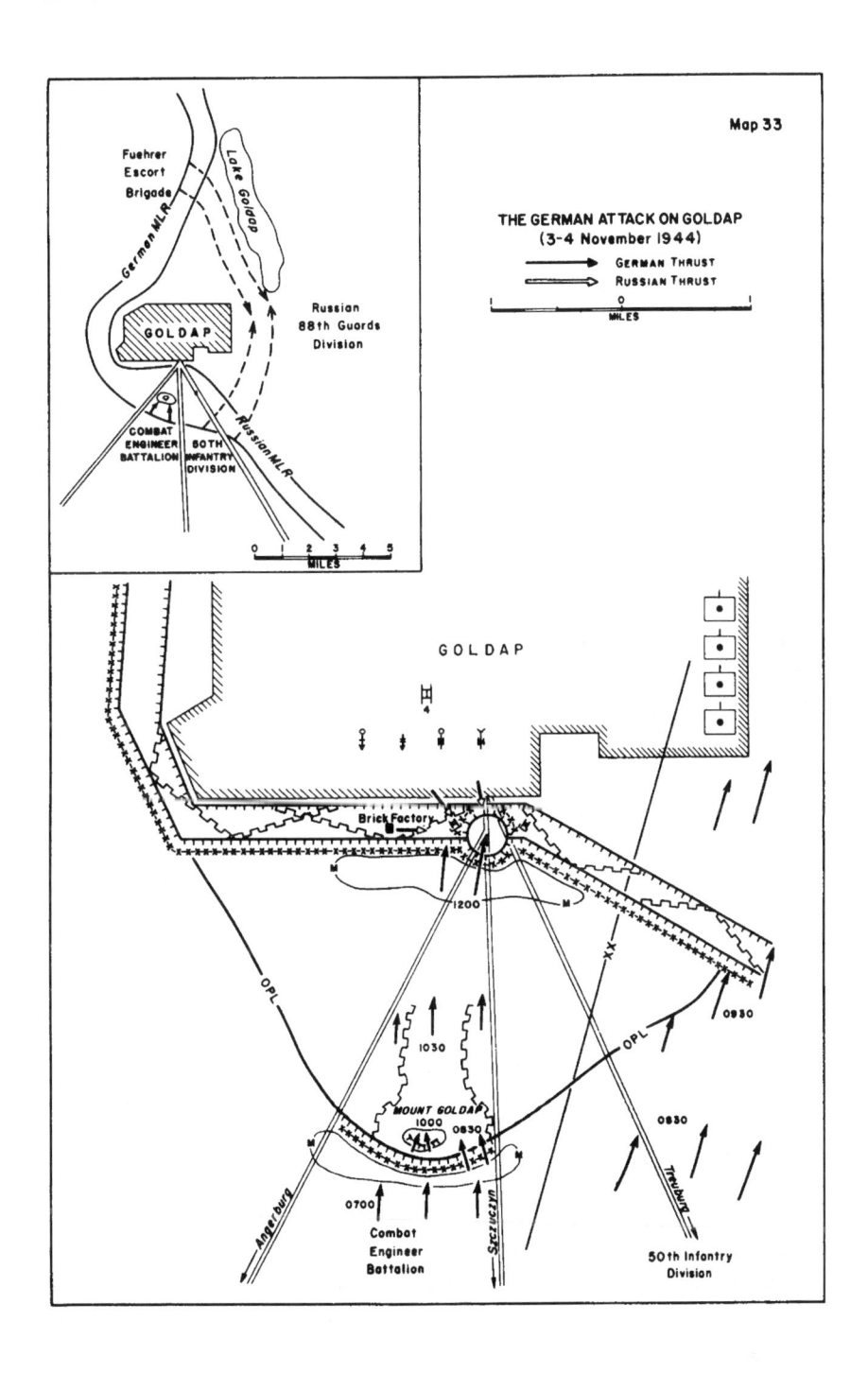

Map 33

THE GERMAN ATTACK ON GOLDAP
(3-4 November 1944)

→ GERMAN THRUST
⇒ RUSSIAN THRUST

elevation afforded a commanding view of the surrounding territory (map 33).

Toward the end of October the commander of Fourth Army was ordered to retake Goldap. The plan he drew up called for an envelopment to be launched early on 3 November with the 50th Infantry Division advancing from the southeast while the Fuehrer Escort Brigade was simultaneously driving down from the northwest. The two attack forces were to pierce the Russian lines at the base of the salient, envelop the enemy garrison in and around Goldap, annihilate the Russians within the pocket, and thus re-establish a straight front line east of the town.

To eliminate any threat to the flank of the 50th Infantry Division from the direction of Mount Goldap, the GHQ engineer battalion directly subordinate to Fourth Army was given the mission of attacking and seizing the forward Russian position from the south. For this purpose the battalion was reinforced by a self-propelled assault gun battery. The attack was scheduled to be launched 90 minutes before the 50th Division was to jump off.

The Russian advance position on Mount Goldap consisted of a continuous fortified line situated halfway up the southern slope between the two roads leading from Goldap to Angerburg and Szczuczyn, respectively. The summit had been transformed into a strong point with all-around defenses. Two connecting trenches interdicted access to the advance position from the rear and thus precluded the possibility of an envelopment. The main position on the southern slope was protected by wire entanglements, while the approaches to the hill were heavily mined, particularly in the vicinity of the two roads.

A force consisting of three infantry companies, each with five machine guns and three heavy mortars, held the advance position. The approaches to the hill lay well within range of four Russian artillery batteries emplaced near the eastern outskirts of Goldap. Their fire was directed by forward observers atop the hill. The flanks of the advance position were connected with the Russian MLR by outpost lines, which could also be directly supported by fire from the MLR.

The Russian MLR, established about 150 feet in front of the southern limits of Goldap, consisted of two parallel fortified lines 500 feet apart. Diagonal connecting trenches crisscrossed the zone between the two lines, permitting the defenders to seal off any hostile penetration. Wire obstacles were placed in front of the outer line.

Every company deployed along the MLR was assigned a 500-yard defense sector. In each, two-thirds of the company strength was employed in the outer line with 1 machinegun emplaced every 50 yards and 1 mortar every 200 yards. The rest of the company was held back in the inner line as a counterattack reserve.

At the fork where the roads branch off to Angerburg and Szczuczyn, the outer line was developed into a strong point, manned by 25 men whose weapons included heavy machineguns and mortars. Two tanks were dug in nearby to provide protective fire. An all-around wire entanglement guarded the strong point. Along the southern outskirts of Goldap the Russians had emplaced a number of heavy infantry weapons and antitank guns so skillfully that they were almost completely hidden from view. Within the town four T34 tanks were standing by as a mobile reserve.

To achieve maximum surprise, the engineers were to attack Mount Goldap on 3 November, without the usual artillery preparation at daybreak. During the preceding night the battalion assembled directly south of the hill. Rain and strong northwesterly winds impeded the Russian reconnaissance and helped to conceal the assembly of the battalion and the concentration of the 50th Infantry Division units on the right. During the last hours before dawn mine-clearing teams of the engineer battalion—unnoticed by the Russians, or so the Germans believed—succeeded in clearing several lanes through the mine field up to within 50 yards of the hostile outposts.

Promptly at 0700 the battalion launched its attack. The intention of taking the forward enemy line in the first assault was not realized. It soon became obvious that the Russians had observed the activities of the mine-clearing teams. However, instead of opening fire immediately, the Russians realigned their machineguns so that they were able to sweep the entire length of the mine lanes. A considerable number of casualties were thus inflicted upon the assault forces. Less than 15 minutes after the attack had been launched, the no man's land in front of the Russian position came under heavy artillery and mortar fire. The attack bogged down in the outpost area.

Even though two German artillery battalions concentrated their fire on Mount Goldap and silenced most of the Russian infantry weapons defending it, the engineers were still unable to advance. By 0800 the four Russian batteries in Goldap had been neutralized by the artillery preparation for the attack of the 50th Infantry Division; the fire from the heavy weapons in the Russian MLR was thereupon diverted against the jumpoff positions of the division. It was then that the engineer troops were finally able to break the hostile resistance and penetrate the positions on the southeastern and eastern slopes of Mount Goldap. Although the hill was not completely occupied by 0830, when the 50th Division jumped off for its attack, the diversionary maneuver of the engineers did tie down the Mount Goldap forces sufficiently to avert the danger of a flank attack.

The Russian commander soon realized that he would be unable to hold the advance position much longer. To avoid unnecessary bloodshed, he ordered the evacuation of the position, beginning at 0900. Covered by fire from three machineguns on the hill's summit, the companies holding the advance position extricated themselves, withdrew along both sides of the hill, and reached their MLR without suffering serious losses. The men in the strong point atop the hill fought a successful rear guard action; however, their resistance was finally broken about 1000 after bitter hand-to-hand fighting with pistols, hand grenades, rifle butts, and bayonets.

Having seized and secured the hill, the engineer battalion was ordered to prepare to join in the attack on the Russian MLR, but to await specific orders before jumping off. The Fourth Army commander intended to hold back the frontal assault by the engineer battalion until such time as the envelopment of Goldap from the east had progressed sufficiently to assure that the maximum number of enemy troops would be trapped within the town. Unfortunately, this plan soon had to be abandoned. At 0930, when the advance elements of the 50th Infantry Division reached the defense belt that skirted the southeast corner of Goldap, they were subjected to such violent flanking fire from the Russian strong point at the road fork that the engineer battalion had to be called upon to resume its attack and reduce this enemy position without delay.

For almost a full hour, beginning at 1050, three German artillery battalions concentrated their fire on the road fork and the immediately adjacent positions. Protected by this curtain of fire and spearheaded by five self-propelled assault guns, two of the engineer companies led the attack toward the main Russian position on a 300-yard frontage. Once again the engineers suffered heavy casualties which were due, primarily, to the vast enemy mine belt that extended in front of the entire position, ranging in depth from 200 to 300 yards. German artillery support proved much too weak to reduce the objective, silence enemy artillery and heavy weapons in the town, and thwart the Russian flanking attack launched from the direction of the brick factory. As a result, the attack ground to a halt 150 yards short of the enemy's outer line.

About 1200, German close-support aircraft succeeded in knocking out the two Russian tanks that were dug in near the strong point. By that time German artillery had stopped the enemy flanking attack and directed its fire against the hostile gun emplacements at the edge of the town. It was only then that the engineers finally succeeded in breaking into the Russian position. In their attempt to widen the gap, the engineers suddenly ran up against a vigorous Russian counterthrust that was supported by the four T34's from within the town. The German assault guns and Russian tanks met at close range. During a violent exchange of fire all but one of the assault guns were put out of action. In furious hand-to-hand fighting the engineer battalion finally succeeded in gaining a secure foothold within the strong point and in neutralizing a 150-yard strip on each side of the road fork. By this action the Russians were prevented from laying effective flanking fire upon the 50th Division's main assault force during the most critical stage of its enveloping attack.

Russian riflemen, taking full advantage of the many connecting trenches between the two lines made repeated attempts to seal off the point of penetration. In the course of the afternoon the Russians launched several counterattacks with forces of varying strength, the largest comprising two companies, in an effort to regain the vital strong point. Although supported by effective artillery and mortar fire from the north and west, these attempts were frustrated. There was no slackening of Russian resistance when, toward evening, the 50th Division finally made contact with the Fuehrer Escort Brigade and closed the ring around the Goldap garrison. During the night the Russians shifted most of their heavy weapons and guns to the eastern part of the town to assist the relief forces driving toward Goldap from the east by a well-timed breakout attempt. Despite the absence of adequate fire support, strong Rusian assault detachments continued their counterattacks on the German-held strong point at the road fork, but to no avail.

The following morning the engineer battalion, which had been reinforced by infantry units during the night, resumed its attack on the inner line. Hardly a single heavy weapon was encountered. Yet, even in this hopeless situation, the Russian riflemen resisted so fiercely that the Germans had to take the positions and connecting trenches one by one. The Russians continued to fire until their ammunition was expended; hardly a man was captured who had not been hit. By noon the engineer battalion was able to enter Goldap, but it was evening before the town was finally mopped up.

During this action the German engineers benefited from the weather conditions, which concealed the build-up and mine-clearing operations from the defenders until shortly before the jumpoff. The cooperation between the Russian infantry and its supporting weapons was exemplary, not only during the fighting in the advance position on Mount Goldap but also later, after the German engineers had breached the MLR. Truly remarkable was the flexibility demonstrated by the Russian artillery, in sharp contrast to its stiff rigidity of former years.

The high state of Russian morale found expression here in the discipline and self-control displayed by the men in the advance position after spotting the German mine-clearing details, in the successful delaying action fought by the rear guards atop the hill, in the determined counterthrusts launched against the German penetrations, and in the courageous, fierce resistance offered by the Russian riflemen

GERMAN BUNKER in the Taiga.

who, particularly during the final phase of the engagement, fought a hopeless battle merely to gain time.

The German engineer battalion, even though victorious in this local action, was decimated by its 2-day commitment as infantry. This was a high price to pay for a diversionary attack that was to contribute to eliminating a Russian salient.

PART THREE
SPECIAL OPERATIONS

Chapter 4
Fighting in Taiga and Tundra

I. General

During the summer of 1941 German forces advancing through northern Finland toward Kandalaksha and Murmansk failed to reach their objective, the Murmansk–Leningrad railroad. After an unsuccessful Russian offensive in the spring of 1942, there followed a period of stalemate which lasted for 2½ years. During this time the German forces north of the Arctic Circle opposed the Russians along two widely separated fronts. The Kandalaksha front to the south was held by two infantry divisions under the command of the XXXVI Infantry Corps, and the Murmansk front to the north was held by one coastal defense and two mountain infantry divisions under the XIX Mountain Infantry Corps. Patrols secured the intermediate terrain (map 34).

Immediately after the Russo-Finnish armistice, which was concluded in the begining of September 1944, the Russians launched an offensive on the Kandalaksha front, followed by another in the Murmansk area a month later.

The actions described in this chapter took place in the land of the taiga and tundra. Primeval forests, lakes, swamps, and rocks are characteristic of the taiga region, which stretches from below the Arctic Circle to the area across which the Russians launched their northern offensive in October 1944. At that time they thrust across the none too distinctly delimited border region where the taiga merges into the tundra. From there to the shores of the Arctic Ocean extends the treeless, mossy tundra.

The terrain factors and weather conditions had a decisive effect on the operations in these regions. Moreover, the assistance given to the Germans by their allies, the Finns, proved to be extremely valuable. Not only did the Finns fight side by side with the German units, they also assisted in the training of newly arrived troops and helped them get adjusted to the peculiarities of the theater. When the Finns dropped out of the war, the position of the Germans became untenable.

The Russians were thoroughly familiar with the requirements of combat in taiga and tundra. During the stalemate they defended themselves with great skill. In 1944 they demonstrated an extraordinary ability to move across trackless terrain and to adapt themselves to its features. Even tanks and artillery traveled over roads that the Germans had previously considered impassable for any vehicle. No less surprising to the Germans was the speed of the Russians in overcoming or bypassing man-made obstacles and barriers. The tactics they used most frequently were enveloping maneuvers. When pursuing withdrawing German units, they often sent encircling forces around one or both flanks of the retreating Germans.

The first three of the following actions took place during the stalemate that extended from the spring of 1942 through the autumn of 1944, while the last one relates to the delaying actions and retrograde movements conducted by the Germans during their withdrawal across northern Finland.

II. A Sabotage Operation Against the Murmansk–Leningrad Rail Line (August 1942)

In the summer of 1942 the German Twentieth Mountain Army was committed in northern Finland. The XXXVI Mountain Infantry Corps held the center of the German front east of Alakurti and opposed superior Russian forces. After the German offensive, whose objective it was to gain control of the vital Murmansk–Leningrad railroad line, ended in failure, both sides established themselves in well-prepared positions, and the situation remained stabilized. The German front was not a continuous line. Between the central and southern corps, and extending north and south of the Arctic Circle, there was a 45-mile gap that was protected by only two Finnish infantry battalions. Operations on both sides were limited to lively patrol activity and small-scale probing attacks.

It was, of course, no secret to the German military leaders that at the time the bulk of Allied lend-lease materiel, including ammunition, motor vehicles, rations, and clothing entered Russia through the port of Murmansk, which is ice-free the year round. From there the supplies were moved to Leningrad by rail. Even the most intensive efforts of German air and naval forces had little effect on the flow of supplies into Murmansk harbor. The Luftwaffe frequently succeeded in cutting the rail line to Leningrad, but the interruptions were only

SMALL UNIT ACTIONS

temporary. With both military and civilian labor forces standing by at all times, the Russians were invariably able to repair the lines and even the damaged tunnels and bridges with surprising ease and speed. The Germans finally came to the conclusion that the only way to disrupt traffic along this important supply artery was to effect a thorough demolition of bridges and tunnels by trained sabotage units.

a. The Special Missions and Sabotage Company (SMS Company). Military operations in the densely wooded terrain, intersticed by numerous lakes, waterways, and swamps, as well as by some very hilly and rocky regions, confronted combat and service units alike with great difficulties. In view of these terrain hazards the idea of launching an all-out attack against the rail line was abandoned, one such attempt having ended in complete failure. Instead, there was a general agreement that this difficult mission could best be accomplished by a highly mobile and specially trained small unit. Such a unit was the so-called Special Missions and Sabotage Company, a GHQ unit attached to army and at that time stationed in the XXXVI Corps rear area.

The Special Missions and Sabotage Company (SMS Company)* was activated in the spring of 1942 as a part of the so-called Brandenburg Regiment. This regiment, operating under the direct control of the Armed Forces High Command, was responsible for the recruiting, organizing, and training of special intelligence and sabotage units of various sizes from companies down to teams and even individuals. Unlike many other special purpose units within the German Armed Forces, these units were manned by hand-picked troops and exceptionally well supplied with weapons and equipment.

The commander of the SMS Company was an exceedingly energetic young officer who possessed superior tactical ability and an intimate knowledge of the Russian language. Each squad had an able and experienced German NCO and an expert Finnish interpreter who spoke fluent Russian. Two out of three of the men were former POW's or deserters from the Red Army, originating from the Ukraine or other parts of Russia and opposing the Soviet regime. The others were so-called ethnical Germans who hailed from southern Tyrol, the Balkans, and the German settlements along the Volga. Three men in each squad had undergone engineer training and were especially proficient in handling and setting explosive charges.

The company was equipped with Russian or Finnish submachineguns. Each platoon had one 80-mm. mortar and each squad one light machinegun. In addition, the company had two 75-mm. field guns

---
*See organizational chart.

Organizational Chart of the Special Missions and Sabotage Company

a. Organization of the Company

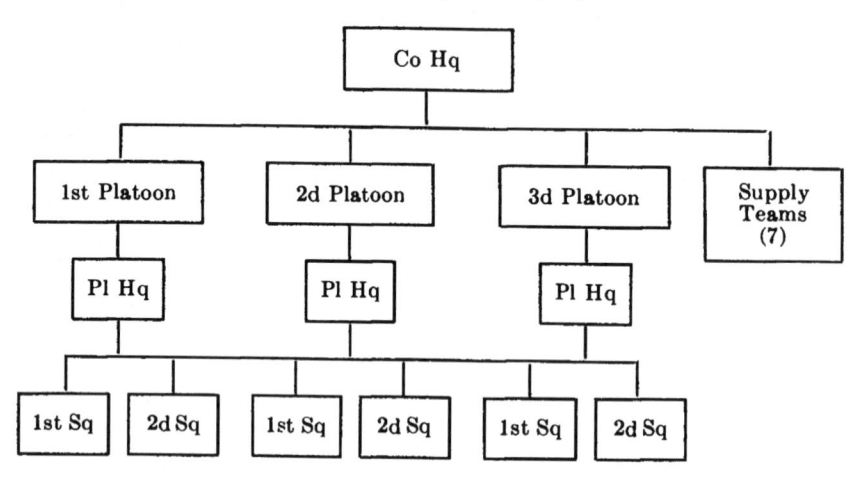

```
                          ┌───────┐
                          │ Co Hq │
                          └───┬───┘
        ┌─────────────┬──────┴──────┬─────────────┐
   ┌─────────┐  ┌─────────┐   ┌─────────┐   ┌─────────┐
   │1st Platoon│ │2d Platoon│  │3d Platoon│  │ Supply  │
   └─────┬────┘  └─────┬────┘  └─────┬────┘  │ Teams   │
         │             │             │       │  (7)    │
     ┌───┴──┐      ┌───┴──┐      ┌───┴──┐    └─────────┘
     │Pl Hq │      │Pl Hq │      │Pl Hq │
     └───┬──┘      └───┬──┘      └───┬──┘
      ┌──┴──┐       ┌──┴──┐       ┌──┴──┐
  ┌─────┐ ┌─────┐ ┌─────┐ ┌─────┐ ┌─────┐ ┌─────┐
  │1st Sq│ │2d Sq│ │1st Sq│ │2d Sq│ │1st Sq│ │2d Sq│
  └─────┘ └─────┘ └─────┘ └─────┘ └─────┘ └─────┘
```

b. Composition of Individual Subunits

Co Hq		Pl Hq		1st Sq		2d Sq	
Co CO	1	Pl Ldr	1	Sq Ldr	1	Sq Ldr	1
First Sgt	1	Hq Sq Ldr	1	Finnish		Finnish	
Messengers	2	Messengers	2	Guide	1	Guide	1
Med NCO	1	Litter Bearer	1	Machine		Engineers	3
Finnish		Finnish		Gunners	3	Sniper	1
Guide & Dog	1	Guide & Dog	1	Engineers	3	Rifle Grenade	
Radiomen	4	Radiomen	2	Sniper	1	Man	1
	—		—	Rifle Gren-		Riflemen	5
Total	10	Total	8	ade Man	1		—
				Riflemen	2	Total	12
					—		
				Total	12		

Supply Teams

Team Ldr	1
Men	2
Total	3

Total strength of the company: 127 Officers and Men.

that could be disassembled and transported in sections. Radio equipment enabled the company headquarters to maintain contact with higher echelons in the year, with each of its platoons, and with one of its intermediate supply points. Attached to the company was a detachment of 18 bloodhounds and watch dogs with 6 Finnish handlers.

b. Preliminary Preparations. In mid-July 1942 the German armies were on the offensive deep in the interior of European Russia. At that time the SMS Company received orders to prepare for a long-range reconnaissance and sabotage operation against the Murmansk-Leningrad rail line. The operation was to take from 2 to 3 weeks and was to be launched early in August. Whereas the long summer days in the Land of the Midnight Sun were favorable for movements and operations, they made the problem of escaping enemy observation all the more difficult.

According to the plan the distance from the point of departure in Kairala to the demolition targets, about 150 miles, was to be traversed by negotiating the lakes and streams of that region. For this purpose collapsible paddle boats and outboard motors, weighing 50 and 20 pounds respectively, were issued to the company. The men were thoroughly trained in the handling and maintenance of both boats and motors at the company's training base near Kairala. During the training period it was quickly discovered that the best safeguard against capsizing, especially when the boats were driven by outboard motor or were being towed, was to lash them together in pairs with poles and heavy rope. However, frequent resort to this expedient was not anticipated since the greatest portion of the route could be covered only by manual propulsion. Furthermore, it was planned to use the outboard motors beyond Tumcha only in the event of an emergency.

To carry out its sabotage mission the company was issued a highly effective explosive charge newly developed by the Finns and equipped with a conventional time fuze. The latter could be adjusted to set off the charge with a delay period of as much as 8 days, thus giving the company ample time to return to its home base safely. During training the company conducted dry runs to familarize every man with the handling and installation of the demolition charges.

The radio operators, too, had to undergo an intensive training course, which included instruction in using the Russian four-element code-group system (the five-element code group was standard in the German Army). It was necessary to adopt the Russian system for this mission in order to avoid recognition which might compromise the plans for the entire operation.

The company commander had two opportunities to reconnoiter the approach route and demolition target points from the air. However, both flights failed to reveal anything that necessitated a change in plans. They only confirmed that there were no Russian troops, labor camps, or permanently inhabited settlements west of Kovda. Finnish liaison officers who served as consultants during the preparations also discounted the possibility of encountering superior Russian forces along the selected approach route, provided the operation plans remained secret.

A Junkers 88 bomber and a Henschel 126 reconnaissance plane were standing by at the Alakurti airfield ready to airdrop supplies and evacuate wounded in the event of an emergency. They were to be contacted by radio and guided to their target area by smoke signals from the ground.

c. Final Preparations. On 25 July 1942 the company commander received the following operations order from the commanding general of XXXVI Mountain Corps:

> Jumping off on 2 August and utilizing available water routes, the SMS Company will move to the area west of Kvoda and will effect demolitions of the Murmansk-Leningrad rail line at two or more points. Excluding a Russian attack, all combat will be avoided. Extreme precaution will be taken to avert arousing enemy suspicion.

The company commander decided to use the route of march previously selected since it necessitated only one portage, across the watershed some 8 miles southeast of Kairala (map 35). To get off to a faster start and to conserve physical energy and motor fuel, the company was to be provided with several assault boats, so that the entire unit could be towed the first leg of the journey.

Some of the items of clothing and equipment normally worn by German arctic troops during the summer had to be discarded to reduce the danger of recognition. They were replaced with Russian-type rubber hip-boots, camouflage jackets, a Finnish dagger, and a small field bag for carrying ammunition and rations. The wearing of cartridge belts and rank insignia was prohibited. Each man carried mosquito netting and a Finnish insect repellent.

Because of weight limitations, neither mortars nor light field guns could be taken along. In place of a mortar, each squad was issued one rifle with a grenade launcher attachment, which had proven very effective in forest fighting. The grenades fired by this launcher had the additional advantage that they could also be hurled by hand during close-in fighting. Beside the submachineguns the company carried

SMALL UNIT ACTIONS

along 3 light machineguns, each with 2,500 rounds of ammunition. The guiding principle was to carry relatively few weapons but more than the bare minimum requirements of ammunition.

The problem of supplying the company was not an easy one. To live off the land exclusively was impossible because the region offered only berries and mushrooms. Much game, including reindeer, elk, black grouse, hazel hens, and polar rabbits, could be found, but to shoot it might well have given the Germans away. However, the lakes could provide ample fish, which would serve as a ration supplement.

It was decided that the company's supply would be handled by seven teams of three men each. These teams were to shuttle supplies forward from Kairala and establish seven supply points along the route. Since the company could carry with it rations and other supplies for the first 6 days, it did not expect to become dependent on the supply teams until after reaching the base camp on Lake Kovd.

A doctor was not available, but an experienced medical technician and three litter bearers, one for each platoon, did accompany the unit.

Before setting out, the company commander requested that two roving reconnaissance patrols, one from each of the two Finnish battalions, provide security up to the Tumcha area. Should any Russians be encountered along the way, these patrols were to distract them by diversionary movements and radio deception.

The following was the projected timetable for the operation:

First day: Proceed to Lake Siyeminki, located at the head of the Kuvzhdenga River.

Second day: Continue to Supply Point 4, west of Tumcha.

Third day: Bypass Tumcha, send out reconnaissance parties, and establish contact with the Finnish roving patrols; then continue to Supply Point 6.

Fourth day: After reaching Lake Kovd, reconnoiter the region around Velikiy Island.

Fifth day: Reconnoiter in the direction of Pazhma Island and establish a base camp there.

Sixth day: Rest.

Seventh and eighth days: Reconnoiter eastward in the direction of the rail line.

Ninth through eleventh days: Commit three demolition detachments, consisting of one platoon each, against three separate points along the rail line. Place and set demolition charges in tunnels and under bridges.

Twelfth day: Return to base camp and rest.

Thirteenth through fifteenth days: Start return trip to Kairala using outboard motors only after reaching Tumcha.

d. The Course of the Operation. Early on the morning of 3 August the company moved out. The paddle boats were lashed together in pairs and towed by assault boats in groups of six down the chain of lakes south of Kairala. Shortly before noon the 3-mile portage was reached. Some time was spent in traversing it, since as many as three trips were necessary to get all the equipment across. By late afternoon the boats were reassembled and paired off. They then moved downstream using the outboard motors whenever possible. After reaching Lake Siyeminki they stopped to rest.

The company continued the advance on the morning of 4 August and all movements went smoothly and according to schedule. Early that evening radio contact was established with the two Finnish patrols, which reported no Russian troops in and around Tumcha.

With the patrols still providing cover, the company proceeded along Lake Sush on 5 August and late in the evening reached Supply Point 6. Meanwhile, the Finnish patrols learned that a Russian patrol had passed through the now-deserted town of Tumcha some 3 or 4 days previously. Since it was a Russian practice to conduct such reconnaissance missions every 10 to 14 days, it could be assumed that they would not be back for another 7 to 10 days.

On 6 August the advance to the next supply point, No. 7, was delayed because the western part of Lake Kovd turned out to be full of bulrushes. One squad was dispatched to Velikiy Island during the evening to learn whether Russian troops or labor details were on the island. Later, the same squad was to act as a covering force while the rest of the company landed on the west side of Pazhma Island and established a base camp. A simple, abbreviated radio code was devised to report the presence or absence of Russian troops. The code consisted of only one or two signals for which the receiving station had to be constantly on the alert.

At 0700 the next morning a flash came that Velikiy Island was clear of enemy forces, while a second message at about 1130 stated that no Russians had been sighted on Pazhma Island either. The company could therefore go ashore and establish a base camp by late evening without fear of detection or interference. Base Camp A was set up on the western side of the island near the small bay into which a brooklet emptied. A cordon of sentries was posted to keep the old fishing village on the east side of the island under close observation. It was assumed that any Russian scouting parties or labor details that might be in the area would take advantage of the blockhouses and running water afforded by the village. Velikiy Island was originally ruled out as a base camp since it was feared that camp fires could easily be spotted by the many fishing parties that were known to frequent the more heavily stocked northern part of Lake Kovd.

According to the schedule, 8 August, the sixth day of the operation, was to be a day of rest. When the first supplies that had been relayed along the route of advance arrived at the base camp, it was learned that one of the supplymen, a member of Supply Team 4, had drowned when his boat capsized. On their own initiative, the leaders of Supply Teams 4 and 5 decided to move Supply Point 5 about 5 miles westward because Team 4, with one man short, could no longer be expected to relay supplies the whole length of its assigned sector. Since fishing around Pazhma Island was good, the company could be adequately fed even if regular rations were delayed.

At dawn, on 9 August, the three platoons each sent out a patrol to reconnoiter the rail bridges and tunnels that were to be blown up. Of the three objectives that were to be involved, the central target was a bridge, which on the basis of aerial photographs was estimated to measure 1,600 feet in length. This bridge could be approached only by boat, and a small island located a short distance to the west afforded an excellent jumpoff point. However, and just because of these advantages, it was also expected that this bridge would be particularly well guarded against sabotage or other attack. This assumption seemed justified in view of the heavy antiaircraft fire that German planes encountered while on bombing missions over the area.

Whereas the approach route to the smaller bridge to the north also seemed quite favorable, considerable difficulties were expected en route to the southern target—for example, the necessity of making two portages. The bridge itself, however, spanned a deep gorge and therefore would probably require much more time to repair than the targets farther north.

The three reconnaissance patrols had succeeded in reaching the immediate vicinity of the objectives in the late afternoon and early evening of 9 August. The explosive charges they had brought along were deposited in protected and well-concealed spots near the targets. During the exceptionally bright night they watched traffic and observed Russian sentries patrolling the rail line and being relieved.

The company commander decided to rest his men on 11 August. During the evening he ordered Company Headquarters and the 2d and 3d Platoons to move to the northwestern tip of Velikiy Island. The following day Base Camp B was established there to shorten the supply line and return route of those two platoons, while Supply Team 7 took over Base Camp A to support the 1st Platoon.

On 13 August additional reconnaissance patrols were sent out. The explosives were moved closer to the target areas and all contingencies

GERMAN BUNKERS on the Kandalaksha front, 1944

were discussed in detail. The company commander ordered the explosive charges placed preferably between the hours of 0100 and 0300 because it was then that the sentries were prone to relax their vigil.

The three sabotage operations were carried out in the early morning hours of 14 August. The 1st Platoon had the misfortune of being spotted by a Russian sentry at 0200, before it was able to place its charges. Although the platoon leader did succeed in pouring gasoline on the bridge and igniting it, he was forced to withdraw after a brief exchange of shots with Russian guards who had meanwhile been alerted by the sentry. During the ensuing melee one of the boats was hit, and its oarsman killed. Another boat capsized, but its occupant was rescued. The Russian guards on the bridge made excellent targets for the German riflemen who picked off 8 or 10 of them.

Shortly after the firing began the Russian guards sounded the emergency alarm, which quickly alerted all posts up and down the line. This was soon followed by feverish Russian radio activity, some of which could be intercepted by the company command post at Base Camp B. When the company commander received a radio message from the 1st Platoon informing him of what had transpired, he ordered the other two platoons to set off their charges without delay. Using its outboard motors after again reaching Lake Kovd, the 1st Platoon returned to Base Camp B at 1700.

The 2d Platoon, committed to the demolition of the main target in the center, succeeded in approaching the bridge, protected by vegetation that lined the southern bank of the long outlet. Guided by their dogs, the three Finns in that platoon quietly overpowered and killed the two Russian sentries at the southern end of the bridge. The southern half of the bridge was then swiftly prepared for demolition at three widely separated points. The presence of the German unit had apparently not been noticed by the Russian guard posted at the middle of the span or by the sentries at the northern end. However, when the general alarm was sounded, guard reinforcements streamed across the bridge on the run and the Germans were no longer able to prepare and place a fourth demolition charge nearer the center of the span. Instead, the charges already in place had to be detonated at once. A skillfully emplaced light machinegun held the Russian sentries at bay until the bulk of the platoon could disengage and withdraw. While the demolition men were pulling back, a 75-yard length of the bridge was blown sky high. Only two of the Germans were slightly wounded, while Russian casualties were conservatively estimated as eight men hit by machinegun fire and several others caught on the bridge when the blast went off. By 0315 the platoon had reassembled and received radio orders from company headquarters to return immediately. Using its outboards the platoon got back to Base Camp B at 1100.

The 3d Platoon encountered some difficulties in approaching its target. After first taking a wrong turn the platoon was further delayed by a strong current. One of the Finnish guides commandeered a fishing boat and the members of the crew disguised themselves as fishermen. The platoon was able to make up the lost time and to reach the bridge in the early evening of 13 August. By 2100 the explosives were in place. The time fuses were set for only a 5-hour delay because the platoon leader wanted to observe the effect of the blasts from a safe distance.

Shortly after the Russian guard relief emerged from its shelter and made its way across the span, at about 0230, the charges went off, collapsing one of the piers and hurling several of the guards from the bridge. When the platoon leader reported the results of his mission to company headquarters, he was ordered to lead the platoon back to Base Camp B, where he arrived by midafternoon.

Soon after 1700, when the three platoons had reassembled, the company, including Supply Team 7, set out on the return trip. Russian reconnaissance planes appeared overhead and strafed the company with machinegun fire. Three men were slightly wounded and several of the boats were damaged.

While moving westward through Lake Kovd, the company's rear elements suddenly heard several motorboats approaching from behind at full speed. Cutting their outboard motors at once, the company barely succeeded in slipping into the reed-covered swamp to the south before six large motor boats swept by in a westerly direction. Each boat carried about 45 Russians armed with automatic weapons.

Contrary to the original plan, the company commander decided then and there to return by way of Lake Vizi in an effort to shake off the Russian pursuers. This change in plans could be communicated only to Supply Team 3 because that team alone was equipped with a radio set. However, all supply teams had been forewarned that, in the event the company failed to pick them up by midnight of 16 August, they were to proceed by the shortest route to the nearest German or Finnish unit.

The mouth of the stream connecting Lakes Kovd and Vizi was found with surprising ease, thanks to the skill of the Finns. The company proceeded under motor power to the western end of Lake Vizi, a journey that took all night. Five boats were lost in the rapids between the two lakes, but their occupants were safely hoisted into other boats.

SMALL UNIT ACTIONS

Russian reconnaissance planes repeatedly circled overhead, but each time the company was able to find cover. On reaching the western end of Lake Vizi, the company rested for several hours on the northern shore, which was farthest removed from the Russian bases.

In the late afternoon, the main body of the company, following close behind the advance guard, was just about to negotiate the watercourse connecting the western tips of Lakes Vizi and Tumcha, when a Russian force of at least four platoons suddenly attacked from ambush positions on both sides of the stream. The men were forced to leave their boats and abandon all equipment, including the radio sets. Most of the men swam to the north, the remaining ones to the south bank. It was fortunate for the company that the point squad had saved a machinegun. Having sized up the situation swiftly, the squad leader set up the weapon on the north bank and soon sprayed the area. As other members of the company reached shore, those whose weapons were still serviceable quickly joined the machinegun crew and brought their fire to bear on the Russian ambush force. Under cover of this defensive screen, the company was able to escape from the Russian trap having lost only five dead and eight wounded. A short time later the men assembled on the south bank of the stream.

From there the journey had to be continued on foot since almost all of the boats had been lost. By midnight the company reached a point about 4 miles northwest of Tumcha where it rested for half a day after establishing an all-around defensive position.

Roving patrols of the two Finnish battalions had been kept on the alert in the area south of Tumcha since the morning of 15 August to cover the return of the SMS Company. When they noticed the circling Russian reconnaissance planes and heard an exchange of fire from the direction of Lake Vizi, they rushed northward and attacked the Russian ambush force from behind, killing or wounding at least 35. Other Finnish patrols picked up Supply Teams 4 and 5, which were making their way westward through the Tumcha area.

In the course of the confusion a member of Supply Team 4, one of the Ukrainians, managed to slip away. Through radio intercept it was later discovered that he had succeeded in joining the Russians near Tumcha. It is safe to assume the reward for his exploits was a one-way ticket to a Siberian penal camp.

During the afternoon of 16 August the company made contact with outposts of the Finnish battalion some 10 miles north of Lake Siyeminki and from there returned to Kairala by evening.

e. The Performance of Foreign Nationals. The ethnic Germans, like the Finns, gave a good account of themselves during the operation. Their tenacity, self-sufficiency, and close kinship with nature proved very valuable. With the exception of the deserter from Supply Team 4, the former Russian nationals gave a good account of themselves. In this operation they were led by reliable German and Austrian cadre personnel, whose presence undoubtedly influenced their performance.

During two subsequent commitments in the XXXVI Mountain Infantry Corps area, however, the company failed to accomplish its mission. In the last instance the majority of the Russian nationals deserted after shooting down some of their officers and NCO's.

III. German Raid on a Russian Strong Point in Northern Finland (February 1944)

During the winter of 1943–44 the XIX Mountain Infantry Corps, occupying the northern sector of the Twentieth Mountain Army, was composed of two mountain divisions and one coastal defense division. The corps was opposed by numerically superior Russian forces. Both the Germans and Russians were holding fairly well-constructed positions for the third successive winter.

One of the two mountain infantry divisions, reinforced by special troops, occupied positions in the rocky tundra terrain about a mile west of the Litsa River, whose course was completely frozen over during the winter and therefore constituted no serious barrier. The tundra region combines the features of subalpine mountain tops and hilly terrain. The relatively minor elevations afford good observation of the intermediate terrain. Bare, rocky ground alternates with mossy patches. With the exception of some scattered, stunted birches the vegetation offers little cover.

The German front line consisted of a chain of unevenly spaced strong points, each organized for all-around defense. In some sectors the intervals between strong points measured up to 1 mile. These gaps were protected by an intricate defense system involving mutual fire support from the strong points and, if necessary, the commitment of local reserves. In general, the MLR was an imaginary line connecting the positions that had been prepared for defensive weapons. Along this line stood sentries, and additional listening posts were manned at night and during bad weather. Only during a state of alert were the positions fully occupied. The distance between the German and Russian lines varied between 1,000 yards and 1 mile.

Both sides limited their activities to intensive patrol actions, and operations in greater than squad strength were a rarity during the winter. In addition to the constant close-range reconnaisance, which was essential for security, especially during the long winter nights

SMALL UNIT ACTIONS

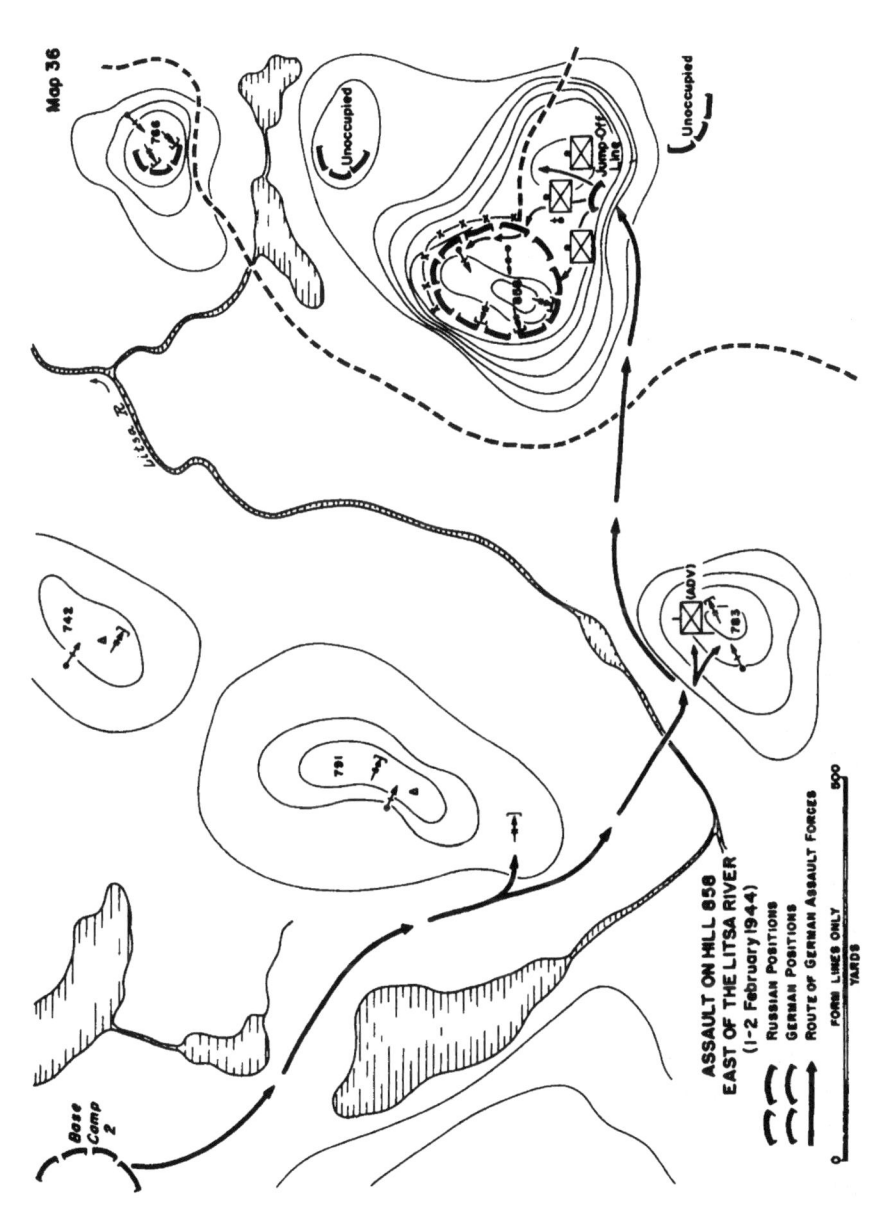

Map 36. ASSAULT ON HILL 658 EAST OF THE LITSA RIVER (1-2 February 1944)

and during snowstorms, both sides carried out raids and probing attacks to gather information, disrupt supply traffic, and keep intact the aggressiveness of the troops.

Early in January 1944 the 1st Battalion, 143d Mountain Infantry Regiment, received orders to prepare and carry out a raid against the

Russian strong point on Hill 858 (map 36). The objective of this raid was to take prisoners and to destroy as many of the enemy defensive installations and shelters as possible. To assure success, the raid was to be preceded by meticulous preparations, for which the battalion was allowed a maximum of four weeks. Hill 858 had been selected because it had not been attacked by the Germans since 1941. The steep western and southern slopes of the hill had been considered insurmountable, especially in winter. The Germans therefore assumed that the Russian garrison, whose outposts controlled the northern and eastern approaches of the hill, felt quite safe in its bastion and would consequently be more liable to relax its guard than troops in other sectors. On the basis of aerial photographs and close reconnaissance it appeared that wire obstacles had been set up only along the northern and eastern perimeter of the strong point. Another factor that influenced the choice of this objective was that German heavy weapons and reserve elements would be able to lend effective support from Hills 742, 791, and 783, which were located in the no man's land between the German strong points and Hill 858.

According to air and ground reconnaissance, the Russian strong point was held by one reinforced platoon. The German battalion commander decided to select a correspondingly small assault force, consisting of 1 platoon sergeant, 3 squad leaders, and 24 men. This force was to be subdivided into an assault squad, composed of the sergeant, 1 squad leader, and 10 men, and 2 supporting squads, each composed of a squad leader and 7 men. The assault force was assisted by reconnaissance elements, a medical team, a machinegun squad with two heavy machineguns, and a mortar squad with one 80-mm. mortar.

The German strong point located closest to the objective was designated Base Camp 2, where one mountain infantry and one engineer platoon were ordered to stand by as reserve forces. Artillery support would be provided upon request.

The raid was to be directed from a forward CP to be established on Hill 783. Between Base Camp 2 and the forward CP contact was to be maintained by telephone and radio. Wire lines would be extended to the assault force's jumpoff line just southeast of the objective. Radio silence was to be imposed during the initial phase of the raid.

Hofer, a battle-tested master sergeant who had proven his ability to lead such raids on previous occasions, was placed in command of the assault squad. He was an excellent mountaineer from the Tyrol and volunteered for this mission. In his mind there was little doubt that, given the right weather and sufficient time for preparation, it

SMALL UNIT ACTIONS

GERMAN SKI COMPANY in the Tundra, May 1944.

would be possible to climb the steep slopes leading to the Russian strong point.

Plans called for the assault squad to be armed exclusively with captured Russian submachineguns, and each man was to carry six magazines of ammunition. The supporting squads were to be equipped with two rifle grenade launchers and 60 grenades, a medium mortar with 48 rounds, and a heavy machinegun with 3,000 rounds. The men were also to carry mines and demolition charges to blow up the Russian installations. In addition, the assault squad was to be issued three Very pistols and flares.

All men were to wear padded winter uniforms and felt boots, except for the members of the assault force, who were to be issued ski boots, whose heavy rubber soles afforded extra traction. Each man was to wear a long white parka with hood, white outer trousers, a woolen cap, and woolen mittens with a hole for the trigger finger. The ammunition was to be carried in outside pockets of their parkas, and a Finnish dagger was to be kept handy. After careful deliberation it was decided not to use skis or wear colored brassards for identification as had been customary on patrol, because speed was less important than remaining unobserved.

The emergency-type rations carried by the assault force was to include combination chocolate-cola candy bars, hardtack, bacon, and dextrose. In addition to the usual supplies, the medical team was to take along a dog sled, two collapsible ski sleds, several reindeer-skin-lined sleeping bags, and some vacuum bottles filled with hot tea.

Before the operation was launched, recently taken aerial photographs were compared with older ones. Apart from a few hitherto unobserved shelters, they revealed no substantial changes in the Russian dispositions. Each man of the assault force was given an opportunity to familiarize himself with the terrain and the disposition of the Russian outposts by observation from Base Camp 2 and the OP's atop Hills 791 and 742. The information thus obtained was collated and formed the basis for panoramic sketches, which were then studied and evaluated in the light of the most recent aerial photographs.

In the German rear area, terrain features resembling the Russian-held strong point were used by the engineer platoon to build a replica of the Russian installations. For almost 2 weeks the assault force carried out a series of dry runs, some of them with live ammunition. During this intensive training period weapons, clothing, and equipment were tested, as were also the various tactical solutions to achieve perfect coordination among the different elements.

The originally proposed plan of dividing the assault force into three separate squads appeared to be the most effective and was finally adopted. During the approach the assault squad was to be split and each half was to be guided to the jumpoff line by one of the supporting squads. The latter were then to occupy their designated positions on the southern and southeastern slopes of Hill 858, while the assault squad reassembled and prepared to move out. Naturally, every man had to be given precise instructions as to the part he was to take in the raid, the success of which depended on maximum precision in timing.

The battalion commander ordered all participating leaders to attend map exercises, where different phases of the adopted and alternate plans of action were reviewed, including possible enemy countermeasures. The nearest major Russian strong point was 1 mile to the rear of Hill 858, so that the intervention by reserves was not expected less than 45 minutes after an alert had been sounded. The powdery snow, averaging over 3 feet in depth, would prevent these reserves from making better time.

After a prolonged freezing spell, during which the temperatures dipped as low as −40° F., the sky was overcast and toward noon of 1 February light snow flurries began to fall. By evening the flurries turned into a regular snowstorm. This was ideal weather for the

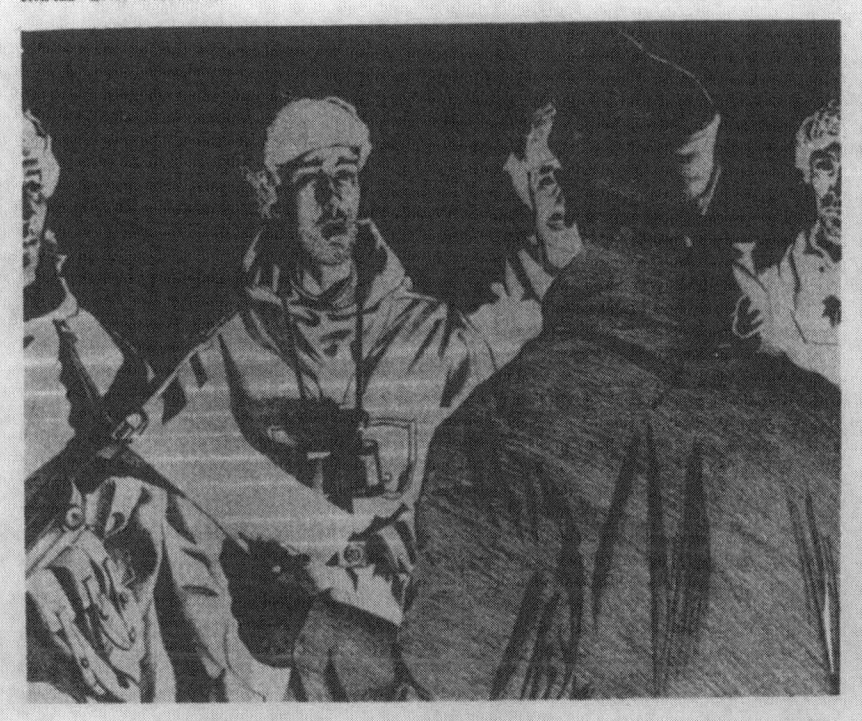

GERMAN PATROL reports in Lapland, 1942.

execution of the planned raid and, since all preparations had been made and the men were well rested, the assault was set for that night.

At 0030 the raiding party left Base Camp 2. The reconnaissance elements, constituting the point, led the way. Following in sequence were the officer in charge of the operation with headquarters personnel to man the forward CP, the medium mortar squad, the assault force proper, the medical team, and the heavy machinegun squad. Each element kept within sight of the one ahead. Part way up the southern slope of Hill 791 the machinegun squad dropped out and moved to a previously designated point from which it covered the advance of the other elements.

Shortly after the raiding party had set out, the snowstorm let up and presently only a few clouds obscured an otherwise clear, moonlit sky. The improved visibility was expected to be unfavorable for the execution of the raid. However, the raiding party continued its march, knowing that once the moon was down, visibility would again be poor. Despite the excellent visibility for the Russians, Hill 783 was reached safely at 0115. As soon as the command post had been established and sentries posted, the assault force proceeded on toward Hill 858. By 0300 the moon had set, and soon thereafter, despite the deep snow and occasional Russian flares, the assault force arrived at the foot of Hill 858, apparently without being observed. Over the steepest portion of the hill's slope the men had to crawl and climb in two single files, a feat that required great effort and skill.

By 0345 all the men were assembled in the jumpoff line. The two supporting squads took up their assigned positions without making contact with the enemy. Hofer and his squad began to work their way toward the road leading to the objective from the east. Concealed by the snow that was banked high on both sides of the road, Hofer hoped to gain access to the Russian compound. When he reached a point about 40 yards from the communication trench that connected the various shelters and emplacements, Hofer saw a Russian emerging from a shelter and walking toward the northeastern part of the compound. Without having noticed the Germans, the Russian disappeared in another section of the trench. Without hesitation Hofer decided to capture the bunker. Just as his squad was getting ready for the assault, Hofer discovered that he had mistaken a stone-reinforced section of the trench for a bunker. He quickly changed his mind, regrouped his squad, and advanced in the direction of the shelters at the northeast end of the compound by moving along the communication trench. One of his men noticed a cable lying in the trench and cut it. Suddenly the squad leader heard the steps of a man coming toward him in the dark. At a given signal the Germans pounced on him and overpowered him. While the squad leader and his men were trying to hold down the struggling Russian in the narrow trench, a second Russian approached unobserved. He saw the scuffle and, shouting for help, made a dash for the nearest shelter before any German could stop him. Since these shouts were bound to alert the Russian garrison and since he had at least captured one prisoner Hofer decided to pull his men back at once and leave the neutralization of the strong point installations to heavy weapons and artillery fire. With the information he had obtained, he would be able to pinpoint their targets.

The withdrawal took place according to plan. First the assault squad evacuated the area taking along the prisoner, then the supporting squad on the left, and finally the one on the right abandoned their positions. The supporting squad on the left did not have time to mine the communication trench and thereby obstruct it as intended. The Russians who had emerged from their shelters on the double were pinned down by grenade launcher and submachinegun fire from the German rear guard, which inflicted heavy losses before following the main body. Hofer was the last man to leave the hill.

As soon as the Russians realized that the Germans were pulling out, they recovered from the initial shock and began to fire light and medium mortars in the presumed direction of the German withdrawal. Since the Russians were unaware of the route the Germans had taken, their fire missed the single-file column retracing its steps down Hill 858.

At 0440 the assault force reached a point about midway between Hills 858 and 783. The sergeant fired a red flare, which both indicated his position and requested fire on Hill 858. The Germans on the surrounding hills were just waiting for this signal. With sudden vehemence the prepared fire of combined heavy weapons and artillery was unleashed, thus facilitating the further withdrawal of the assault force. The Russians also fired flares and lit up the no man's land between the German and Russian strong points with long-burning signal rockets. In addition to the Russian mortars firing from Hill 858, heavy machineguns on Hill 766 now joined in and raked the Litsa Valley. Their fire was well adjusted and German counterfire failed to silence them. The Russian mortars also directed well-aimed projectiles on Base Camp 2.

The withdrawing assault force took advantage of every terrain feature while traversing the northern slope of Hill 783 and crossing the Litsa. Up to that point it had not suffered a single casualty. When it was moving up the slope of Hill 791 from the bottom of Litsa Valley, the end of the column was suddenly hit by a hail of machinegun fire from Hill 766. Five men were wounded and, when a 120-mm. mortar shell scored a direct hit on the machinegun squad on the south slope of Hill 791, the Germans suffered six additional casualties.

The last elements of the assault force reached Base Camp 2 at 0530, by which time all the wounded had been brought back safely and given first aid. Fifteen minutes later the Germans ceased firing and the Russians followed suit soon afterward.

This action is typical of the small-scale fighting that took place in northern Finland from 1941 through 1944. Meticulous preparations and painstaking efforts usually led to negligible results. In this instance the German raiders did achieve surprise and were able to capture a prisoner, but they found out that the Russians on Hill 858 were on the alert, despite the fact that this strong point had not been attacked in 3 years. Interrogation of the prisoner provided little information, except that the garrison on the hill had recently been relieved by fresh troops. If a lesson was to be learned from this raid, it was that even the most careful preparation could not guarantee the success of such an operation.

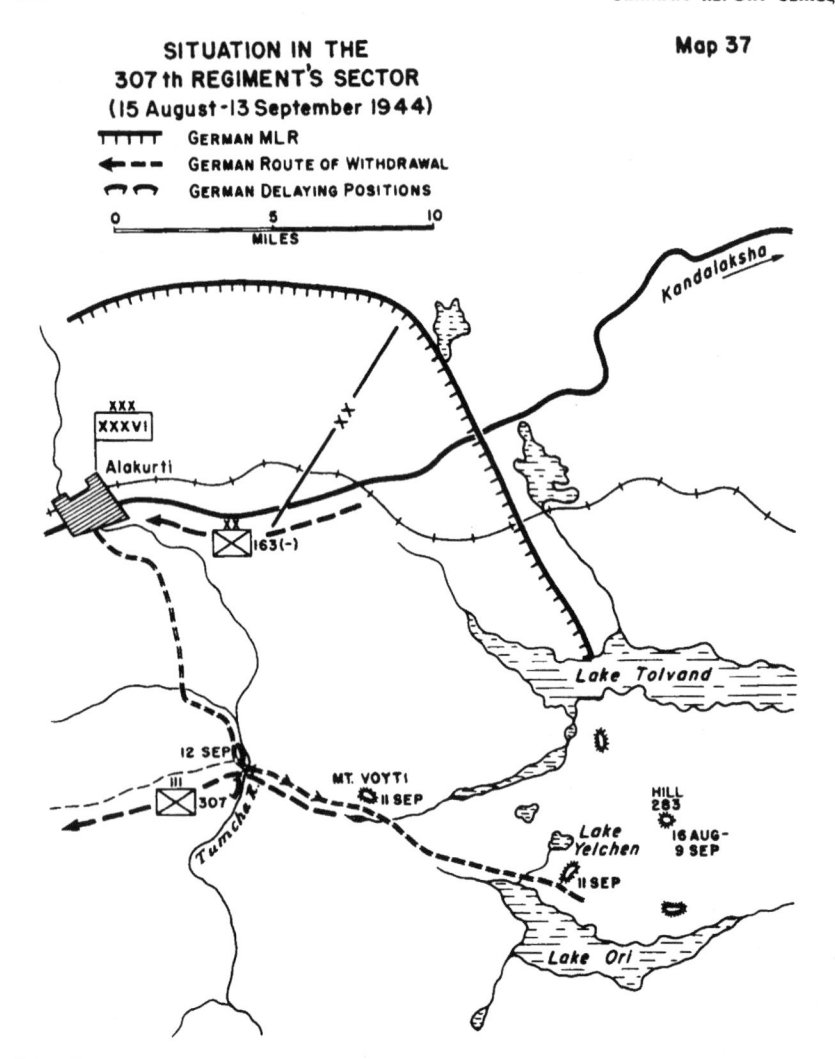

**SITUATION IN THE
307th REGIMENT'S SECTOR
(15 August–13 September 1944)**

⊤⊤⊤⊤ GERMAN MLR
←−− GERMAN ROUTE OF WITHDRAWAL
⌒⌒ GERMAN DELAYING POSITIONS

0   5   10
MILES

Map 37

IV. The Last German Offensive Operation in Northern Finland (August 1944)

In the late summer of 1944 the Germans were preparing to evacuate their forces from northern Finland. The Russians, who anticipated such a move, brought up new divisions with the intention of cutting the Kandalaksha–Rovaniemi railroad and highway west of Alakurti and the vital Alakurti–Vuorijarvi–Salla road. The German 163d Infantry Division, forming part of the XXXVI Corps, was responsible for the defense of a large salient extending from a point approximately 11 miles northeast of Alakurti to the primeval forests west of Lake Ori (map 37).

The 163d Division's mission was to secure the vital German lines of communication during the impending withdrawal. Between Lakes Tolvand and Ori the German defense line was formed by a number of fortified strong points consisting of blockhouses and bunkers protected by wire entanglements. Each strong point was manned by one or two rifle platoons supported by mortars and heavy machineguns. Roving patrols of up to squad strength maintained contact between the strong points, and several intermediate sentry posts were established. The Russians had developed a similar defense system opposite the German positions.

The terrain across which this German front extended features lakes, swamps, primeval forests, rocky plateaus, and occasionally dominating hills. The stands of timber, consisting in this region primarily of tall firs and stunted pines, are relatively sparse. On the other hand there is a dense growth of blueberry and cranberry shrubs over wide areas. Huge boulders and decaying tree trunks make the region even more difficult to negotiate. Inhabiting the forests are bison, elk, reindeer, bear, and grouse. The few inhabited localities in this region were many miles behind the German lines.

Whereas during the winter the Germans had relatively little difficulty in maintaining security in this region since new tracks were immediately recognizable in the virgin snowscape, they were unable to keep the area under observation during the summer. An encounter with a Russian patrol had to be expected anywhere at any moment.

Digging a foxhole was almost impossible because only a thin layer of dirt covered the rocky subsoil. As an expedient blockhouses and bunkers were built, but these made inviting targets for antitank guns. Stone parapets offered little protection against any but the smallest caliber projectiles and greatly increased the number of casualties from rock fragmentation.

In this region every movement took a disproportionate amount of time. Weapons, equipment, and every other item of supply had to be carried over narrow trails that had been gradually blazed across the wilderness. Two-wheeled carts could be used only over stretches where roads had been laboriously cut. It took hours to evacuate casualties to the nearest first aid station, and as many as 12 men were needed to escort 1 casualty—4 litter bearers, 4 relief bearers acting as guards, and 4 others to carry the rations, equipment, and other baggage. The old Finnish proverb, "At the creation of time the good Lord did not think of hurrying," is characteristic of the spell cast by nature on human activities in this region.

Most of the time the German company commanders, platoon, and even squad leaders were completely on their own; hence, any mistake on their part was all the more costly. The implementation of an order took an infinitely long time and it was equally time-consuming to enforce any change in plans. The responsibility of junior leaders went far beyond what was generally expected of men of their rank.

When properly clothed, the German troops bore up fairly well in winter, even when temperatures dropped to −40° F. In the summer, however, when the mercury occasionally rose to 95° F. in the shade, any activity at all in those humid swamps was sheer torture. The Germans therefore preferred to occupy high ground, where there was some relief to be had from the heat and the swarms of mosquitoes that plagued them everywhere else. The Russians were apparently little affected by temperature or insects and could spend many days in the swampland without slowing down in their effort.

On 13 August, after all had been quiet along the 307th Regiment's front for several months, Russian riflemen supported by mortars suddenly attacked Yelchen, a well-fortified German strong point named after tiny Lake Yelchen near the northwestern tip of Lake Ori. One of the Russian prisoners taken during the inconclusive action that ensued disclosed that he belonged to the 67th Rifle Division and that his unit had only recently moved into this area.

Lieutenant Colonel Schmitt, the commander of the 307th Infantry Regiment, who was responsible for the defense of this sector, decided to improve his positions before the Russians could launch an offensive. For this purpose he concentrated some of the forces at his disposal for an attack on Hill 283, which dominated the area between Lakes Tolvand and Ori. With the Germans entrenched on top of the hill, a Russian thrust between the lakes could be delayed until reinforcements were brought up from another sector.

Schmitt had no detailed information regarding Russian strength and dispositions on Hill 283. German reconnaissance patrols probing the hill defenses had recently been repulsed. No hostile artillery fire had so far been encountered in the area.

On 16 August the 1st Battalion of the 307th Regiment reached Strong Point Yelchen according to plan. The artillery battalion, which was supposed to support the attack with its light howitzers, experienced great difficulty with the road and was forced to stop more than 2 miles short of its objective. Instead of occupying its designated emplacements just west of Yelchen, the guns went into position in an area barely within range of Hill 283.

During the night of 16–17 August the 1st Battalion moved out under cover of darkness and reached the immediate vicinity of Hill

283 just before dawn. Since the artillery battalion was not ready for action and the attack could not be postponed without losing the element of surprise, Schmitt ordered the battalion commander to launch the assault without artillery preparation. The Russians were taken completely by surprise, but rallied quickly and defended themselves fiercely. It was not until Schmitt had moved up reinforcements that a report reached him at his CP at Yelchen, stating that the Russians had been driven back from Hill 283 after leaving behind 89 dead.

During the next 2 days Schmitt could not obtain a clear picture of the situation on Hill 283 because signal communication between there and Yelchen had broken down. He therefore decided to join a supply column that was bound for the hill. This column comprised no less than 170 pack carriers and escorts, the minimum needed to provide the 1st Battalion with ammunition and a 2-day supply of canned rations.

During the afternoon of 20 August, after several hours of strenuous marching, Schmitt arrived at the 1st Battalion's CP. There he found out that the summit of the oval, shrub-covered hill was in Russian hands and that the Germans were pinned down in shallow hollows, behind rocks, and behind the sparse growth of trees on the west side of the hill. He was told that the battalion had been unable to flush out the Russians during the initial attack. Unable to dig into the rocky ground, the hapless German infantrymen were exposed to mortar fire and ricochets from the ground and trees.

There was no doubt in Schmitt's mind that another attempt had to be made to clear and secure the hilltop. Reconnaissance patrols were then sent out. The information they brought back served as a basis for discussion of the assault plan between Schmitt and the battalion commander. The next day Schmitt returned to Yelchen to coordinate the artillery fire that was to precede the assault. During the evening hours the howitzers adjusted their fire by high-burst ranging.

After a brief but intensive preparation the infantrymen jumped off at 0500 on 22 August. In the difficult terrain they had to cross to reach the hilltop, the infantrymen made slow progress and were thus unable to take full advantage of the softening up achieved by the artillery fire. They failed to make a single penetration into the Russian defense system. Instead, they were forced to withdraw to their line of departure. The battalion commander himself was among the seriously wounded.

The attack on Hill 283 was the last German offensive operation in this region.

GERMAN INFANTRY, 1944.

SMALL UNIT ACTIONS

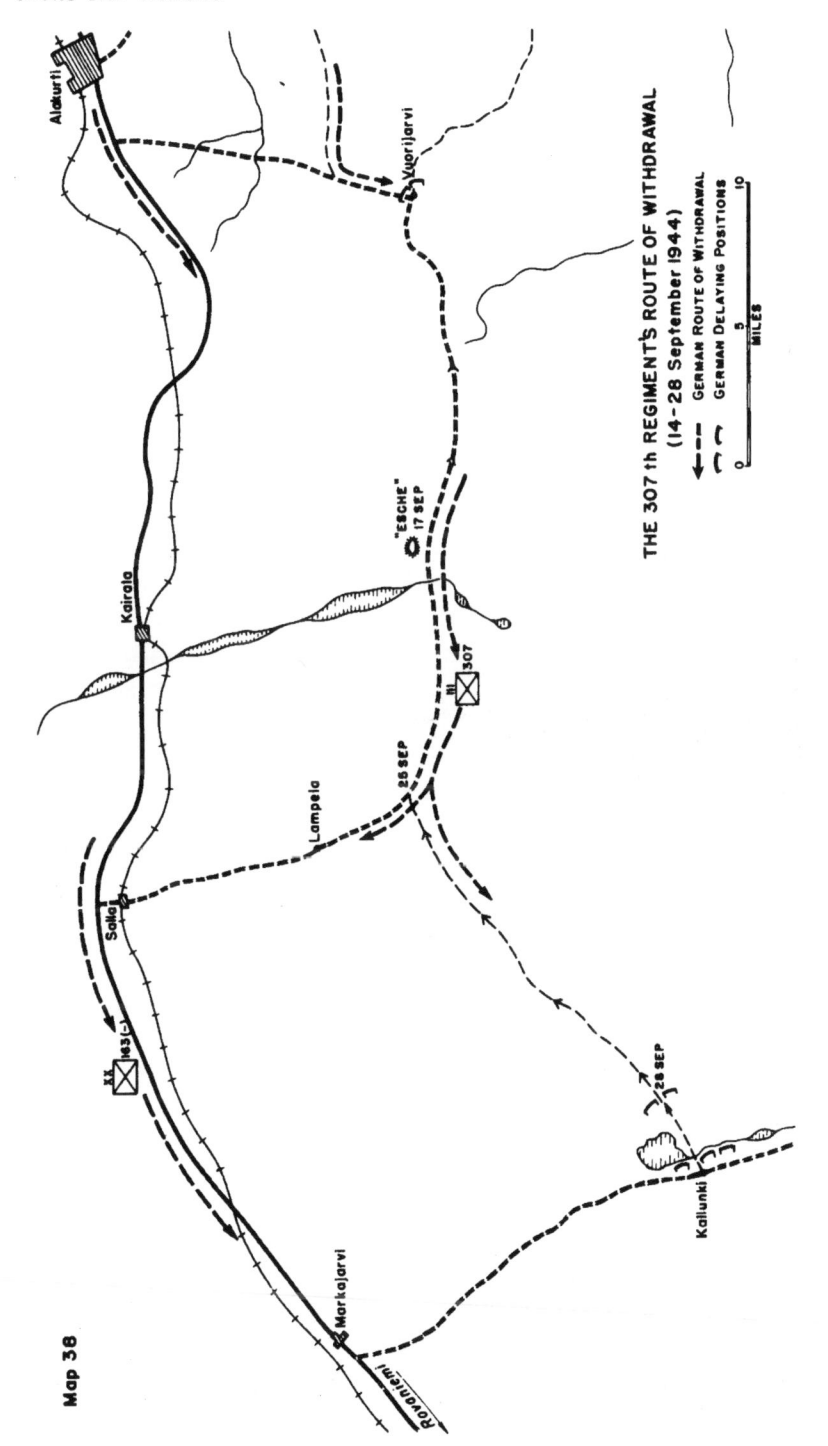

THE 307th REGIMENT'S ROUTE OF WITHDRAWAL
(14-28 September 1944)
--→ GERMAN ROUTE OF WITHDRAWAL
--⌒ GERMAN DELAYING POSITIONS

Map 38

V. German Retrograde Movement Through the Taiga (September 1944)

During the last days of August and the beginning of September there was little change in the situation along the 307th Infantry Regiment's sector between Lakes Tolvand and Ori. The 1st Battalion was clinging to its precarious positions on the west side of Hill 283, facing the well-entrenched Russians on the summit. German patrols observed feverish construction work and the felling of trees on the Russian side of the hill, but were unable to obtain any clues as to Russian intentions, since all of the enemy's activities were carried on by night (map 38).

On the morning of 9 September Russian artillery suddenly opened fire on the German hill positions. Consternation and surprise in the German ranks was great because in more than 2 years of localized warfare the Russians had never used artillery in this region. After a short preparation three tanks emerged from the Russian fortifications on the hill, their guns firing pointblank at the German infantrymen. Helplessly exposed to this new threat, the Germans abandoned the hill without waiting for orders. In the process the battalion suffered few casualties, but its radio set and other valuable items of equipment were lost.

The news of the loss of Hill 283 did not reach the regimental commander, Lieutenant Colonel Schmitt, until the battalion turned up at Strong Point Yelchen in the late afternoon. He immediately requested division headquarters to send some antitank weapons, which had hitherto been considered excess baggage in this theater.

On 11 September Russian forces began to attack Yelchen with small arms and mortar fire. Instead of maintaining strict fire discipline the German garrison expended its ammunition so fast that it was forced to abandon the well-constructed position much sooner than intended.

Encouraged by these unexpectedly quick successes, Russian assault detachments in company and platoon strength tried to keep the retreating Germans off balance. One of these detachments caught up with the march column of the artillery battalion that was moving from Yelchen to the strong point on Mount Voyti. After some initial confusion the artillerymen put up a staunch defense, firing on the approaching Russians at only 50 yards range. The battalion thus escaped annihilation, its only materiel losses being two guns that had to be destroyed during the brief engagement to prevent their capture.

By evening Voyti was the only strong point east of the Tumcha River still in German hands. The blockhouses at the foot of Mount Voyti were held by the weakened 1st Battalion, which had fought its way back from Yelchen during the day. The garrison was equipped with small arms and heavy weapons, but had neither artillery nor any of the recently requested antitank guns. All other regimental units had safely crossed the Tumcha and were moving toward Vuorijarvi (map 38). Every hour counted since the slow German march columns would never reach Salla intact unless the men at Voyti could hold off the mobile Russian assault detachments. After the premature evacuation of Yelchen the fate of the entire 163d Division hinged upon the sustained defense of Voyti and the approaches to the Tumcha River.

That night the Russians made their first attempts to seize Voyti. Once again the Germans were amazed to see Russian tanks driving across country that they had considered tankproof for the last 3 years. The Russian armor broke through the outer defense ring, and the battle for the blockhouses raged by the light of burning sheds. Three of the tanks were disabled by mines, but their guns continued firing at the German defenders. Calling over the telephone from his CP on the west bank of the Tumcha, Colonel Schmitt asked the battalion commander to hold out promising the early arrival of a relief force which he had dispatched upon being notified that the Voyti garrison had come under attack. The relief force, a reinforced engineer platoon, reached Voyti just in time to rescue the garrison and conduct it safely to the Tumcha River. To block the only road leading to the river the engineers emplaced roadblocks and mines that they had prepared for this purpose during the preceding months. Schmitt hoped to delay the advancing Russians long enough to permit the main body of his regiment to withdraw beyond Vuorijarvi.

When the engineer platoon reached the Tumcha at dawn, it joined the other German elements who had previously crossed to the west bank. The engineers thereupon blew up the only bridge that spanned the deep and rapid river. As Schmitt and the rear guard watched the demolition, they suddenly came under the fire of two Russian tanks which had somehow managed to keep up with the Germans despite roadblocks, mines, and demolitions.

During the next few days the 307th Infantry Regiment withdrew beyond Vuorijarvi according to plan. The Russians crossed the Tumcha and gained access to the roads west of the river. They were thus in a favorable position to envelop and destroy major elements of the withdrawing German columns. As a countermeasure Schmitt decided to employ rear guard units to defend improvised delaying positions at favorable points along the escape route to Salla and Rovaniemi.

One such delaying position was established at "Esche" near the chain of lakes that extends southeastward from Kairala. The position was held by Company B of the 307th Regiment. The company commander had orders to remain in place until he received specific instructions to withdraw.

When the Russians reached "Esche" on 16 September, they enveloped the position on both sides and one infantry battalion supported by tanks began a siege of the German garrison. In the course of the afternoon and night the Russians launched no less than seven separate assaults, but each time they were thrown back with heavy losses.

Upon being notified that the strong point was surrounded and hard pressed, Schmitt organized his 3d Battalion into a relief force. Because of the necessary preparations the battalion's departure was delayed until evening, by which time radio communication with "Esche" had broken off. Schmitt sent out a patrol, but it failed to get through to the encircled force. After every other means had proved unsuccessful a reconnaissance plane attempted to drop a message to the embattled company, ordering it to try to break out.

When the relief force got to within a mile of "Esche," it clashed with Russian advance elements that had managed to bypass the German position. Instead of relieving the "Esche" garrison, the 3d Battalion was forced to withdraw in the face of superior Russian forces. Schmitt had given up all hope of rescuing Company B when, shortly after dawn on 17 September, he was notified of the contents of an intercepted Russian radio message revealing that the company had broken out. This unexpected news was confirmed early that afternoon when the exhausted men reached the German lines. The company commander reported that 16 men had been killed and 25 wounded.

The company commander told how by a stroke of luck the airdropped order to break out had fallen within the lines of the beleaguered unit. After waiting for darkness to set in, Company B had made a diversionary attack to the northeast and, taking advantage of the initial Russian confusion, had slipped out of the pocket and escaped to the west.

During the second half of September, while the main body of the 163d Division was withdrawing along the main highway, the 307th Regiment was ordered to use a path that traversed the otherwise impassable primeval forest from a point southeast of Lampela to Kallunki. However, since this path could not sustain any vehicular traffic, all regimental vehicles were dispatched to Salla. Reinforced by a bicycle company and an engineer platoon, those elements of the 307th that were to follow the forest path were ordered to emplace obstacles along the way and establish a defensive position northeast of Kallunki upon their arrival in that village.

On 25 September the regiment started its march along the barely visible path that twisted its way through the boulder-strewn primeval forest. The engineer platoon, at the tail of the column, did what it could to make pursuit difficult for the Russians.

Upon arriving at Kallunki in the late afternoon of 26 September, Schmitt set up his CP and reported by radio to division headquarters. To his message he added that he would eat his hat if the Russians reached the Onkamo position within the next 72 hours. It turned out that his optimism was unjustified, for the very next morning Russian advance elements attacked the German delaying position with mortars and light mountain howitzers. Schmitt thereupon requested that an artillery battalion be dispatched from Maerkejaervi to bolster his weakened force.

During the following night an incident occurred that illustrates the sort of nervous strain to which the Germans were subjected during their withdrawal through the taiga. The bicycle company, previously reduced to platoon strength in a series of tough engagements during which it lost its commanding officer, was holding an outpost line in the forest in front of the Onkamo position. At 0200 the acting commander and his men suddenly turned up in the battle position, reporting that they had been outflanked by strong Russian forces. According to the lieutenant all indications pointed to a Russian enveloping attack in battalion strength. However, combat reconnaissance patrols, sent out that night and the following morning to verify this alarming report, failed to locate any Russian forces at the points he had indicated. The only traces of activity that could be found were numerous reindeer tracks, which led to the final conclusion that the battle-tested men had fled from a herd of reindeer.

During the entire retrograde movement through the taiga the Germans were amazed at the ease and speed with which the Russians surmounted natural and man-made obstacles. Along paths, which—according to German unit commanders who had spent several years in the taiga and tundra—could be negotiated only by infantry forces, Russian tracked and wheeled vehicles would suddenly make their appearance and surprise the German rear guards. Against harassed German units that had lost most of their equipment during the difficult withdrawal across northern Finland, the fresh Russian troops launched a series of limited flanking thrusts, alternating them with bold wide enveloping maneuvers. By the beginning of November 1944 the last German troops had either escaped to Norway or had been taken prisoner in Finland.

Chapter 5

Russian Operations at River Lines

I. General

The Russians were fully cognizant of the tactical principles involved in river-crossing operations. In their efforts to reach the enemy-held bank of a river and establish a bridgehead, they usually selected a point that was most difficult to defend and where relatively light resistance could be expected. Once they had established a bridgehead, they held it at any cost.

Characteristic of Russian operations at river lines were the careful preparations that, although often causing considerable delay in the start of the operation, were excellently concealed. Many a time the German defenders were caught by surprise. During the first 2 years of the war such operations failed frequently because the Germans still had sufficient manpower and materiel for speedy counterattacks. Moreover, some of the Russian lower echelon commanders lacked experience in exercising proper control over the different small units and detachments that had infiltrated across a river. The efforts of other arms and services, such as armor, engineers, and tactical air force, were not sufficiently coordinated with those of the infantry. During this phase of the struggle the Russian leaders often failed to demonstrate enough initiative to take advantage of the opportunities they had so painstakingly created.

The first action in this chapter took place 2 months after the German invasion of the USSR. At that time the Russians were attempting to delay the German advance by every means at their disposal, and river crossings were little more than battle reconnaissance by infiltration. A study of the operation is significant mainly because the Russians employed unusual methods which they subsequently refined to the high degree of perfection achieved in the chapter's last action, occuring in February 1945.

II. Battle Reconnaissance by Infiltration (August 1941)

During the last 10 days of August 1941 the German offensive on the southern front ground to a halt after reaching the Dnepr River. The

Russians, dug in along the east bank, were still conducting limited counterattacks near Cherkassy.

While one German infantry division was preparing to force a river crossing at Cherkassy, another division was deployed along a wide front with the primary mission of protecting the assault division's northern flank. North of Cherkassy a part of the latter division, the 1st Battalion (Reinforced), 196th Infantry Regiment, was committed on a broad front and in considerable depth between Dakhnovka and Svidovok. Its mission was to defend the river line against Russian crossing attempts (map 39).

Facing the 1st Battalion was a reinforced Russian rifle regiment. Its defenses were fortified by log-reinforced intrenchments with machinegun emplacements, and by primitive, unconnected trenches. The positions were heavily manned and an entire battalion was held in reserve behind the center of the line. Forward artillery observers and security elements had established themselves on the islands in midstream. The Russians had a threefold mission. They were to defend the river against German attempts to cross, observe any signs of enemy intentions, and maintain contact with a partisan brigade that operated from the forest behind the German lines west of the river.

The Russian regiment was composed of seasoned fighters. The troops were well rested, having been in the area and out of action for some time. Supplies of rations, weapons, and ammunition were adequate. As for morale, the veterans of the unit had a fatalistic attitude and the replacements, most of whom had been members of the Communist Youth Organization, were utter fanatics.

The German battalion was at 80 percent combat strength. This highly trained and battle-tested unit was well supplied with all essentials. Although suffering from fatigue because of the constant vigil it had to maintain aling its thinly held front line and its rear area, the men's morale was high.

During the night of 21–22 August, three men, residents of Svidovok and Dakhnovka, swam across the Dnepr with the aid of fascine-type rafts made of reeds and twigs, and reached the Russian regimental command post. They brought information about German troop dispositions, including the assumed location of command posts and heavy weapons.

Upon receipt of this information the Russian regimental commander decided to send reconnaissance patrols across the river in an effort to gain more details. As an initial step, the covering forces on the three islands were reinforced. From his reserve battalion the regimental commander then selected 40 men who appeared to be best suited for the task of gathering information behind enemy lines. Two reconnaissance detachments, each composed of 1 officer, 3 noncommissioned officers, and 16 men, were organized. Each man was armed with a submachinegun and three hand grenades, and each wore a light-weight fatigue uniform and straw shoes. The men ranged in age from 16 to 30 and were all excellent swimmers.

Standing by on the east bank of the river were eight flatbottomed boats to carry the patrols to the hostile shore by way of the islands. Each boat was manned by two native fishermen who alternately propelled and steered by means of a scull oar, taking full advantage of the current.

On 23 August the following regimental orders were issued to the reconnaissance patrols:

The west bank of the river is thinly held by German forces. According to reports from Svidovok and Dakhnovka, the various enemy outposts are as much as 300 yards apart.

German local reserves appear to be limited. The assumed location of positions as reported by the civilian informers is indicated on the attached map.

The regiment requires exact information regarding the location of positions and composition of forces in Sectors *a* and *b*. It is essential that some prisoners be taken and brought back for interrogation.

The operation will be protected by the covering forces on the islands under careful observation of the artillery observers. Upon completion of the mission the reconnaissance patrols will return to the islands.

After these orders were received the plan of action was formulated. At 0300 on 24 August the detachments proceeded to their jumpoff positions on Islands X and Z and remained there until evening. To avert premature detection the men carefully concealed themselves and their equipment, particularly the boats. H-hour was set for 2200. The entire operation was placed under the command of Captain Orlov, with Lieutenants Novikov and Mirskiy in charge of Patrols X and Z, respectively.

Final briefings were held during the day. The civilian informers were present and expressed full confidence that success was assured, provided the west bank could be reached without arousing suspicion.

Late on the evening of 24 August the regimental advance command post moved to the river bank directly opposite Island Z. A signal platoon provided blinker light communication with the islands.

a. Patrol Novikov. At dusk on 24 August the boats slipped quietly

RUSSIAN POW's, 1941.

into the river at the northern tip of the islands and prepared to cross to the hostile shore. The boats from Island X pushed off at 2145 and headed toward the west bank fronting Sector *a*, close behind one another. The scull straps were wrapped in rags; not a sound was to be heard. Within 5 minutes the dark outline of the shore became visible. After another 5 minutes all 4 boats had touched the bank, which rose sharply some 15 to 20 feet and overhung the river in spots.

Lieutenant Novikov climbed up, looked around, and, finding the area unoccupied, placed a wooden marker at a well-concealed point.

At a signal from Novikov the men climbed up the embankment in single file. A security detail of five men was then detached and ordered to remain near the landing site. The rest of the patrol cautiously probed inland about a hundred yards before turning south.

Around 2300 the sound of approaching voices and footsteps was heard. The patrol quickly took cover and hugged the ground. Soon four Germans passed close by. At a hand signal from Novikov the Russians jumped the German soldiers and sought to disarm and capture them as noiselessly as possible. One of the Germans, however, succeeded in firing several bursts with his submachinegun while another shouted, "Russians, Russians!" In the ensuing hand-to-hand fighting, which lasted but a minute, all four Germans were killed. When it was all over, one member of the patrol lay dead and four were wounded, one so seriously that he had to be left behind.

The noise of the encounter had alerted the Germans. Soon orders were being shouted, and heavy footsteps could be heard approaching from several directions. The Russians quickly made their way back to the river. When they were only some 50 paces from the bank, German flares went off all around them and machineguns opened up at close range, forcing them to hit the ground. German soldiers were coming on the run from the east, and the patrol was forced to make a desperate lunge for the river. One Russian was cut down by a machinegun burst, but Novikov and the rest got to the river safely, slid down the steep embankment, hit their boats, and shoved off. German flares fired over the water illuminated the boats, and an exchange of fire soon followed. One of the boats was hit and its sculler killed, but the rest of its complement was able to cling to another boat and thus succeeded in reaching Island Y safely.

Despite the fact that the reconnaissance patrol had not been able to carry out its mission in full, the Russians did determine that there were definite gaps between the German positions and that roving contact patrols were maintaining a close watch. The situation seemed to warrant further reconnoitering.

b. Patrol Mirskiy. After Patrol Z had reached the west bank fronting Sector *b*, Lieutenant Mirskiy marked the landing point with a white cloth which he concealed under a bluff. He then proceeded to reconnoiter the immediate environs of the river bank and found no Germans within a 50-yard radius. Leaving the bulk of his force behind, Mirskiy took five men and felt his way southward in search of the enemy positions. After advancing about 150 paces he smelled the aroma of tobacco smoke. Mirskiy cautiously crawled forward while the others covered him. Within a few minutes he reached a low wire entanglement that appeared to be several yards in depth. A few yards farther and he heard very faintly the sound of conversation and the tapping of metal on metal.

Carefully Mirskiy crept back to the five-man detail and then joined the rest of the party. After assigning 5 men to provide security from the south, he led the bulk of the patrol northward, parallel to the river and about 150 yards inland.

The Russians, stealthily feeling their way through the thick bushes, had proceeded only a short distance when suddenly a German machinegun opened fire from the vicinity of the landing point, which was now to the right rear of the patrol. Simultaneously, loud noises were heard as German flares illuminated the entire area. To avoid being cut off Mirskiy quickly doubled back toward the landing site. Hand grenades were exploding all around and a German machinegun fired from point-blank range. The Russians quickly dispersed and tried to make their way back to the river. Intermittent firing from the south indicated that the security detail was still engaged by the German roving patrol.

Eleven members of the Russian patrol succeeded in reaching the river and assembled at a point to the north of the landing site where they waited patiently for the rest. Meanwhile, the Germans were carefully searching the area. An hour passed. The other nine, including Lieutenant Mirskiy and Sergeant Petrov, had still not returned, so Sergeant Rudin ordered two men to pull the boats upstream, which they did under the protective cover of the high, overhanging river bank. The remnants of the patrol then embarked and reached Island Z without further incident. From there they returned to the east bank later the same night.

The findings of this patrol, like those of the first, were inconclusive. Although wide gaps were found to exist in the German lines, they were closely watched by numerous contact patrols. Some of the enemy positions were not found at the places where the civilian informers had indicated, the Germans having probably realigned their forces in the meantime. One thing, however, was certain: another similar undertaking was necessary, preferably one of longer duration. In view of the possibilities of concealment offered by the tangled brushwood atop the west bank, it seemed most desirable that future reconnaissance activity be conducted in daylight after the necessary forces had crossed over and found hiding places the preceding night.

c. Scouts Succeed Where Patrols Had Failed. The Russian commander immediately decided to send additional elements to reconnoiter the German positions. This time contact was also to be sought with the partisan brigade in the forest. The three civilian informers were instructed to return to Svidovok and Dakhnovka to establish a system of communication between the partisan brigade and the regimental CP on the east bank. By means of simple, prearranged smoke signals from chimneys in the village the agents were to transmit information regarding the arrival of German reinforcements, troop movements, and the location of command posts. In addition, detailed written reports were to be sent back by couriers periodically dispatched from the east bank.

From the rifle regiment 10 soldiers, above average in intelligence and familiar with the region, were selected as the scouts to perform this mission. They were furnished with fascine rafts and assigned numbers. Scouts 1 through 5 were assigned Sector *a*, the others were to operate against Sector *b*.

The scouts were ordered to swim across the river during the night and seek cover in the bushes and under the bluffs along the west bank; crawl forward by daylight, hidden by the bushes and swamp vegetation, carefully observing the immediate environs and beyond for German troop dispositions, location of heavy weapons, and command posts; seek out and mark paths suitable for infiltration according to conventional procedures adopted by partisans; establish contact with trustworthy civilians in Dakhnovka and Svidovok and, if practicable, with the partisans themselves; and, finally, not to engage the enemy except as a last resort.

In the pitch darkness of the evening of 25 August, while a light rain was falling, the 10 scouts set out from Island X. Each man wore a shirt and trousers and had a knife tied around his neck. Fastened to his fascine were a native-type denim jacket and trousers, straw shoes, a pistol with 25 rounds of ammunition, a strip map, and a pencil—all in waterproof wrapping.

Scout 1 reached the west bank undetected. In a well-concealed hiding place he changed his clothes, then crawled up the embankment to survey the situation. No enemy troops were in sight. He took cover in the thick underbrush a short distance from the river and remained still while he observed three successive German patrols passing close by.

At daybreak he noted a German mess detail approaching from a position about 150 yards to the south where several machineguns were emplaced. After the Germans had returned to their position, the scout followed their footpath and soon discovered a command post and a heavy mortar emplacement nearby. He proceeded several hundred yards farther but around noon decided to work his way northward closer to the river. While pausing to observe a machine-

SMALL UNIT ACTIONS

gun nest, he had his first close call. Thinking that they had seen suspicious movements in the bushes, the Germans combed the area. The scout, however, was able to escape detection by turning off and moving quickly in a westerly direction. In the excitement he lost his pistol, which, together with several other clues, the Germans were to find the following day.

After dark he found a hiding place at a point northeast of Svidovok and remained there for the night. The next morning, 27 August, he noticed men and women with pails of water and bundles of straw and wood, escorted by a German soldier, making their way from the village to the nearby heavy machinegun positions. Shortly thereafter the scout saw them returning unescorted and took this opportunity to join them, thus gaining entrance to the village unrecognized and unmolested. After having eaten, he contacted a villager who was considered an anticommunist by the Germans. The two men discussed means of communication. Remaining in the village until 1 September, the scout took advantage of every opportunity to gather information. By professing a hatred of Stalin and a desire to fight on the side of the Germans, he even gained access to a German field kitchen, where he worked in return for his meals.

Through wives of partisans who lived in the village he endeavored to make contact with the partisan brigade in the adjacent forest. Accompanying some of the women when they went to fetch wood, he met with partisan representatives for the first time. They exchanged information regarding enemy forces and positions and agreed upon methods of transmitting messages. Upon conclusion of the discussions the scout was given a report which he was to deliver to the command post upon his return.

On 2 September the scout started on his return trip. He again joined a group of women who were carrying wood and water to the German positions. Once outside the village he concealed himself in some brushwood and, having assured himself that the coast was clear, crawled to a blind spot between two German positions. Toward dusk, as a heavy fog was settling over the area, he made his way to the river and gained the other side in safety.

The results of this reconnaissance mission were so satisfactory that the Russians were able to launch an effective attack against the German command post in Svidovok and the heavy weapons emplacements the very next day.

Scout 10 had reached the west bank in much the same manner as Scout 1. The next morning, 26 August, he started out, following a ditch which ran northwestward from the river. When he came within sight of two heavy machinegun positions and some German soldiers getting water from the ditch he took cover and watched. From his hiding place he heard shots and shouting from somewhere to the north. A dog that had been barking in the vicinity suddenly appeared over the crest of the embankment. Shortly thereafter the scout heard the sound of Germans who were closing in from all sides. Without hesitation he threw himself into the ditch where the water came well over his head. While the Germans were making an intensive search of the area, he kept himself submerged, breathing through a hollow reed he had picked along the ditch.

After what seemed to be about half an hour the scout raised his head just enough to permit him to look around. Having assured himself that the immediate danger of detection had passed, he set out again, swimming or wading as the depth of the water warranted. Soon he abandoned the ditch and crawled through the swamp and underbrush in a westerly direction until he reached a steep slope overlooking a pond. Here again he heard the barking of a dog. Without a moment's hesitation the scout jumped into the pond where he remained for more than an hour, either partially or completely submerged.

When he was satisfied that it was safe to proceed, he climbed the slope and took cover in the undergrowth. Numerous German reconnaissance patrols and ration details passed close by. Toward dusk he fell in some distance behind one of the ration details that was heading south. Reaching the fringe of the forest, he climbed a tree and concealed himself until the next morning. As it grew light he was able to spot German machinegun and mortar emplacements from his perch in the tree. He climbed down, struck out southward keeping close to the woods, and soon approached the village of Dakhnovka. From his hiding place in a cornfield he watched the village until evening. After nightfall he struck up a conversation with a group of women who, as they revealed, were taking food to their husbands who belonged to the partisan brigade in the forest. After identifying himself to them, the scout arranged with the women to pick him up on their way back to the village the following morning.

When he reached Dakhnovka in the company of the women the next morning, he was directed to a barn that was to serve as his hideout. Later in the day the scout met with an agent who warned him about the strict security measures enforced by the Germans and brought him some women's clothing for use in an emergency. The agent also told him that there was no chance of crossing the ditch and reaching the river directly from the village since the area was too closely guarded and off limits to all civilians. The scout informed him that arrangements had been made to parachute crates of carrier pigeons to the partisans and that it was the responsibility of the partisans to transport the pigeons to the village. Since the scout remained in the village until 3 September, he had ample opportunity to obtain information about the German garrison, including the location of the company command post and the emplacements of a howitzer platoon.

On the evening of 3 September, in the company of the women, he made his way out to the partisans in the forest and was met by the supply officer of the partisan brigade, with whom he discussed means of message transmission. The two men agreed that the most suitable courier route from the forest to the river was the one the scout had followed and marked.

The next day, using the same route over which he had come, the scout started back. By evening of 5 September he reached the bank where he had landed and from there swam to the east bank by way of Island Z.

Information gathered by all 10 scouts was collated and evaluated. As a result of this intelligence, Russian artillery was able to place vital German point targets under effective fire.

d. Russian Couriers Infiltrate During Diversionary Combat Patrol Actions. The crowning feat of the operation was to be the establishment of a regular courier service between the Russian forces on the east side of the Dnepr and the partisan brigade in the forest on the west bank. To make it easier for the couriers to get through, combat patrols were to be committed in simultaneous feints against Svidovok and Dakhnovka in an effort to tie down German forces and divert their attention.

The undertaking was planned and directed by the Russian regimental commander and was supported by concentrated artillery fire from the east bank of the river. To carry out the feints, two detachments, each consisting of 50 sailors from the Dnepr flotilla, were organized into combat patrols. Two couriers were attached to each patrol. Three large rowboats and several smaller river craft were made available to transport the troops across the river. The sailors were armed with light machineguns, automatic rifles, submachineguns, and pistols. Dressed in denim jackets and trousers and wearing straw shoes, each courier carried a pistol, 50 rounds of ammunition, a waterproof strip map, and a container with 1 carrier pigeon. Each courier was given a copy of the following order for transmittal to the partisan brigade.

Supreme Partisan Headquarters, Ukraine   6 September 1941

  1. Effective at once and in accordance with orders from Army

Headquarters, Colonel N. N. is relieved from command of the . . . Partisan Brigade and transferred to Supreme Partisan Headquarters, Ukraine. Major M. M. will assume command of the brigade.

2. Radio sets will not become available for issue until several weeks hence.

3. From this date until 13 September carrier pigeons will be dropped from aircraft at the designated time and place upon the flashing of the prearranged "all clear" light signals.

By Command of the Supreme Partisan Commander, Ukraine.

(Signed)   General X. X.

During the night of 6–7 September the villages of Svidovok and Dakhnovka, as well as points in between, were raked by a heavy artillery barrage. Landings were effected between 0030 and 0100.

When, during the preceding day, the Germans noticed that the civilian populace was forsaking the villages for the open fields, they became suspicious and took precautions that held down their subsequent losses considerably.

After hitting the west bank in the Svidovok sector, Assault Detachment *a* advanced some 400 yards inland. The German reserves that had been concentrated in this area met the attackers and hurled them back in furious hand-to-hand fighting lasting an hour. Meanwhile, the couriers were working their way through the German lines and, although one was discovered about 3 hours later and promptly killed, the second, skirting the village by a wide margin to the northwest, succeeded in making his way to the partisan camp in the forest by evening.

In the Dakhnovka sector the Germans were actually waiting in ambush for Detachment *b*; consequently, the assault was frustrated from the very outset. Both the couriers, however, succeeded in getting ashore. As one of them attempted to slip through the German lines near the village, he was trapped by a German patrol and shot on the spot. The second courier, following the previously charted route along the ditch, reached the partisans without incident.

In the course of this combined action, involving both combat patrols and couriers, 38 Russians were killed or wounded while the defending German forces suffered only 7 killed and 8 wounded.

In general the Russians displayed great ability in negotiating major water barriers by the most primitive means, often by swimming. The Germans therefore had to regard with the utmost suspicion every bundle of reeds and twigs that was seen floating in a river, no matter how harmless or natural it looked.

SMALL UNIT ACTIONS

It was a Russian practice to attack at several points simultaneously, even if only to insure the successful execution of the very smallest mission regardless of the cost involved. In such situations, where a continuous line could not be maintained by the defending Germans, gaps in the line were permissible, but only in such places where a clear field of vision and fire was assured. The use of a trip wire warning system and of numerous contact patrols was essential.

Since the Russians were capable of negotiating waterways, swamps, and trackless forests with considerable ease and since German observation of Russian activity was often restricted, the use of hounds frequently proved effective.

As a rule, Russian troops collaborated closely with the civilian populace of German-occupied areas and took full advantage of all means of deception. Close German surveillance of civilians with thorough and frequent house-to-house searches were therefore mandatory. By the same token, fraternizing with the Russians, whether

Map 40

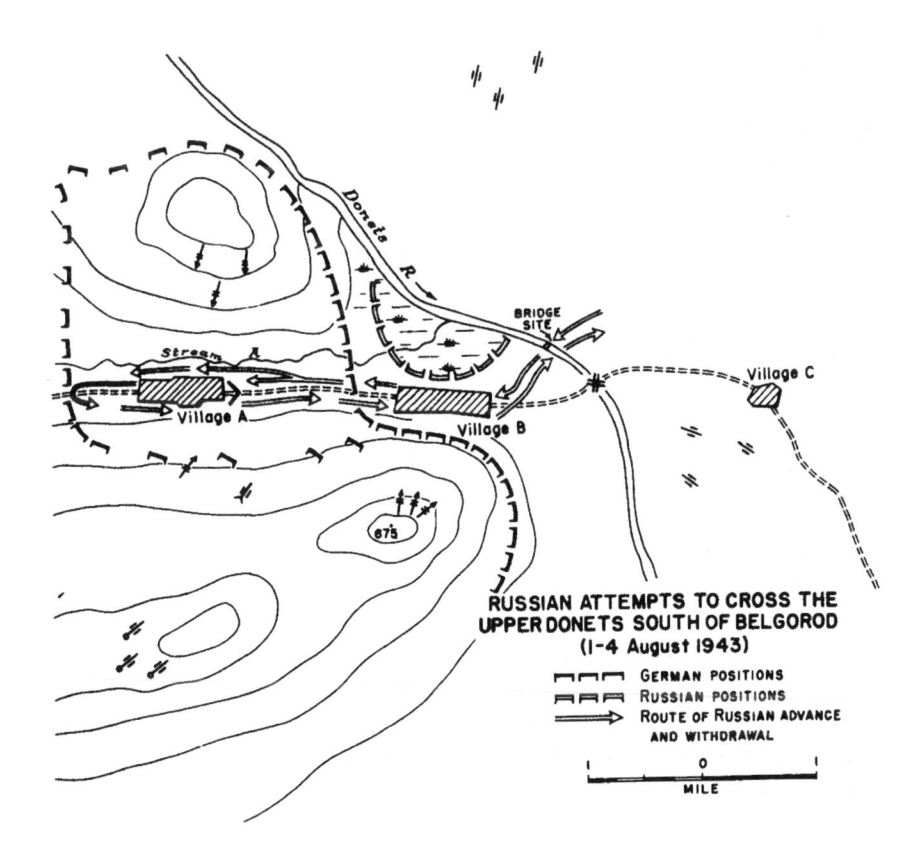

RUSSIAN ATTEMPTS TO CROSS THE UPPER DONETS SOUTH OF BELGOROD (1-4 August 1943)

military or civilian, and taking them into their confidence often proved foolhardy and dangerous for the Germans. The frequent changing of command posts and billeting areas drastically reduced the danger of German troops becoming too friendly with the civilian populace.

III. A Unique Underwater Bridge (August 1943)

This action illustrates the persistence with which the Russians carried out a river crossing in the face of overwhelming odds. No sacrifice in human lives or materiel seemed too great to reach an objective that had been designated by a ruthless commander.

The last major German offensive in Russia, Operation ZITADELLE, was launched on 5 July 1943 with Kursk as the objective. After its failure the badly mauled German divisions limped back to their line of departure west of the Upper Donets below Belgorod, where they moved into their well-constructed former positions and awaited a Russian counteroffensive, which was not long in coming. The German 320th Infantry Division, which held the salient opposite Village C, was at 45 percent of its T/O strength (map 40).

The German artillery and heavy weapons positioned in the hills southwest of Village B were zeroed in on a former bridge site and readied for night fighting. Ridge 675, which afforded excellent visibility, had been transformed into an impregnable bastion. Shellproof dugouts, deep shelters, and communication tunnels protected the gun crews against the heaviest counterbattery fire. The exits of the tunnels facing the river were excellently camouflaged. Machineguns were emplaced in these exits, ready to open fire should the enemy attempt to cross at night. Their field of fire covered the Russian concentration areas and also the approach routes on both banks of the river. The firing data of all weapons had been carefully computed and checked. Small searchlights had been emplaced along the ridge to illuminate the immediate outpost area, but their range did not extend beyond that of the infantry weapons. The Russians were unaware of these meticulous preparations since the German defenders had so far made no use of them.

After closing up to the Donets, Russian infantry patrols on 1 August crossed the river about a mile upstream from the demolished road bridge and infiltrated the German positions in that sector under cover of a heavy barrage. The next day the patrols were followed by several companies, which succeeded in gaining a toe hold but encountered such fierce German resistance that they suffered crippling losses. The remnants of the Russian landing party were driven into a swamp close to the river bank. In this swamp the Russians estab-

RUSSIAN INFANTRY mopping up while German tank burns, 1943.

lished a bridgehead, which they held stubbornly and reinforced during the succeeding two nights.

Shortly after dusk on 2 August German observers on the ridge overlooking Village B heard sounds from the meadows along the adjacent east bank. These left no doubt that the Russians intended to erect a substantial bridge across the river. The night was clear and quiet, and one could easily recognize the sound of sawing and hammering. Apparently the bridge construction was well under way. Russian artillery shelled the German positions on the west bank in an attempt to mask the noises of the construction work.

The German division commander decided not to interfere immediately but to deliver a decisive blow at the most effective moment. Several batteries were to mass their fire on the bridge site and smash the construction work after it had progressed sufficiently. At the designated time, just before midnight, all pieces fired simultaneously upon the bridge site and then stopped as abruptly as they had started. In the light of the burning lumber on the east bank near the bridge site, the observers on the ridge saw the silhouette of a bizarre tangle of beams and pillars. The partially completed bridge was a shambles in the midst of which wounded men were screaming for help. Shadows of scurrying figures, presumed to be medical aid men, were moving up and down.

Scarcely half an hour had passed when the German observers noticed that full-scale construction activity was being resumed at the identical point. Intensive hammering and sawing induced the German artillery commander to fire another concentration shortly after midnight. The result was equally devastating, but this time the bursts of the projectiles were followed by silence, interrupted only by explosions from a few ammunition dumps that had caught fire after having sustained direct hits. Soon the fires died down and, after a while, the Russians once more resumed their efforts as though nothing had happened. Obviously, the bridge had to be finished by dawn.

To prevent them from realizing this intention without expending too much ammunition, the division commander ordered one 210-mm. howitzer battery to deliver intermittent harassing fire on the bridge site. Flash observation indicated that the projectiles landed on or very close to their target. In the course of an hour the effect of each round could be deduced from the Russians' pattern of reaction. Whenever a projectile did major damage, a prolonged work stoppage would occur; whereas after a near-hit the hammering resumed immediately. The German commander realized that under these circumstances the Russians might still be able to complete the bridge by dawn despite the harassing fire.

He therefore decided to employ some of the hidden machineguns to rake the construction site with bursts of fire at short intervals. Judging by the screams of those who were hit and the immediate suspension of the bridging operation, the rapid precision fire of these weapons had a devastating effect. Despite obviously high losses, the Russians tried to continue the construction, but had to slow down and finally give it up entirely.

At periodic intervals, the German howitzers resumed their harassing fire to discourage the Russians from resuming their project and to complete the destruction. Only when day broke was it possible to obtain a true picture of the results achieved during the night. A horrible sight presented itself to the observers. Splintered rafters pointed skyward, and in between hung grotesquely mutilated bodies of the daring men who had scorned death in an effort to accomplish their mission. Even more mangled corpses were strewn about in a wide circle around the bridge site or lay partially submerged in the mud holes formed by shell craters. The whole area was littered with smashed vehicles, dead horses, and all kinds of ammunition and equipment.

The Russians seemed to have vanished from the scene of their failure. After this fiasco the German division commander believed that, for the time being at least, the threat of a river crossing had been eliminated. This assumption seemed all the more justified because during the day the Russians made some gains in the adjacent sector to the north and would undoubtedly seek to exploit these advantages. Had the Russian engineers succeeded in completing the bridge, the enemy command would certainly have seized the opportunity of launching a thrust through the valley toward the Belgorod–Kharkov highway, with the result that the entire German front along the Donets would have collapsed.

In the 320th Division sector all was quiet on 3 August. As soon as darkness fell, however, the Russians resumed their preparations at the same place as before. Although the Germans had not expected this renewal of activities at the same point, their defense system was intact and they intended to make good use of the experience they had gained the preceding night. Almost immediately they began to lob howitzer shells and fire machinegun bursts at the same target as before. The machineguns were by far the most effective antipersonnel weapon, while the artillery fire was directed against vehicles and equipment. Despite heavy losses, the Russians refused to be discouraged and doggedly continued their river-crossing attempts. Just before midnight they apparently gave up the bridge construction project and stopped working. The sound of track-laying vehicles coming from the east bank gave the impression that prime movers had been moved up to recover the disabled vehicles, stores of supplies, and bridging equipment.

In this instance the Germans arrived at entirely erroneous conclusions. To their great surprise the sounds of the tracked vehicles did not diminish as dawn approached. On the contrary, the noises came closer and grew louder. When the Germans turned on their searchlights, they noticed that what they had believed to be prime movers were actually tanks which had somehow crossed the Donets under the cover of darkness. While dawn was breaking, the lead tanks reached the outskirts of Village B, through which they drove with their guns firing against the German fortified line west of that village. That was the prearranged signal for a general attack, for immediately afterward Russian artillery opened fire on Village B from the east bank. Shells rained down upon Ridge 675 and the other hills situated on both sides of the valley of Stream A; they were obviously intended to neutralize the dominating positions of the German defense system. The Russian bridgehead force in the swamp also came to life.

The Germans immediately replied with artillery fire aimed at the Russian forces in the valley and east of Village A. This barrage, in addition to the numerous previously established obstacles and mine fields, stopped the Russian advance until there was sufficient light to permit more accurate firing. In the full morning light the Germans were finally able to assess the situation fairly accurately. The Russian lead tanks had cleared the road block east of Village A and, closely followed by infantry echeloned in depth, had advanced to the center of the village. Other tanks had followed through the gap and, turning south and north, had started to reduce the Village A fortifications by attacking one German strong point after another. Elements of the bridgehead force assisted the tanks in this operation and soon reached the northwestern outskirts of the village. Furious antitank and machinegun fire aimed at them from the overlooking hills, however, interdicted any further advance.

Fighting stubbornly, the German garrison gradually withdrew westward. To continue the advance, the Russian forces in Village A needed assistance, which failed to arrive because the support elements had been intercepted and pinned down by artillery fire before they could reach the village. During the morning a few tanks and combat patrols probed westward but failed to advance beyond the last houses of the mile-long village. While harassed by lively machinegun and artillery fire, the main body of the Russian infantry force, some two or three battalions, attempted to establish flank protection from the north and south.

GERMAN ASSAULT GUN attacks behind smoke screen.

By noon the attack had bogged down everywhere; Russian forces were hemmed into a long and narrow pocket, from which they could neither advance nor retreat without suffering heavy losses. Their situation was the more hopeless since all attempts to bring in reinforcements were thwarted by a curtain of fire laid down by the Germans on the hills dominating the road leading from the Donets to Village A.

Not until dark could the Russians hope to move up sufficient troops to resume their attack. A renewal of the attack would constitute a grave threat to the German defenders, who had been obliged to employ every available man and weapon to stop the Russian advance. Obviously, the Russian forces west of the Donets had to be eliminated before the day was over.

The German commander withdrew one engineer company, nine assault, some antitank, and antiaircraft guns from the sector north of Village A and assembled the force about 4 miles west of the village. Shortly before 1300 this task force launched a frontal counterattack on both sides of the road, supported by fighter-bombers.

The engineers were particularly eager to reach the Donets and find out just how the Russians had managed to cross the river with a large number of medium tanks without the aid of a bridge. This question was uppermost in everyone's mind. It puzzled the German division and corps commanders, who were familiar with that part of the Donets and who were convinced that the river was too deep to be crossed by tanks. During Operation ZITADELLE the Germans had had to build a 70-ton bridge near Belgorod before their tanks and assault guns could get across.

At dawn on the 4th, observers on Ridge 675 had seen tank tracks leading to the eastern approaches of the river, disappear in the water, and reappear on the western shore. Hence the Germans first concluded that amphibious tanks had made a sudden appearance on the front. However, since the Russian tanks encountered in the fighting around Village A were ordinary T34's, this possibility had to be ruled out.

How then did the Russians get these tanks across the Donets without a bridge at a point where its depth had recently been measured at close to 10 feet? Although the T34 undeniably surpassed any European tank in cross-country mobility and had often accomplished astonishing feats, the German experts agreed that no tank could have crossed the Donets on its own.

The riddle was not solved until many more hours of heavy fighting brought the German task force back to the river bank. The Russians still offered very stubborn resistance. Their infantry, supported by tanks, clung to each foot of ground, and each house in Village A had to be retaken in costly hand-to-hand fighting.

The assault guns spearheaded the German counterattack and engaged in furious duels with the T34's. Still enjoying numerical superiority, the tanks stubbornly held their ground, allowing the assault guns to approach to within close range. In the course of the action some of the assault guns suffered direct hits, but they continued firing as long as their guns remained intact.

German planes bombed and strafed the Russian forces, who were also hit by artillery shell fire from the surrounding hills. The infantry began to waver, but the T34's continued to offer strong resistance. Their stubborn refusal to yield succeeded in delaying the German counterattack. In the late afternoon the last Russian tank fell victim to the remaining German assault guns and, with that, resistance finally collapsed.

Darkness was falling as the Germans reached their former positions along the eastern edge of Village A. Assault-gun sections and engineer patrols, in pursuit of the routed enemy, reached the point of the river where the Russian tanks had effected their crossing that morning. Even at close range no sign of a bridge could be found. It was only when soundings were taken in the river that the riddle was solved.

About 20 inches below the water's surface, the engineers came upon a bridge. On various occasions during the campaign the Russians had built underwater bridges in an effort to conceal river crossings from German air observation and to protect the bridges from premature destruction. Consequently, the bridge as such did not cause so much of a surprise as did the fact that it had been built despite devastating fire in an incredibly short time. Upon closer inspection of the underwater bridge the mystery began to unravel itself. The Germans discovered a bridge built of "bridge tanks," a standard item of Russian equipment, which featured a special superstructure mounted on a conventional medium tank chassis. Other tanks could drive over the adjustable flat top and thus negotiate antitank ditches and small water barriers with relative ease. In this instance the Russians drove two rows of "bridge tanks" into the river by leap-frogging them all the way to the west bank. Planks were laid across the superstructures to join the two rows of tanks and were secured by heavy ropes. The Russians did not seem to attach much importance to the fact that a few tanks overturned and plunged into the water in the process. The main thing was that the bulk of the tank force reached the other side.

This unique improvisation, which served its immediate purpose despite its obvious shortcomings, would have been even more effective if the Russian attack had been successful. In the event the Russians could have recovered the submerged bridge tanks from the river bottom and salvaged them. As it turned out, however, German engineers blasted the underwater tanks the following night and condemned them to their watery grave.

IV. The Swamp Bridgehead (June 1944)

During the following years the Russians perfected their river crossing methods. In this action, which took place during the summer of 1944, the Russians displayed their ability of crossing rivers unobtrusively. Starting with the infiltration of individual soldiers, they gradually formed a bridgehead, almost unnoticed by the Germans. For this purpose they chose the most unfavorable point for such an operation, and as a result the Germans tended to ignore their presence on the near shore. Persisting in their preparations for several weeks, the Russians created the prerequisites for enlarging their initial bridgehead. When the Germans finally realized the danger, it was too late for effective counteraction. Confronted by insurmountable terrain difficulties, they were unable to drive the Russians out of the area. Several weeks later the Russians used the bridgehead as a jump-off position for an all-out offensive. This example is typical of Russian tactics. It should serve as a warning against underestimating the

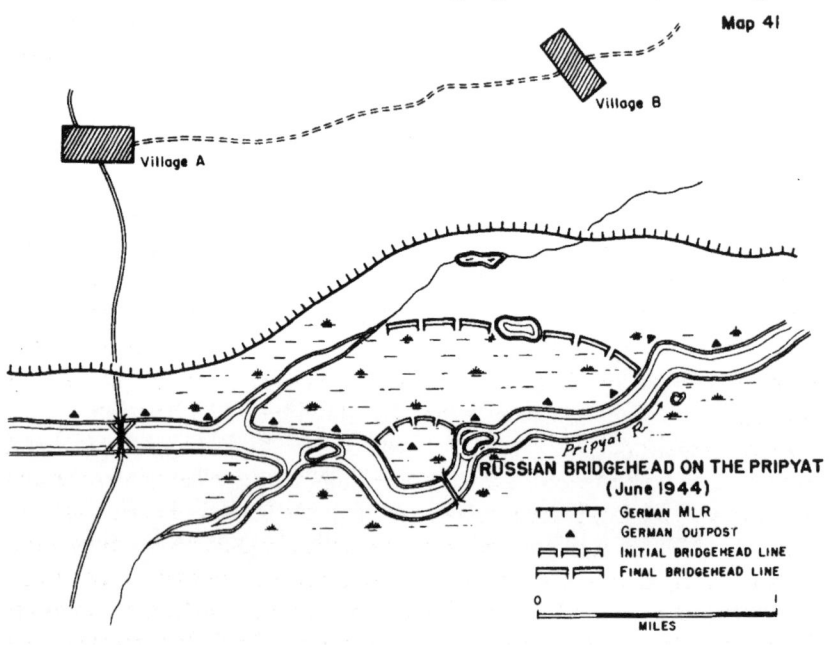

Map 41

RUSSIAN BRIDGEHEAD ON THE PRIPYAT
(June 1944)

- GERMAN MLR
- GERMAN OUTPOST
- INITIAL BRIDGEHEAD LINE
- FINAL BRIDGEHEAD LINE

importance of small unit actions that initially appear completely innocuous.

During June 1944 a German infantry division had taken up defensive positions along the north bank of the Pripyat River. The sector between Villages A and B was defended by an infantry battalion (map 41). In this area the Pripyat River was bounded on both sides by extensive swamps and a maze of small streams and tributaries, stagnant pools and lakes. Marshy river banks were overgrown with reeds and underbrush up to 6 feet in height. Only in the area near the road leading south from Village A across the Pripyat were the banks dry and relatively devoid of vegetation. The road bridge was out, but since the river at this point was shallow and the bed was sandy, it could be forded with comparative ease.

Originally the German MLR was to run close to the north bank. However, since terrain conditions did not allow for establishing fortifications and the vegetation obstructed a clear field of fire and since, furthermore, the Germans believed that no human being could stay for any length of time in the stagnant swamp, the MLR was set up along the line indicated on the map. Near the river bank proper, outposts manned by three or four men were established on platforms built on piles driven into the murky swamp.

At first the Germans observed only weak Russian patrols. However, these patrols gradually grew in strength and number. The Germans expected that the Russians would attempt a crossing at the bridge site, where terrain conditions favored such an undertaking. But, realizing that German resistance would be strongest on both sides of the bridge site, the Russians decided to establish a bridgehead at the most unlikely point—in the worst swamps east of the bridge. At the outset the Russians established a foothold on two small islands that the Germans had left unoccupied because they were too swampy. Several days passed. Then, one morning, the Germans observed a few Russians along a strip of the north bank opposite the islands. They infiltrated into the undergrowth and reeds, although the water reached their chests. The Germans did not attach much importance to this discovery because they thought the Russians could not possibly stay there, and therefore they saw no threat from that direction.

This turned out to be a serious mistake. The Russian bridgehead was gradually reinforced, and three or four nights later the garrisons seized the nearest German outposts. A subsequent German counterattack failed because the swamp was extremely difficult to approach. Moreover, the German unit making the counterattack was placed under very accurate flanking fire by Russian snipers sitting in trees on the river islands. Since the Russians could not be dislodged from the north bank by small-arms fire, the Germans tended to accept the situation as inevitable. The general feeling persisted that no major danger threatened the German positions from that direction.

The subsequent conduct of the Russians in their tiny bridgehead was typical of Russian combat methods of 1944. Mostly under cover of darkness, they made persistent efforts to improve their bridgehead positions by building corduroy roads, high observation posts, and wooden platforms. Exposed to German fire, the Russian soldiers moved around in the swampy terrain, often with water up to their chests. Within the limits imposed by the shortage of ammunition, the Germans did their best to make the position untenable and to dislodge the Russians from their bridgehead. However, the dense vegetation favored infiltration tactics and hampered observed fire.

At that time the Russians began to build an underwater footbridge. This bridge, about 6 feet wide, consisted of previously assembled trestles. During the night these were put in place in the river, with the planking about 4 inches below the surface of the water. This presented no technical difficulties because of the very slow current of the Pripyat River. The bridge was thus invisible to the German observers. Its existence was not suspected by the Germans until a few Russian antitank guns suddenly appeared on the north bank of the river. Russian prisoners subsequently confirmed the existence of an underwater bridge and supplied information about its construction. Despite repeated attempts the Germans failed to destroy this bridge.

In 2 weeks the Russians had thus created an adequate jumpoff base for further operations. One foggy morning they attacked the German outposts in the immediate area of the river bend. They suddenly employed artillery and a few close-support aircraft to neutralize positions in the German MLR and to prevent movement of reserves. Thus far, Russian artillery had been conspicuous by its absence in the fighting along the river, probably because the Russians wished to draw as little attention as possible to the bridgehead operation.

As a result of this attack, the Germans were pushed back to the edge of the swamp. Content with this success, the Russians took up defensive positions along the perimeter of their newly won bridgehead, which was protected in part by a river inlet and a body of stagnant water. Since neither tanks nor assault guns could be employed in the swampy terrain, all German counterattacks were unsuccessful. The Russians consolidated the bridgehead during the following days and then used it as one of the jumpoff bases for their large-scale summer offensive.

V. The Oder Crossings (February 1945)

The following action, which took place during the last phase of the war, led to the formation of a Russian bridgehead which was to assume decisive importance a few weeks after its buildup. The procedure followed by the Russians was at variance with that in the preceding example. In this instance the Russians formed the bridgehead in a single day by executing a well-timed pincers attack. Before the main crossing, strong Russian elements made a diversionary assault farther up the river. This secondary attack achieved the double purpose of forcing the Germans to commit their reserves and of compelling them to fight on two fronts as soon as the main attack force had crossed the river. In this instance the two attack forces coordinated their operations and received effective ground and air support. In evaluating this action it should be remembered that the

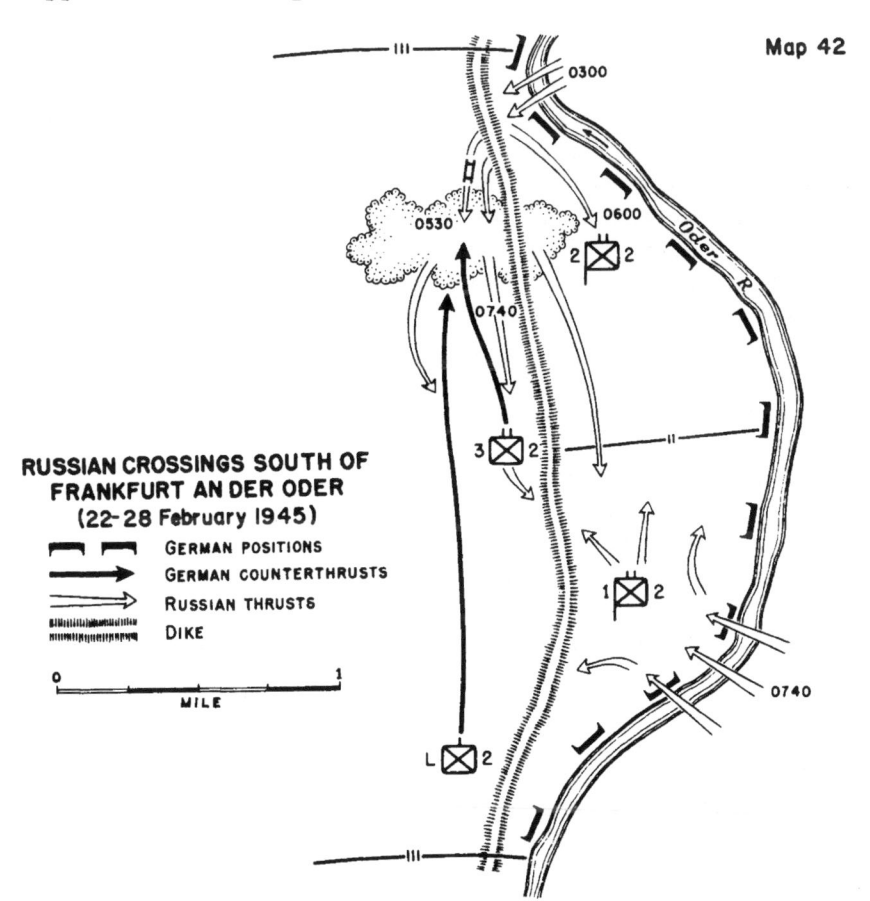

Map 42

RUSSIAN CROSSINGS SOUTH OF FRANKFURT AN DER ODER
(22-28 February 1945)

GERMAN POSITIONS
GERMAN COUNTERTHRUSTS
RUSSIAN THRUSTS
DIKE

German troops facing the Russians were improvised units organized in times of extreme emergency.

In early February 1945, after the collapse of the German front in Poland in January, the Russian advance ground to a temporary halt east of the Oder River. An improvised German infantry division was deployed on the west bank south of Frankfurt an der Oder. The 2d Grenadier Regiment of this division, composed of such diverse formations as security guards, SS units, Volkssturm battalions [*Ed.:* People's militia units, hastily assembled during the last year of the war], as well as training classes from a military school, was assigned a 4-mile sector along a river bend that formed a salient approximately 10 miles south of Frankfurt. The 1st and 2d Battalions took up positions directly behind the river bank, while the 3d Battalion was committed along a dike that formed the chord of the salient and dominated the open terrain between the dike and the river bend. The 2d Grenadier Regiment was supported by a light artillery battalion, two field howitzer batteries, and one rocket launcher battalion. Their observation posts were located in the forward positions, near the battalion CP's, and on the dike (map 42).

In mid-February Russian tank and motorized spearheads attempted a surprise crossing of the Oder River near Frankfurt but failed. After that, the Russians waited until their infantry was able to close up to the mechanized units. On the night of 22 February several Russian reconnaissance patrols attempted to cross the river unobserved, but were intercepted and repulsed by the two battalions on the west bank. A series of small-scale engagements took place during the following nights, but the German regimental commander felt certain that no Russian patrols had infiltrated his sector and that the enemy did not intend to force a crossing in that area.

The night of 27-28 February was marked by poor visibility, rain, and strong west winds. Despite the bad weather, Russian reconnaissance aircraft were exceptionally active, and the droning of their engines could be heard throughout the night. The entire regimental sector up to the dike received sporadic harassing fire.

At 0300 a strong Russian patrol crossed the river at the north end of the salient on pneumatic rafts without being observed by the Germans, broke into the positions of the 2d Battalion's left wing, silenced the defenders, and sealed off both flanks of the 200-yard penetration. The storm and the noise of the aircraft engines drowned out the sounds of the fighting, so that neither the adjacent units nor the staff at the battalion CP were aroused.

Within the hour a Russian rifle battalion with antitank guns, howitzers, and five light tanks was put across the river at the same

SMALL UNIT ACTION

German 88-MM. GUN knocks out Russian tanks.

point on ponton ferries. The Germans were unaware of the existence of the bridgehead until 0400, when they suddenly heard the noise of Russian tanks starting their engines. The 2d Battalion commander alerted his reserves, but their counterattacks against both flanks of the bridgehead failed to dislodge the Russians.

To block any further advance of the bridgehead force, the regimental commander ordered Companies I and K to assemble near the center of the woods while it was still dark. At 0530 the two companies were suddenly attacked by a force driving from the north. The five tanks had broken out of the bridgehead and, supported by infantry, were advancing on the west side of the dike. In their attempt to block the Russian thrust, the two German companies suffered heavy casualties in bitter hand-to-hand fighting. Although the fire from the Russian tank guns was far from accurate, it paralyzed the resistance of the inexperienced German troops. At 0600 a platoon of Russian infantry turned eastward and attacked the 2d Battalion CP from the rear, forcing the German staff to evacuate in haste.

At dawn the regimental commander evaluated the situation. The Russians held the eastern half of the woods. A few German pockets of resistance were holding out directly south of the woods. Sporadic bursts of fire were still heard from the woods. The remnants of Companies I and K were out of contact with regimental headquarters. At its new command post the 2d Battalion staff had no control over its subordinate units in the river positions.

In this emergency the regimental commander ordered Company L, the only unit still in reserve, to move from its position near the southern end of the salient and block any further Russian advance. He notified division headquarters of the critical situation and was promised reinforcements. One battalion was to be moved to his sector to launch a counterattack against the Russian bridgehead, but its arrival could not be expected before noon. Meanwhile, the regimental commander directed the artillery battalion to shell the Russian forces assembled in the woods.

While the attention of the Germans was diverted to the threat from the north, the main attack force was preparing to cross the river opposite the 1st Battalion sector. At 0700 approximately 25 Russian batteries opened fire on the positions of the 1st and 2d Battalions on the west bank, on the German observation posts atop the dike, on Company L moving north, and on the artillery positions in the rear. At 0740 the main attack force, consisting of two infantry regiments, began to cross the Oder and gained an immediate hold on the west bank. Simultaneously, the force that had made the initial assault assembled in the woods and thrust southward, effectively supported by artillery fire from the east bank of the river. The Russian forces pushed back the remnants of the 3d Battalion, including Company L, eliminated those German observation posts on the dike that had survived the artillery preparation, and cut off the German forces holding out in the positions along the river bank. This thrust prevented the two battalions from withdrawing to previously prepared positions along the dike.

Under these circumstances the main attack force had no difficulty in clearing a 1-mile stretch of the west bank and mopping up the area east of the dike. During the following days the Russians consolidated the bridgehead, which became one of their principal assembly areas for the last major offensive of the war.

In this action the Russians demonstrated their proficiency in achieving surprise, selecting crossing sites advantageous for the establishment of a bridgehead, supporting with artillery fire the force that made the initial assault, and coordinating the secondary attack with the main crossing. The two-pronged attack across the Oder was based on a detailed and well-integrated plan. Surprise was obtained by maintaining secrecy and deceiving the Germans as to the point of main crossing. Thorough reconnaissance preceded the initial landings, which were based on information gathered by patrols that had crossed the river during preceding nights. The Russians knew the locations of the German command posts, artillery observers, and reserves. The main crossing site was at a considerable distance from the one selected for the initial assault. The Russian artillery on the east bank of the Oder gave excellent support throughout the attack; its forward observers stayed with the advance elements of the initial assault force and pinpointed targets. By diverting the attention of the defenders and attracting their reserve forces, the initial assault force assured the success of the main crossing.

Chapter 6
Forest Combat

I. General

Combat in forests, whatever the size of the forces originally committed, eventually assumes the characteristics of small unit actions. Dense wooded areas form a curtain between elements of any unit having a common objective and inevitably split them into smaller and smaller groups as the general situation becomes increasingly obscure.

Terrain in which it is difficult to maintain contact and control makes great demands upon the mettle of troops and upon the effectiveness of their leadership. The mental strain of forest combat is severe, particularly on inexperienced soldiers. The sound of every shell seems louder in wooded areas, and the prolonged periods of close combat inherent in forest fighting shatter the nerves and sap the strength of even well-conditioned forces.

The German lack of experience in fighting in forests was a great disadvantage in the Russian campaign. The German troops, trained to depend on the massed fire of all the combat arms, had to adapt themselves to terrain where the infantry had to carry the main burden. And even the infantry was limited to the use of the rifle, machine pistol, hand grenade, mortar, and the *panzerfaust*. [*Ed.:* Recoilless antitank grenade and launcher, both expendable.] The machinegun had but limited effect in dense woods, and suitable observation and firing positions for artillery in the forests of European Russia are rare.

The Russian, on the other hand, innately possessed characteristics which served him well in forest fighting. His physical strength, his ability to get along with few comforts, and his natural ability as a woodsman led him to seek combat in the forest as keenly as the German sought to avoid it.

II. Initiation Into Forest Fighting (July 1941)

During the first weeks of the Russian campaign, one of the German infantry divisions forming part of Army Group North was moving across Latvia in the direction of Leningrad. After crossing the

FOREST FIGHTING IN LATVIA
(13 July 1941)

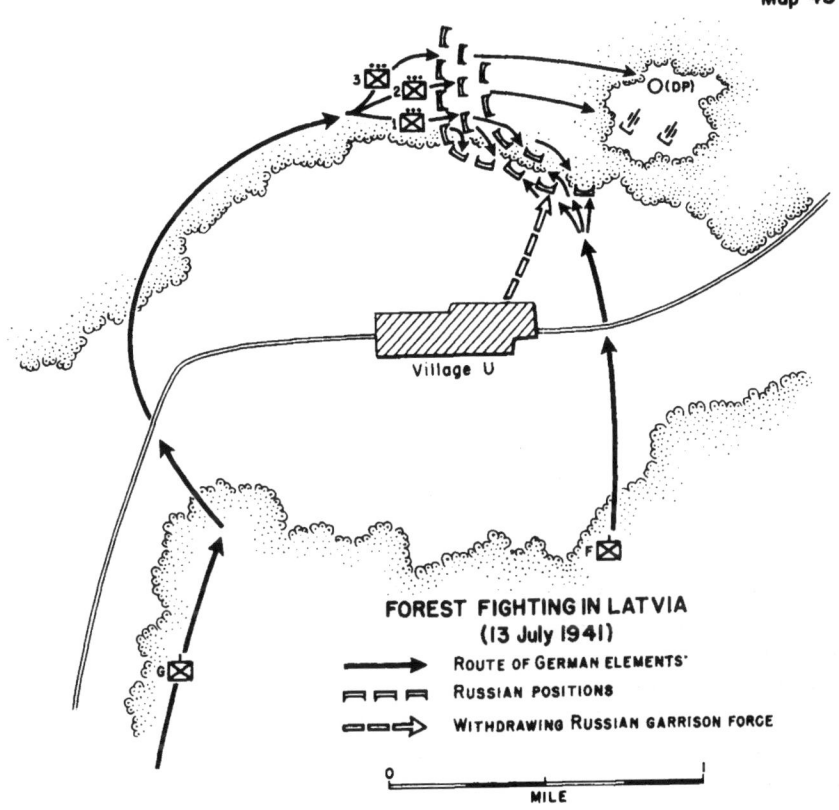

- ➙ ROUTE OF GERMAN ELEMENTS
- ▭▭▭ RUSSIAN POSITIONS
- ⇢⇢⇢ WITHDRAWING RUSSIAN GARRISON FORCE

Dvina at a point about 30 miles north of Dvinsk, the advance guard of the lead regiment encountered light Russian resistance. On the morning of 13 July, when the going became increasingly difficult, the regimental commander decided to commit two battalions abreast. Advancing in extended formation, the two battalions reached the edge of a clearing in the dense forest where the road selected as axis of advance turned eastward (map 43).

This clearing was ellipse-shaped and measured about 2 miles in length and 1 mile in width. In the center was Russian-held Village U, which lay astride the German route of advance. German reconnaissance elements observed Russian movements near what looked like prepared positions at the northeastern edge of the clearing. Several guns fired from emplacements located behind these positions.

When the regimental commander arrived at the southern edge of the clearing, he gathered all available information and suggested an immediate halt in the division's movement. After evaluating the situation he decided against a frontal attack on the village. Instead, he ordered Company G, commanded by Lieutenant Meyer, to sweep around the clearing in a wide enveloping move through the woods north of the road and to neutralize the enemy positions, thereby reopening the division's route of advance. Company F was to act as a decoy by simulating an attack from the southern edge of the clearing without actually emerging from the forest.

It was necessary for Company G to cross the open terrain through which the road led southwest of the village. Despite intermittent Russian artillery fire Meyer, with about 100 men, reached the opposite edge of the forest without suffering casualties. The commander of the Russian garrison in the village observed the company's movement and, recognizing the danger of being outflanked, hurriedly withdrew his troops to the positions at the northeast edge of the forest.

Meyer and his men moved cautiously along the forest's edge, keeping out of the enemy's view. Around noon, at a point due north of the village, the Germans suddenly ran into enemy fire from within the forest. A patrol sent out by Meyer reported that the Russian positions extended northward into the forest, thus covering the right flank of the defense forces and that members of the patrol had drawn fire from individual snipers and outpost detachments concealed in foxholes and slit trenches.

On the basis of this information, Meyer decided to split his force, committing the 1st and 2d Platoons in a frontal assault while holding the rest in reserve. As soon as the attack got under way, however, he realized that he would have to employ the 3d Platoon on the left of the assault force, because the Russian positions extended even farther back into the forest than he had at first presumed.

While Company G was regrouping, pandemonium suddenly broke loose. Mortar shells exploded on the ground and against tree trunks and branches. Machinegun bullets whizzed through the air, ricocheting from trees and off the ground. Hand grenade fragments flew in all directions. Russian snipers, who had permitted the attackers to bypass them, suddenly came to life and fired on the Germans from behind. Wild shouts rang through the forest.

This inferno of fire and noise was too much for the German infantrymen, who were inexperienced in close-in forest fighting. The men were so terrified that they stopped in their tracks and sought cover. The attack bogged down. While the German infantrymen hugged the ground, it occurred to them that the din made by the Russians was entirely out of proportion to the actual effectiveness of their fire. Meanwhile, Meyer had crawled to each one of the platoons and given instructions to his NCO's. The platoon leaders rallied their men, formed assault detachments, and urged each man to outdo the Rus-

GERMAN RIVER CROSSING, 1942

sians in creating terror and confusion. Upon a given signal the Germans began to shout wildly and fire their weapons as rapidly as they could. Bolstered by the sound of their own yelling and the noise of their weapons, the men of Company G resumed the attack.

A hard struggle ensued, for the defenders resisted to the end and had to be ferreted out man by man. After 2 hours of fighting the 1st Platoon was able to penetrate the defense belt and turn against the rear of the Russian positions along the forest's edge. Thereupon the defenders' resistance collapsed, and the two other platoons made their way to the small clearing where the Russian artillery batteries were emplaced. The Germans overpowered the artillerymen, capturing the guns and an ammunition dump before the Russians could destroy them.

Company F joined Meyer and his men in mopping up Russian nests of resistance at the forest's edge, and by late afternoon the German division was able to resume its advance.

The psychological factor in closein fighting is particularly pronounced in the case of a unit experiencing this type of combat for the first time. Since sound tends to be augmented in wooded areas, a concentration fired by different kinds of weapons along with ricocheting projectiles and loud shouting is bound to have a telling effect on the nerves of troops advancing through a forest. Close combat is always nerve-racking, but especially so in forests, where it often rages for extended periods and at very close quarters. Since a defender can conceal himself very effectively behind trees and in underbrush, the attacker is easily overcome by a feeling of uncertainty and utter helplessness.

It is then that leadership assumes crucial importance. In the above action Meyer's ability to evaluate the situation promptly, to exercise strong personal leadership, and to solve the problem by countering

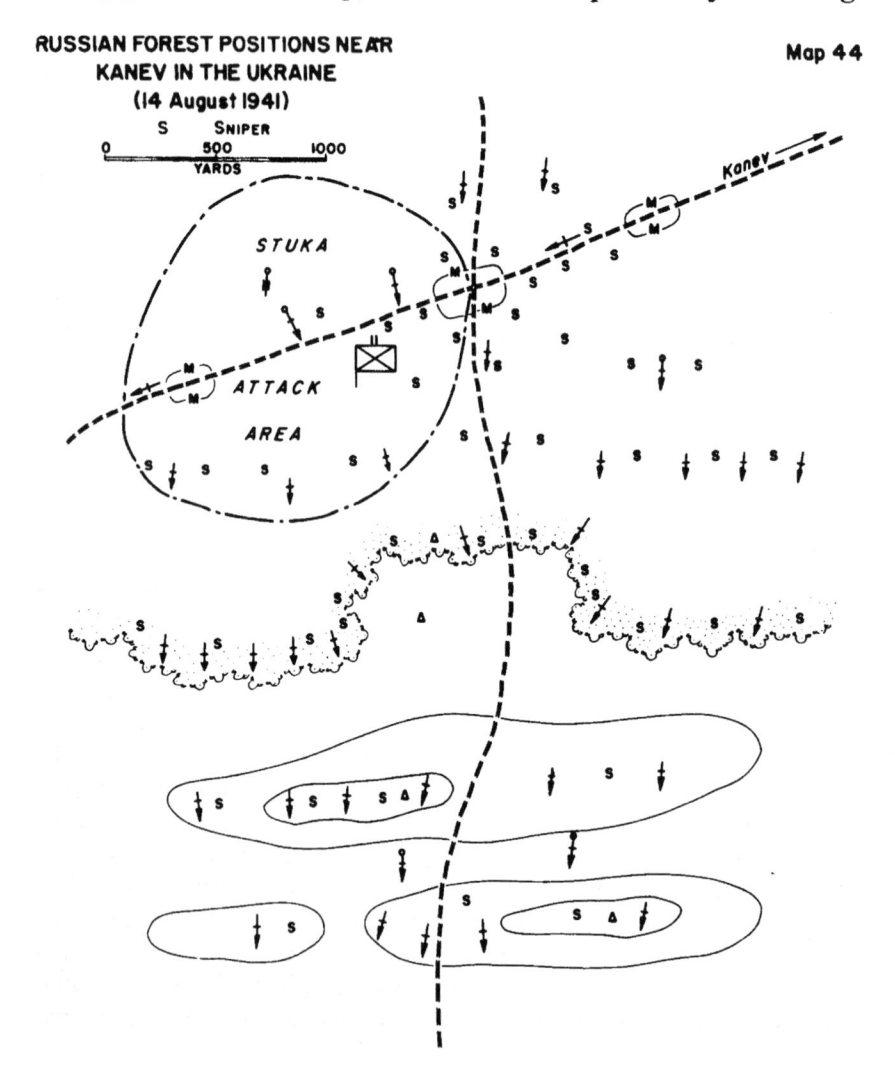

RUSSIAN FOREST POSITIONS NEAR KANEV IN THE UKRAINE (14 August 1941)

Map 44

noise with more noise and fire with massed fire enabled Company G to turn the tide in a contest that might otherwise have been lost.

III. Russian Defensive Position Near the Edge of a Forest (August 1941)

Defensive positions established near the edge of a forest or just within it can be neutralized most effectively by a well coordinated air-ground attack. In August 1941 the Germans succeeded in doing so about 5 miles southwest of Kanev. At that time the Russian forces were being pushed back toward the Dnepr by German infantry divisions thrusting from the west and the south. A Russian battalion forming part of an infantry brigade had been ordered to dig in south of a crossroad leading to Kanev and to hold out to the last man. The battalion had no artillery support, but was equipped with heavy mortars and infantry cannon. The German 169th Infantry Regiment, which was part of the 68th Division moving up from the south, was to capture the crossroad and establish contact with the German forces driving toward the Dnepr from the west. The German regiment was at only 65 percent of its T/O strength, whereas the Russian battalion was almost completely intact.

In organizing their defense the Russians set up two lines of combat outposts, the first line occupying two adjacent ridges about 1,000 yards in front of the MLR at the southern edge of a woods, the second on a ridge about 500 yards behind the first. Each outpost line was manned by one rifle platoon, with one sniper and two machineguns per squad. Between the two lines of outposts the Russians sited two light mortar squads. Infantry cannon and heavy mortars supported the outposts from behind the MLR, the forward observers for these pieces being stationed on the ridges (map 44).

The Russian main battle position was organized with two rifle companies, each having one platoon at the edge and two platoons echeloned in depth within the forest. The crossroad proper was defended by the remaining elements of the company assigned to the outpost positions. The positions along the edge of the forest consisted of groups of two to six foxholes, each well camouflaged. A number of snipers were posted in trees at the edge of and within the forest. The positions in the forest were dug in almost straight lines and were so well concealed that they could be spotted only at very close range. At several points the Russian machine gunners and snipers had cleared narrow fire lanes, but none of these was higher than twenty inches from the ground, so that approaching Germans would be unable to recognize them. The defenders did not have sufficient time to set up live or dead abatis. They laid wooden antipersonnel mines in three fields across the road leading to Kanev from the west. Some of the riflemen were dug in under wood piles, each entrance being concealed from the outside.

Wire lines connected the battalion CP with company CP's, heavy weapons positions, and outposts. Two observation posts were set up in the clearing where the north-south road entered the forest. They were dug in under tree trunks, and their wire lines to the firing positions were buried 10 inches deep in the ground.

At 0900 on 14 August the 1st Battalion of the 169th Infantry Regiment approached the forest from the south. Although the battalion commander did expect Russian resistance within the forest, he was unaware of the strength of the defensive positions. The German advance guard had come to within 1,000 yards of the first ridge when the Russians suddenly opened up with machinegun, mortar, and small-arms fire. The battalion commander thereupon deployed his unit for a concerted attack on the first ridge and called for artillery support. The German fire, zeroed in on the first ridge, was too much for the Russian defenders, and, after a short period of hand-to-hand fighting, the German infantry captured the first outpost line. When the two light mortar squads located between the two outpost lines tried to withdraw, German machine gunners and riflemen took them under fire and wiped them out.

At 1030 the second outpost line was still holding fast; Russian machine gunners and snipers pinned down the Germans on the opposite ridge. Russian infantry cannon and heavy mortars in the main battle position within the forest laid interdictory fire on the low ground between the Germans and their next objective. German observers on the first ridge pinpointed targets for their heavy weapons and artillery, under cover of whose fire the infantrymen slowly inched their way forward. Although the distance to the second Russian outpost line was but 500 yards, the Germans had to struggle for a full hour before they could ascend the ridge. When they finally reached the top, they were unable to advance any farther in the face of the well-aimed Russian fire from the forest.

While the German battalion was reorganizing for a final thrust, this time against the Russian MLR, its commander requested division headquarters to initiate a dive-bomber strike against the nerve center of resistance near the crossroad. Around noon a dive-bomber force loosed its destruction on the forest area, where it silenced the Russian cannon and mortars and smashed the CP and the wire net. As the German artillery joined in the fray the 1st Battalion resumed its advance, meeting but sporadic resistance at the point of entry into the forest opposite the bombed area. The forward line was deserted. In the positions deeper within the forest the advancing Germans found

SMALL UNIT ACTIONS

dead and wounded Russians and many discarded weapons. Here and there tree snipers fired at them, whereupon German machine and submachine gunners sprayed the trees. The 1st Battalion mopped up the forest as far as the crossroad and then turned east along the road to Kanev. It took some prisoners, but a number of Russians defending the rear positions managed to escape. One Russian commissar, who had been shooting down his retreating countrymen, blew his head off with a hand grenade as some German troops were closing in on him.

The mine fields failed to delay the Germans. The one west of the crossroad was detonated by German artillery fire and the others were

German 20-mm. ANTIAIRCRAFT GUN used in ground fighting, 1942.

detected after prisoners had given away the location. The Russians had gone to considerable trouble to conceal the mines, placing some of them under fresh tire tracks. Without the information obtained by immediate interrogation of the prisoners, these mines would no doubt have caused heavy German casualties. It was also learned from prisoners that the infantry cannon company had been commanded by a woman.

Some of the snipers and observers were so well concealed that the Germans bypassed them and did not discover their hideouts until the forest was combed out. Here and there Russian soldiers were being pulled out of their hiding places more than an hour after the main body of the battalion had continued its march to Kanev.

The speed with which the Russians had established their excellent positions at the edge and inside the forest amazed the Germans. In the course of just one night they had dug themselves in and camouflaged their positions and weapons with great effectiveness. Upon contact with the German battalion, the Russians might have prolonged the struggle if they had pulled back their outposts instead of sacrificing them on the ridges. These men and their weapons might have been far more effective had they been employed within the forest.

The forest gave strong assistance to this Russian battalion, which lacked both artillery and air support. Had this unit been employed in open terrain, the Germans would have overrun it in no time, as was the case with so many other Russian infantry units during the early phase of the campaign.

IV. German Defense of a Forest Strong Point (February 1942)

In the early months of 1942 the divisions of Army Group Center made desperate attempts to halt the Russian counteroffensive west and southwest of Moscow. After participating in the heavy fighting southwest of the Soviet capital, the German 15th Infantry Division, each of its regiments reduced to three or four decimated companies, limped westward in the direction of the Bolshaya Shanya River, behind which it was supposed to make a stand along a newly established defense line about 40 miles east of Vyazma (map 45).

At the beginning of February typical Russian midwinter weather prevailed with temperatures averaging −22° F. Under a blanket of 2 feet of snow the ground was solidly frozen to a depth of 3 feet. Since the construction of defensive positions under such weather conditions was bound to take considerable time, the division commander had ordered his regiments to conduct a series of delaying actions and defend every inhabited locality along the route of withdrawal.

SMALL UNIT ACTIONS

Map 45

GERMAN DEFENSE OF A FOREST STRONG POINT SOUTHWEST OF MOSCOW (1-6 February 1942)

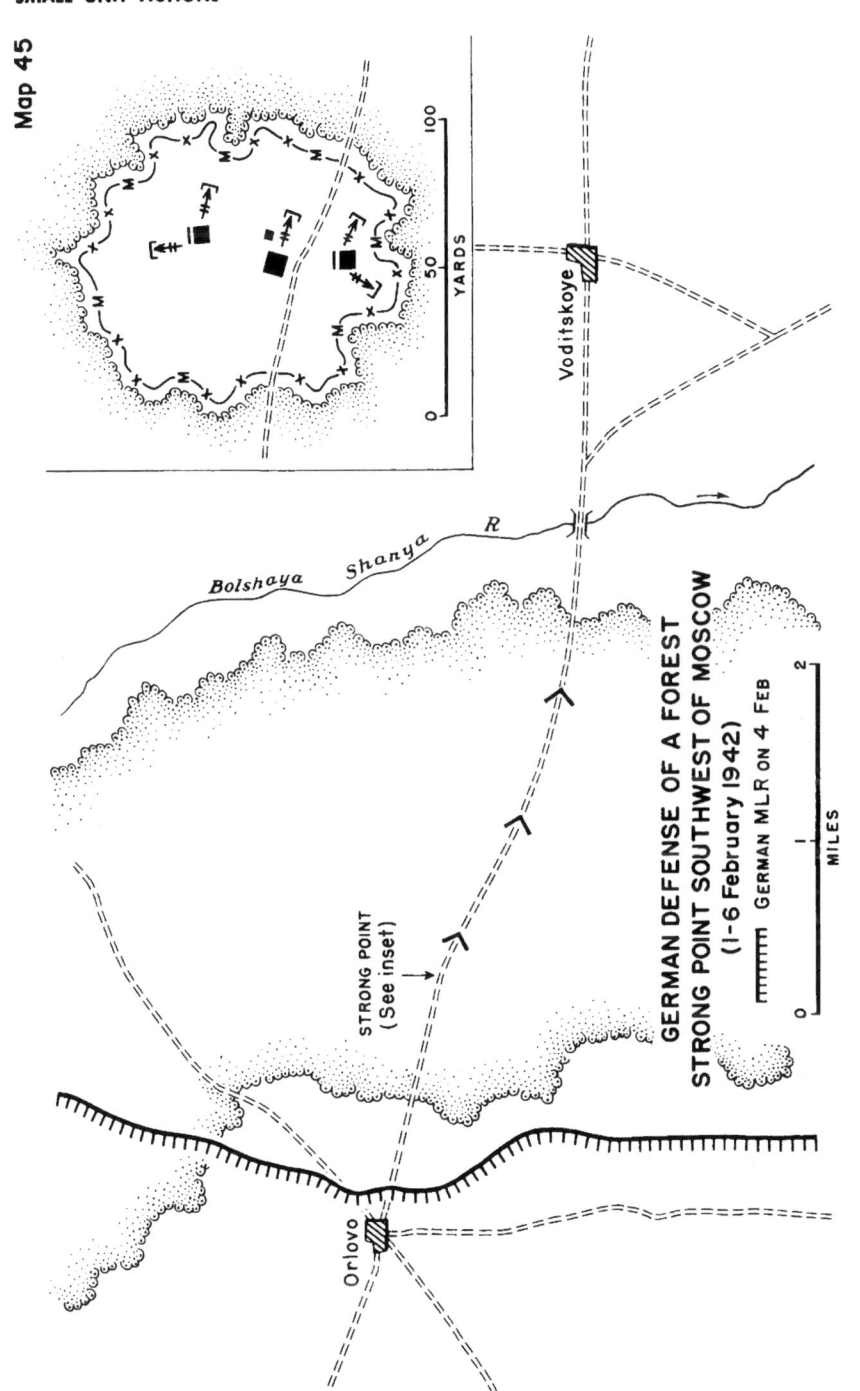

⊥⊥⊥⊥⊥⊥⊥ GERMAN MLR ON 4 FEB

On 1 February the 81st Regiment, part of the 15th Infantry Division, was holding Voditskoye against strong attacks by well-equipped elements of the 1st Moscow Guard Division. The regimental commander doubted that his weak forces would be able to hold out there more than 2 or 3 days. Since the defense line just east of Orlovo was not yet ready and Voditskoye was the last inhabited locality blocking the Russian advance, he ordered Company C to convert into a strong point the ground surrounding a forester's cabin, located some 1,000 yards due east of Orlovo. The company consisted of 1 officer and 25 battle-weary men, who, like most Army Group Center troops, were short of winter clothing. Ammunition was ample, but rations were limited to 10 ounces of bread a day per man. To assist Company C with the construction work, a platoon of 20 engineers and 30 men from service units were to be dispatched from Orlovo.

The forester's cabin was a log structure with a thatched roof. Nearby stood a shed. These structures were situated along the Voditskoye-Orlovo road in the center of a clearing about 100 yards in diameter. The forest consisted of a dense stand of young pines.

With the addition of a heavy machinegun section, telephone and radio operators, and a forward artillery observer, the forest garrison was increased to 35 men. Since it was impossible to accommodate all of the men in the cabin and the shed for any length of time, the company commander decided to construct two additional shelters on the other side of the road. Company C had no proper entrenching tools nor were there any explosives available to break up the frozen ground. The company commander decided to improvise and had the men clear two small areas in the snow and light log fires. These were maintained for 36 hours to thaw the ground sufficiently to permit the use of their primitive Russian shovels. The only drawback to this procedure was that the fires attracted the attention of Russian fliers. To offset this disadvantage, decoy fires were lighted in adjacent parts of the forest.

After the excavation work was finished, heavy logs were placed over the two holes and covered with the excavated clay, which then froze solid thus forming a shellproof outer hull. Stoves made of discarded metal containers were used to heat the shelters. To provide insulation the interior of the cabin, the shed, and the two dugouts was reinforced with clay. Embrasures were provided on all sides of the structures.

The trees at the edge of the clearing were sawed off and barbed wire was strung along the stumps. Antipersonnel mines were attached to the wire and covered with a light layer of snow. Three roadblocks were prepared, but were left open along the approach road leading from the river through the forest.

These preparations were accomplished within 3 days. By the afternoon of 4 February all was in readiness. This was none too soon since the regiment holding out in Voditskoye was being hard pressed by the Russians. That very evening the regimental commander issued orders to withdraw to the fortified line east of Orlovo. After the regiment had safely passed the newly established forest strong point, its garrison closed the roadblocks and emplaced mines in front of them.

The following day the garrison heard the sound of detonations that came from the direction of the roadblocks. While the company was completing its last-minute preparations, the artillery observer requested that a barrage be laid down in front of the second and third roadblocks.

The night of 5–6 February passed quietly. As dawn was breaking, observers within the strong point noticed ghostlike figures clad in white and silhouetted against the trees at the clearing's edge in the immediate vicinity of the wire entanglement. Mine explosions drowned out the sounds of the first bursts of German and Russian rifle fire. The attackers' brief delay outside the wire entanglement provided the Germans with sufficient time to take the machineguns from the warm shelters and emplace them in the prepared positions. The Russians cut the wire at three points, where they had formed assault detachments. When, at a given signal, they stormed into the clearing, they were annihilated by pointblank machinegun fire. Within a matter of minutes artillery fire hit Russian reinforcements that had just arrived near the clearing, forcing them to flee in wild disorder. The Russian raid had miscarried at the cost of 40 dead and 10 wounded; the German defenders did not suffer a single casualty.

Company C's morale was high as a result of this engagement. During the following days the Germans successfully defended the forest strong point against repeated assaults; the Russians finally gave up their attacks at this point of the front.

Once again the Russians had demonstrated their ability to endure extreme cold. Even during such severe winter weather they were able to spend several weeks in the open and remain in fighting trim. The forest was their ally, affording protection against the biting wind and providing fuel in unlimited quantities.

Interrogation of the wounded Russians revealed the incredible hardships they had experienced during the winter offensive that saved Moscow. Since most inhabited localities had gone up in flames, the Russians were almost completely deprived of shelter. Headquarters staffs were occasionally set up in the cellars of burnt-out buildings, but the troops remained in the open. Whenever they were not on the move, they assembled around fires in the forest. The prisoners also told of how some of the Russian companies spent their nights in the bitter cold. A company of men would line up along a long rope which was then wound up like a skein of yarn. Thus pressed closely together and warmed by the heat of each other's bodies, the men would sleep while standing on their feet. Every hour the skein would be unwound and then rewound in such a manner that those on the inside would form the outer ring and those who had been exposed to the cold wind would benefit from the relative comforts of an inside position.

V. Russian Infiltration Tactics (October 1942)

The Russians' skill in infiltrating positions in wooded terrain presented the Germans with many a difficult problem. They were experts at making their way through narrow gaps in the front and gaining a foothold in seemingly impassable swampy forests. The Russian methods usually followed the same pattern. During the first night a few men would infiltrate the German lines and vanish in the forest. During the second night reinforcements would bring the force up to platoon strength. In this way, providing no countermeasures were taken, a whole battalion, complete with staff and signal communications, could be lodged in the rear of the German lines within 1 week. In many instances wide sectors of the German front caved in because the responsible commander had disregarded the apparently insignificant infiltrations that had occurred under his very nose.

In the summer of 1942 the German 129th Infantry Division was defending a wide sector approximately 10 miles southeast of Rzhev. Despite heavy Russian pressure lasting for several weeks the division had held fast until mid-August, when the village of Dubakino on the division's right was lost after a brief engagement. After withdrawing from Dubakino, the weak German garrison reassembled a few hundred yards to the west and established an outpost line on the easterly edge of a swampy woods (map 46).

The high level of the ground water prevented the Germans from setting up a continuous defense line. Every night individual Russian soldiers infiltrated into the forest at points that the Germans considered impenetrable because of the dense undergrowth and swampy ground. The Russians formed detachments which on successive nights proceeded to attack the German outposts one by one

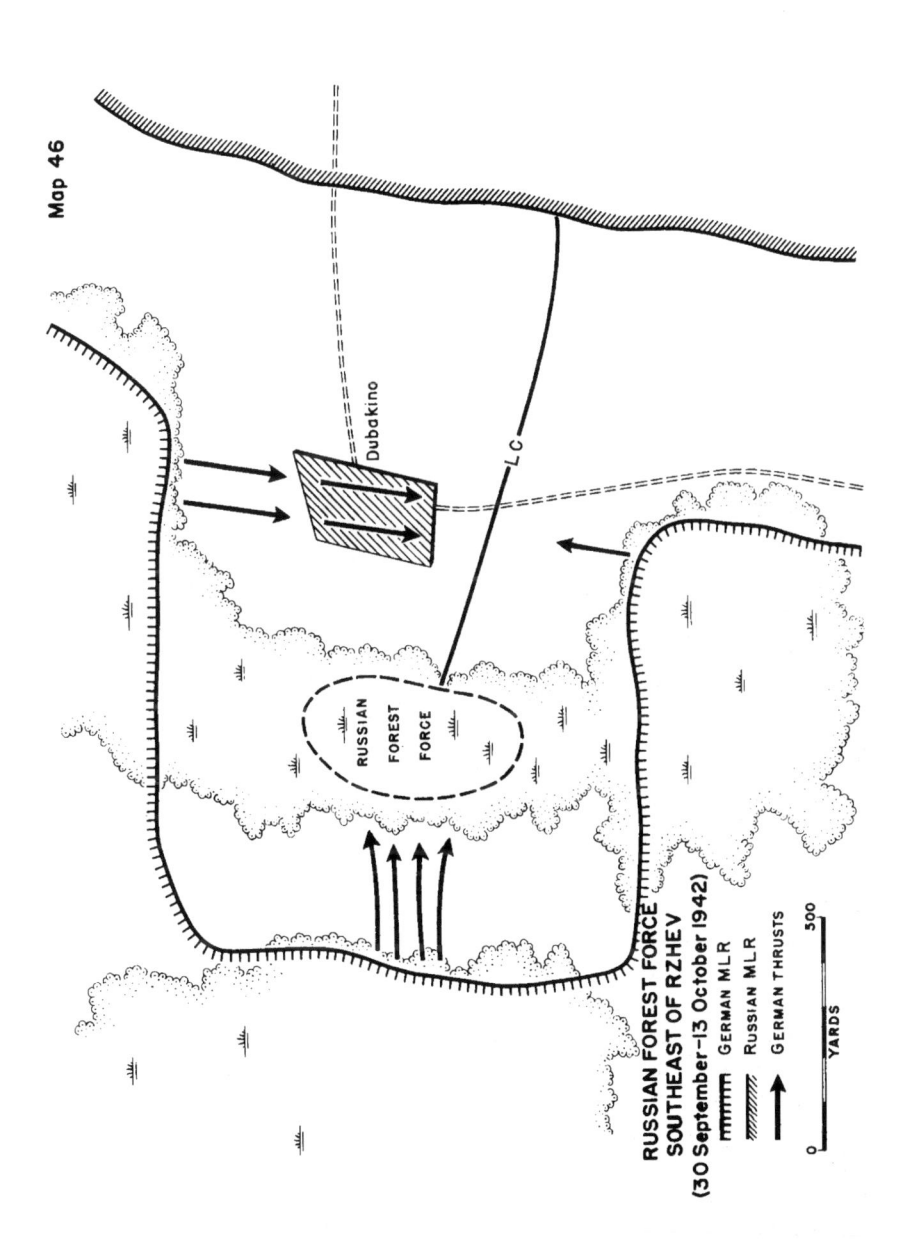

RUSSIAN FOREST FORCE SOUTHEAST OF RZHEV
(30 September–13 October 1942)

GERMAN ARMORED INFANTRY Advancing Through Forest.

from all sides, annihilating them. By this method the Russians gradually enlarged the area in their possession with a minimum of effort.

Since the Germans were unable to comb out the forest, their position became untenable and they were forced to withdraw westward to the eastern edge of another woods. There, on slightly higher ground, the terrain permitted the establishment of a continuous defense line from which they could watch the Russian-held portion of the woods across a 300-yard-wide clearing. Reconnaissance patrols attempting to determine the strength of the Russians in the woods were met by small-arms fire and had to return without information.

By mid-September the battle around Rzhev subsided, and the division commander was able to withdraw the 427th Regiment from the line. He gave the regiment the mission of eliminating the Russian salient west of Dubakino. In drawing up his plan of attack the regimental commander intended first to cut the Russian communications to the rear to prevent any further build-up or an attempt by the forest force to withdraw eastward. Once this had been accomplished, one battalion was to launch a frontal attack and annihilate the Russians in the pocket.

To implement this plan two infantry companies of the 1st Battalion were moved to the northern shoulder of the salient and an engineer company was assembled at the opposite shoulder to form the other arm of the pincers. After a 60-minute preparation starting at noon on 30 September, the two infantry companies jumped off and captured Dubakino in the face of light resistance. The engineers, however, advanced only 200 yards, and then came under flanking fire from the east that pinned them down about 200 yards short of the village. Even though the encirclement of the forest force had not yet been completed, the 3d Battalion, supported by an assault gun battery, launched its attack scheduled for 1400. After crossing the clearing, the self-propelled assault guns stopped near the forest's edge to support the advancing infantry forces. The latter, however, were unable to penetrate the woods because of heavy Russian mortar fire and the great number of wooden box mines at the few points of access to the woods. Russian small-arms fire weakened the ranks of the attackers, who were unable to identify the Russian positions in the dense forest.

By the end of the first day of the attack the two arms of the pincers had failed to make any further progress. The remnants of the 3d Battalion had withdrawn to their line of departure. During that night and the one following the Russian forest force received reinforcements and supplies through the gap in the German line. The pincer forces were unable to stop these movements because of the danger of hitting friendly forces on either side of the gap. Artillery fire against the moving and unidentified targets proved ineffective.

Before resuming the attack the regimental commander requested reinforcements from division headquarters, and on 2 October he received a battery of 210-mm. howitzers amply supplied with ammunition. Upon the arrival of these guns he withdrew the pincer forces to their jumpoff positions at the salient's shoulders to prevent their suffering casualties from the saturation fire that was about to be laid down on the Russians in the woods. When the artillery fire had lifted after 1 hour, the reinforced 3d Battalion made another frontal attack against the forest force. Again, Russian mortar and small-arms fire drove back the attackers with serious losses. The artillery bombardment had obviously had little effect.

The regimental commander thereupon decided to revert to his initial plan of cutting off the forest force from the east before launching another frontal attack. During the next 10 nights the pincer forces systematically worked their way toward each other in a series of coordinated small-scale attacks. A few prisoners taken in the course of the fighting stated that the pocket force had been ordered to hold out to the last man, but the Germans were unable to obtain from them any information as to the Russian strength or dispositions.

On 13 October the gap was finally closed, and the 3d Battalion launched its third daytime attack against the Russians who were presumed to be in the pocket. It encountered extremely light resistance and was slowed down mainly by the swampy terrain and mine-clearing operations. After passing through the woods the battalion linked up with the troops in Dubakino. Only 20 Russians, those who formed the rear guard of the pocket force, were captured.

The strength of the pocket force, which had caused more than 250 German casualties and had then managed to escape the trap by withdrawing, was never determined. Extensive field fortifications were found in the woods. A force of as many as 600 men might conceivably have manned them, but there was no way of knowing whether the positions had been fully occupied. Every slightly elevated patch of ground in the woods was honeycombed with trenches and foxholes, which were camouflaged well enough to defy detection from more than a few yards distance. Most of the trenches were covered by underbrush and were interconnected by underground passages. The defense system, being adapted to the terrain to make use of what solid ground there was in the woods, was not laid out according to any tactical plan. The German artillery shells had disappeared in the swampy ground, leaving no traces except for a few mutilated tree trunks and broken branches.

GERMAN ASSAULT GUN advances ahead of infantry, 1942.

Map 47

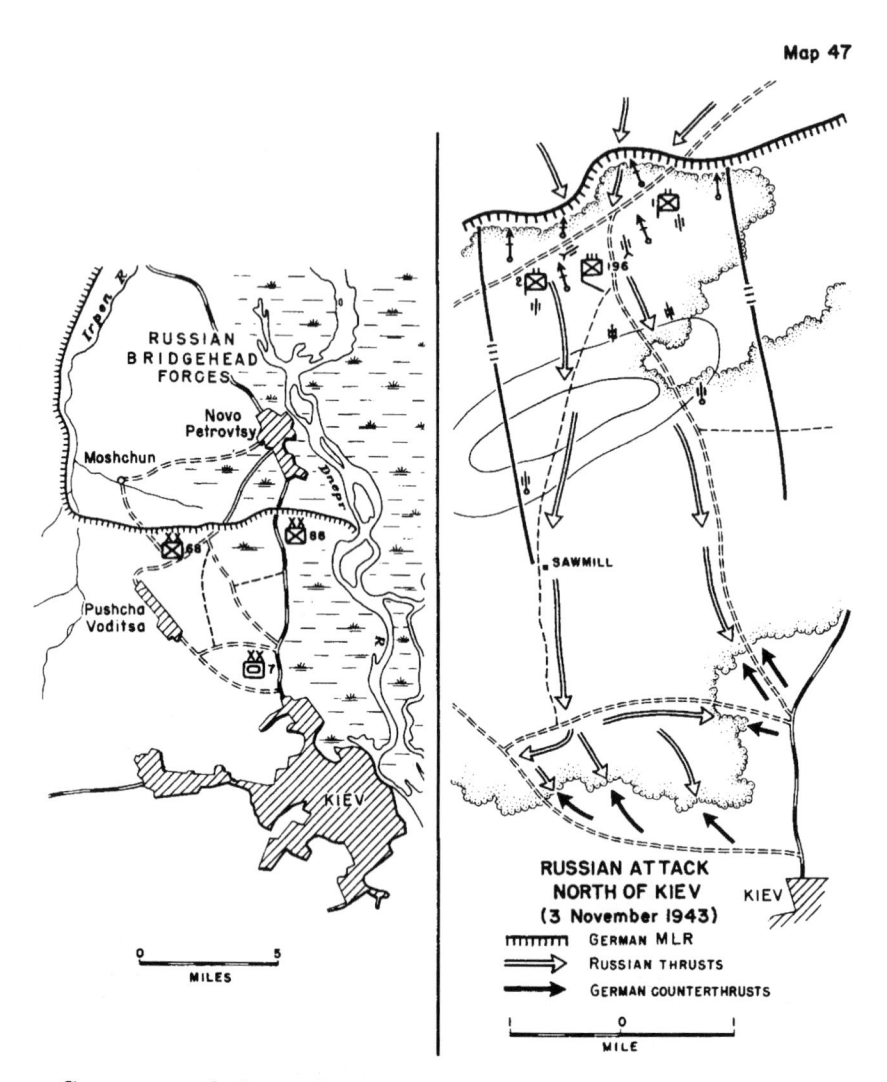

RUSSIAN ATTACK
NORTH OF KIEV
(3 November 1943)
⊥⊥⊥⊥⊥ GERMAN MLR
⇨ RUSSIAN THRUSTS
➡ GERMAN COUNTERTHRUSTS

Contrary to their usual procedure the Russians had abandoned their territorial gains, but only after having derived every possible advantage from the possession of the woods. In this instance the Russians not only infiltrated the German lines, but—by their unnoticed withdrawal—also showed how adroit they were in extricating themselves from almost complete encirclement.

VI. Russian Attack Through a Forest (November 1943)

Armored units are usually ineffective in forest fighting, but the Russians did use small groups of tanks in support of infantry forces whenever ground conditions permitted. Toward the end of October 1943 German air reconnaissance provided information indicating that the Russian bridgehead on the west bank of the Dnepr north of Kiev was being constantly reinforced. Armored and infantry units were pouring across the river over ponton and underwater bridges or being shuttled across by ferries. The weak Luftwaffe was unable to delay the progress of the build-up.

The bridgehead forces were denied access to Kiev by the German 68th and 88th Infantry Divisions, which held an approximately 10-mile-wide sector extending from the Dnepr to the Irpen River (map 47). The Russian forces were at full strength, well trained, and amply supplied with the necessities of war. The 68th Division was a battle-weary formation whose infantry strength had shrunk to 40 percent of its prescribed T/O. The 1st and 2d Battalions of its 196th Infantry Regiment held positions south of a large clearing in the forest that stretched across the division's sector. Mine fields protected the battalions' boundaries with adjoining units and blocked the road leading through the German MLR southeastward to Kiev. The MLR was established at the forest's edge, and mortars, antitank guns, and cannon were dispersed over an area up to 1 mile to the rear. The 105-mm. howitzers and 150-mm. guns took up positions in front of and behind a low, wooded hill located 2½ miles behind the MLR.

During the last days of October the Russian forces in the bridgehead conducted many reconnaissance patrols and probed the sector of the two battalions, sending out combat patrols in varying strength. At the same time they had advanced their outposts to within 500 yards of the German MLR and had established a number of new positions, many of which were only dummies. The Russian artillery used smoke shells during its fire for adjustment, so that the Germans would not be able to spot the gun emplacements in the forest before the start of the Russian attack.

Because of the steady build-up in the bridgehead and, particularly, the intense activity opposite the 1st and 2d Battalions, the division commander expected a Russian attack along the road to Kiev. On 31 October, however, when the Russians intensified their artillery fire on the area south of Moshchun, it seemed more likely that they would attempt to break through to Kiev at a point west of the 196th Regiment's sector. Russian combat patrols exerted strong pressure along the entire forest front during the next 2 days, thus leaving the Germans in doubt as to the point of main effort in the impending attack.

At the beginning of November the weather was sunny and exceptionally mild for late autumn. The following actions took place in a high stand of deciduous and coniferous timber. The ground was fairly dry and passable for armored vehicles.

The night of 2–3 November was quiet, but at 0600 the following morning the Russian artillery suddenly laid down a heavy barrage on the 1st and 2d Battalion sectors. The German MLR and the edge of the forest immediately behind it was subjected to murderous fire for an hour and a half. By interspersing smoke shells frequently the Russians reduced the visibility within the forest to less than 50 yards. The MLR at the forest's edge was blanketed by particularly heavy smoke; hence, the German observation posts and fire-direction centers were unable to function.

At 0730 the fire was suddenly shifted to the adjacent sectors and to the area in the rear of the two battalions. At the same time, Russian infantry began to infiltrate the battered MLR of the 196th Regiment, which was now defended by only a few isolated nests of resistance. The first wave of Russian tanks, forming a point of main effort opposite the center of the 196th Regiment's sector, drove past the partly detonated mine fields and approached the forest's edge in extended formation with all guns ablaze. Immediately behind the tanks, and in some instances between them, came Russian infantrymen carrying submachine guns, automatic rifles, and hand grenades.

The second wave, following at 300 yards distance, consisted of tanks and infantrymen, the latter equipped with machineguns and light mortars. Upon reaching the forest's edge, the tanks overran the remaining pockets of resistance and the infantrymen wiped out the few Germans who had managed to survive. Then the infantry regrouped and entered the forest, protected by the tanks which had stopped at the edge. Entering in wedge formation the Russian infantry units in the 1st Battalion's sector advanced southwestward along the Novo Petrovtsy-Pushcha Voditsa road toward the fork where the road to Kiev branches off. Upon reaching the roadfork, the infantry units requested the tanks to move up close behind them. As they pushed into the forest, the tanks took care of any nests of resistance that the infantry had not immediately been able to overcome. During this phase of the action the infantry advanced slowly but methodically and maintained close interunit contact.

Whereas the 2d Battalion forces in the forest were able to delay the Russian advance by fighting a stubborn delaying action, the 1st Battalion gave way, thereby forcing the battalion to its right to make a hasty withdrawal. In the face of such light resistance as was encountered, the Russian infantry columns of the first two waves shifted from massed to extended formation and began to comb out the forest. Assault detachments in company strength, equipped exclusively with submachineguns, followed behind the skirmish line. Russian tanks moved up and wiped out any German strong points in the forest that continued to resist after being enveloped by the infantry. The tanks, which had first moved through the forest in open formation, assembled near the roadfork and drove down the road leading southeast to Kiev in close column, stopping only when their assistance was requested by the infantry. The German antitank guns and howitzers were encircled by Russian infantry detachments, which pinned down their crews with small-arms fire. Most of the first- and second-wave infantry units bypassed these isolated German weapons, leaving their destruction to the tanks or infantry formations of the third wave.

The Russian attack forces in the 2d Battalion's sector proceeded in the same manner, but their progress was much slower because the infantry was supported by only five tanks. Upon reaching the abandoned CP of the 196th Regiment, the Russians halted for 15 minutes to regroup their forces. Meanwhile the main tank column continued its advance along the road to Kiev, and the infantry forces east of that road rested and regrouped upon reaching a path leading eastward in the direction of the Dnepr.

By 1000 the Russian infantry in the 2d Battalion's sector had reached the top of the hill. The five tanks were at that moment moving along the forest road leading south to the sawmill. In the 1st Battalion's sector the advance continued in the direction of Kiev. Toward noon the Russian forces emerged from the forest on a broad front, the eastern end of which was only some 2 miles from the suburbs of Kiev. The 68th Division's commander had moved his reserves to block the road to Kiev and had called for assistance from the 7th Panzer Division to ward off the threat from the north. Ten Russian tanks were destroyed immediately after having emerged from the woods, whereupon the remaining tanks withdrew into the forest with the infantry following in their tracks.

The Russians had taken little more than 4 hours to penetrate and fight their way through the 5 miles of German-held forest. The combined-arms tactics of the Russian tanks and infantry proved very effective. An unusual amount of smoke grenades was used by the Russians during the preparation fire. These grenades were detonated by impact fuzes of the delay rather than the supersensitive type to prevent the projectiles from being set in action by striking the tree tops.

The German division commander, who knew that an attack was imminent, might have taken advantage of the delay in the start of the assault by shifting the MLR of the two battalions from the

GERMAN TANK rumbles through Kiev.

forest's edge to the interior of the woods. By leaving only security detachments in the MLR positions, he could have simulated the presence of the full defense force and saved manpower for defending the forest proper.

VII. German and Russian Combat Tricks

a. A German Decoy Diverts Russian Aircraft (Winter 1941-42). During the desperate struggle in the Rzhev area in the winter of 1941-42, the Russians employed several outdated biplanes to conduct night raids against German installations, to drop propaganda leaflets, and to supply encircled Russian units. Since the nightly harassing raids robbed the German defenders of their much-needed rest, the commander of a German infantry regiment decided to trick the enemy into dropping his bombs where they could cause no damage. He ordered his engineers to hang several lanterns on 6-foot poles set up in an isolated area. A wire connected the lanterns, and a man about 800 yards away manipulated the wire in such a way that the lanterns swayed back and forth. From the air this motion produced the effect of a number of men walking on the ground and carrying lanterns in their hands. On the following night the Russian aircraft appeared as usual. Upon spotting what appeared to be a rewarding target, they immediately released their bombs which exploded without causing any damage except for the destruction of a number of lanterns. After this ruse had been successfully employed for a number of nights, higher headquarters refused to supply any more lanterns because of excessive expenditure. However, when a bomb landed squarely on the billets of the division commander two nights later, the order was rescinded, and lanterns were again available in unlimited quantities.

b. The Dummy Drop Zone (January 1943). During the fighting near Demyansk in January 1943 a German infantry regiment succeeded in encircling elements of several Russian divisions in its rear area. Within a short time the Russians began to airdrop supplies to their encircled forces. A German radio intelligence detachment intercepted a Russian message transmitted to the units in the pocket, ordering them to lay out a drop zone with four fires. During the following night the fires should form the letter T; letters were to be changed every night.

The German regimental commander decided to take advantage of this information and prevent the Russian units in the pocket from receiving badly needed supplies. To this end he established a dummy drop zone outside the pocket. Russian prisoners of war who served the division as laborers were ordered to fill four shell craters forming the letter **T** with dry wood, which was then soaked in gasoline. The laborers had scarcely completed the task when the noise of approaching aircraft became audible. The piles of wood in the pits were quickly set afire. Upon noticing the fires on the ground, Russian aircraft dumped their cargo of ammunition and rations over the German drop zone. This deception was successfully repeated on three successive nights, and the encircled forces were thus deprived of supplies. They were forced to surrender a few days later.

On other occasions the Germans were equally successful in deceiving Russian aircraft, provided that they observed the correct procedure. First, the number of fires and the letters they formed in the drop zone had to correspond to the prearranged signal. If the fires on the ground were not correctly laid out, the Russian pilots became suspicious and were likely to drop a few bombs instead of the desired supplies. Second, the fires had to be built in shell craters or pits according to Russian methods and not on flat ground.

The slow-flying Russian cargo planes were vulnerable to small-arms fire while making their approach run to the lighted drop zone. No tracer ammunition was to be used for this purpose. In their eagerness to recover the airdropped supplies, the German soldiers often did not wait until all Russian aircraft had departed. In one instance, a noncommissioned officer was severly injured when he was hit by frozen sides of bacon.

c. Russian Traps (February 1943). Near Demyansk in February 1943 the German forces in the MLR were greatly understrength, and Russian reconnaissance patrols were often able to infiltrate. They would cut a wire line connecting outposts with the rear and prepare an ambush for the German troubleshooters, who usually arrived within a short time. As a rule, the wire repair team consisted of two men, whose attention was concentrated on the task at hand. While the two were engaged in repairing the damaged wire, the Russians would catch them off guard, overpower them silently, and take them away. At that time the German manpower shortage was so pronounced that usually no infantry detachments were available to protect the troubleshooters.

Another incident occurred on a particularly dark night, when one of two German infantrymen manning a machinegun momentarily left his post to investigate a suspicious noise. Five Russians belonging to a reconnaissance patrol jumped at the soldier who had remained at the machinegun, threw ground pepper into his face, pulled a bag over his head, and disappeared with him into the night. When he heard the noise, the other man ran back to the machinegun and fired several bursts in the direction in which the Russian patrol had vanished. On the following morning the bodies of a Russian officer and two Russian enlisted men were found in the immediate vicinity of the outpost, as was the body of the abducted German machine gunner. Two severely wounded Russians were discovered a few yards away. Among the Russian officer's papers the Germans found an elaborate plan of attack based on preliminary reconnaissance information, indicating that during the four preceding nights the officer had observed the German outpost area from behind a disabled tank at only 30 yards distance from the German machinegun crew.

d. German Sound Deception (November 1944). During the fighting along the Narev River in November 1944 the commander of a German infantry regiment requested from higher headquarters the dispatch of a sound truck equipped with recordings simulating the approach, assembly, and the attack of an armored division. Each record ran for 12 minutes. As soon as the requested equipment arrived, a shelter was constructed on a reverse slope so that the sound truck would be protected from enemy view and fire. Observers, equipped with telescopes, were to scrutinize the Russian positions to determine the emplacements of their heavy weapons and artillery. A fire plan was prepared according to which the heavy weapons of the three German battalions in that sector were to alternately fire at specified targets in order to confuse the Russians. Division and corps intercept units were alerted. The time for the deceptive attack was set for the late afternoon of a hazy November day, when visibility was at a minimum.

Soon after the start of the German fire, which was perfectly coordinated with the sounds of approaching armor, the Russian heavy weapons began to reply. A little later the artillery went into action. As the noise of the approaching German tanks grew louder, the Russian unit commanders became more and more alarmed and sent out frantic calls for help. This radio traffic was observed by the German intercept detachments, which were thus able to plot the location of the enemy command posts.

Thirty-seven minutes later a Russian artillery shell scored a direct hit on the cable which linked the loudspeaker to the sound truck, thus putting a sudden end to the performance. However, by this time the deception had achieved its purpose. The Russian forward positions had been identified, 11 mortar and 7 antitank gun emplacements had been determined, and a great number of artillery pieces had been located by flash and sound ranging. On the following day the identified Russian weapons were taken under fire and destroyed.

Chapter 7

Antipartisan Warfare

I. General

Guerrilla warfare is as old as time itself. During more recent times this type of operation has assumed an ever greater importance in military and political planning. That the study of partisan and antipartisan combat methods is an absolutely essential element of any up-to-date military training program is obvious. Based on practical German experience in Russia, the following examples are certain to stimulate interest in this subject.

Partisan operations do not conform to any hard and fast tactical doctrine or principles that have general applicability. The partisan fighter is unpredictable and unscrupulous. His weapons are usually simple in design and limited in number. They achieve deadly effectiveness in the hands of a tough, crafty group of individuals who operate almost entirely independent of normal logistical support. Proficient in camouflaging their activities, these men spread a reign of terror over the civilian population of their own country.

Success in antipartisan warfare is not a matter of observing certain rules or applying standing operating procedures that have proved effective in particular instances. Rather, it is contingent upon carefully gathering all facts for evaluating the partisans' command structure, intelligence system, mobility in occupied territories, and relationship to the civilian population. The more examples from practical experience that are available for analyzing these factors, the better prepared will be those who might be called upon to lead the fight against partisans. The study of these examples will condition the future leaders and arouse their imagination, thus preparing them for missions that, under the present conditions of warfare, are likely to be assigned to any military commander.

It is in this spirit that the following small unit actions should be read. Far more important than the application of proper tactics, however, is the adoption of a sound overall policy guaranteeing the successful conduct of antipartisan operations. This policy must develop appropriate propagandistic, economic, and political measures

GERMAN MOTORIZED COLUMN takes a break on the road to Minsk, July 1941.

designed to turn the civilian population of occupied areas against the partisans and to obtain its cooperation in the antipartisan struggle. The enforcement of such a policy is the responsibility of the top-level command. It must be planned before the first bomb is released over enemy territory and must be applied when the first soldier sets foot on enemy soil.

During their initial encounters with partisans, combat troops usually tend to underestimate the importance and effectiveness of these irregular forces, principally because their equipment consists solely of small arms. What a dangerous fallacy! In most instances partisans are energetic and relentless men driven by a fanatic belief in their cause. Weak individuals drop from their ranks long before seeing action. The partisans' will to resist and their resolve to inflict damage, regardless of infractions of international conventions, compensate for deficiencies in equipment.

II. The First Encounter (June 1941)

The partisan activity that the Germans encountered immediately after the invasion of Russia was entirely unexpected. German officers who had fought against the Russians in World War I remembered that, when overrun or cut off, the Russians of that day stoically accepted their fate as prisoners of war. In World War I it was not unusual for two or three German soldiers on bicycle or horseback to escort as many as 500 Russian prisoners to a distant collecting point. Small groups of captives were often sent to the rear in the custody of the ranking prisoner. Independent operations by isolated or by-passed groups were practically unknown.

In relying on their experiences from World War I, the Germans overlooked the fact that the Russian Army of 1941 was not a mere continuation of the armies of the Czars, but rather a force born of a long and bitter revolutionary struggle in which the end justified any means. Since the time of the Russian civil wars the partisan fighter had become a legendary figure.

It took but a few days to shock the Germans into the realization that the Russian soldier of 1941 followed concepts different from those of his forebears of World War I.

The Germans learned that isolated Russian soldiers considered it their duty not only to continue the struggle as partisans but also to enlist civilians in their cause. If an isolated group had an energetic leader, its fighting spirit would be rekindled immediately after the initial shock, and harassing action behind the German lines would invariably follow.

Map 48

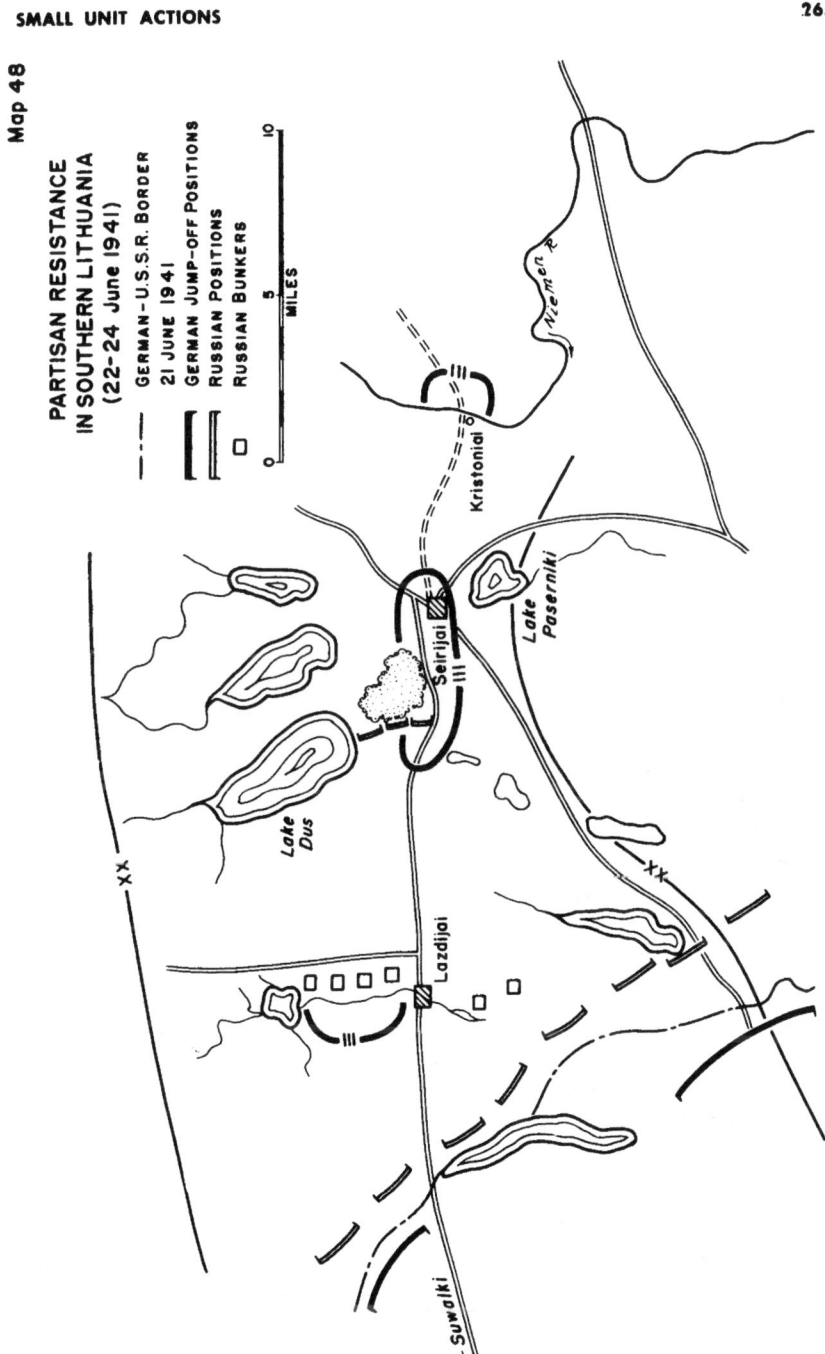

PARTISAN RESISTANCE
IN SOUTHERN LITHUANIA
(22-24 June 1941)

--- GERMAN–U.S.S.R. BORDER 21 JUNE 1941
GERMAN JUMP-OFF POSITIONS
RUSSIAN POSITIONS
□ RUSSIAN BUNKERS

The Germans met strong partisan resistance on the very first day of the Russian campaign.

At 0305 on 22 June 1941 the German V Corps invaded Russia from the area east and northeast of Suwalki. The spearhead division of the corps was to break through the Russian front in an operation along the Suwalki–Lazdijai–Seirijai road and, to complete the first phase of its offensive, establish a bridgehead across the Niemen River near Kristoniai (map 48).

The Russian border defenses were quickly overrun by the assault division, which then committed two regiments against the newly constructed fortifications near Lazdijai. The regiment on the right wing broke into that town by 1000, pushed through a narrow passage south of Lake Dus, and established a bridgehead across the Niemen by late afternoon. The distance from the line of departure to the bridgehead was 40 miles by air. The regiment on the left did not penetrate the bunker defenses in its area until the next day.

On the evening of the 22d the division was spread out over a wide area. The leading regiment, together with the reconnaissance battalion and most of the divisional artillery, was astride the Niemen. One regiment was tied down north of Lazdijai, and the reserve regiment, which had followed the lead regiment, was at the outskirts of Seirijai. By dark the entire division area was quiet.

About 2200 the firing of small arms was heard, but neither from the bridgehead nor from the Lazdijai area. It came from Seirijai, the area of the reserve regiment.

At the division command post it was first believed that, in the excitement of the first day of battle, German units were firing on each other in the dark. Soon, however, division headquarters was informed that elements of a German bridge column had been ambushed near the forest west of Seirijai and that traffic west of Seirijai was blocked. A short time later the reserve regiment reported street fighting against armed civilians in Seirijai.

This report was at first doubted. Until 1939 the area had been part of Lithuania, and its transfer to the USSR under a German-Russian agreement was strongly opposed by the local population. It appeared incredible that Lithuanians should suddenly have taken up the Russian cause. There was more likelihood that isolated Russian soldiers were continuing to offer resistance. About midnight, nevertheless, the commander of the reserve regiment reported intermittent fire from the forest and stated that armed civilians were actually participating in the fighting.

The regimental commander was ordered to flush the forest at dawn on the 23d. On the assumption that the force in the forest numbered only stragglers and lightly armed civilians, regiment assigned but one battalion to the mission. Following the same line of thought, the battalion commander felt that one company with the support of a heavy machinegun section would be adequate.

After proceeding a short distance into the forest, the company met strong resistance and had to go over to the defensive. A second company was committed without improving the situation. The third company also bogged down, and the operation ended in failure. This failure did clarify the situation. It showed that the force in the forest had been greatly underestimated.

The Russians had achieved a success greater than they probably realized. From the forest they were able to dominate a large area. No bypass around it, protected from Russian observation, was available to the German vehicles, and consequently communications within the division area were interrupted and supplies to the bridgehead regiment beyond the Niemen were cut off. The reserve regiment, one-third of the division's fighting power, was tied down. To solve this serious situation, division ordered the entire reserve regiment plus one artillery battalion committed against the forest stronghold on the 24th.

The attack plan was to destroy systematically the forest force, sector by sector, after breaking the enemy resistance with artillery and heavy weapons fire. For the assault proper two infantry battalions were echeloned in depth, elements of the third battalion sealed off the edge of the forest, and the remaining troops of the third battalion remained in Seirijai, which was without defense from the south and north.

The attacking battalions met stubborn resistance. A concentration of heavy weapons, mortars, and artillery within the dense woods was difficult and their fire did not always attain the desired effect. Not until the regiment moved its 37-mm. antitank guns to point-blank range were the first partisans overcome. Because it was necessary to use these time-consuming tactics, the forest was not in German hands until evening.

After the fighting was over, the Germans found that some 400 to 500 Russian soldiers, cut off by the German break-through, had formed the nucleus of the forest force. The majority of the force, however, were Russian civilians who had settled in the area after the USSR occupied Lithuania. Some civilians had joined the partisans voluntarily, others under duress. Most of the Russian soldiers had discarded their uniforms and obtained civilian clothing.

The entire force was under the command of a Russian field grade officer who had also organized the ambush in the town of Seirijai.

It was estimated that about one-fourth of the partisan force, including the commander, had escaped. Some must have made their way across the Niemen, because subsequently several German officers and men disappeared without a trace as the division continued its eastward advance. In one such instance a German field grade officer vanished shortly after leaving the division command post. In spite of a thorough investigation, nothing was ever found of the officer, his driver, or his vehicle.

The principal lessons learned by the Germans in their first encounter with partisans in Russia, were:

1. Partisans give no quarter and it is therefore a mistake to employ second-rate or weak forces against them. If casualties are to be held to a minimum and time is to be saved, the antipartisan forces must be as strong as possible and equipped with weapons, such as tanks and guns, that are not available to the partisans.

2. In order to encircle partisan forces, a tight ring must be thrown around the entire area. Russian partisans did not continue a hopeless engagement, but attempted to disperse, to disappear individually from a pocket, or, if necessary, to break out, and reassemble in a previously designated area. If partisan elements slip through a cordon too weakly manned, they are certain to resume operations in another location after a short while.

III. The Forest Camp (December 1942)

During the winter of 1941–42 the railway line and highway connecting Gomel with Bryansk constituted the principal arteries over which an important sector of the German central front received its supplies. In the vast swampy forests west of Bryansk the Germans were never able to subdue the partisans for any length of time. The partisan forces were much too strong, and their combat losses were quickly replaced by local manpower. They were well equipped with automatic weapons and ammunition from the supply dumps that the Russians had been forced to abandon during their hasty retreat in the summer of 1941.

Under the direct control and close supervision of Moscow, the partisan forces in the Bryansk area coordinated their activities with the operations of the regular Russian forces. The orders of the partisan leaders were obeyed implicitly by the inhabitants of the many remote villages where German patrols were seen only on rare occasions. Over a period of several months the Germans heard of only one case of noncompliance with a partisan leader's orders. In this instance the mayor of a small village had refused to deliver to

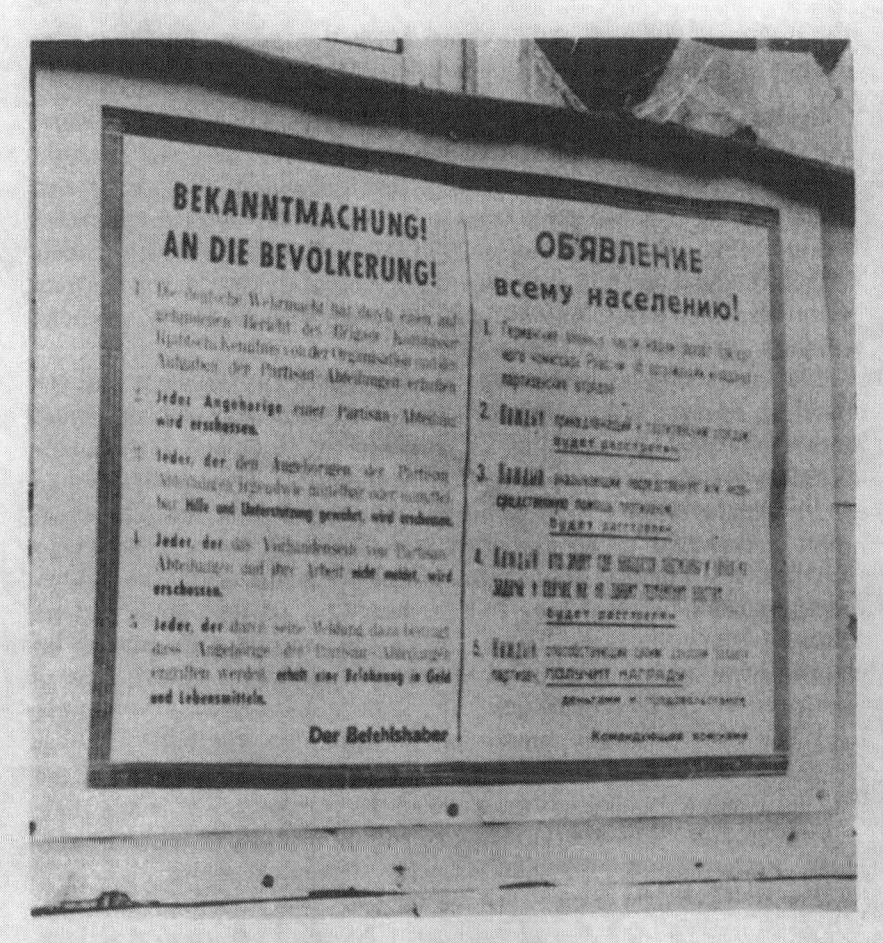

GERMAN POSTER warns of death penalty for any partisan or anyone assisting him, August 1941.

the partisans the last cow that was left in his community and offered to substitute some sheep. A few days later he appeared at the nearest German outpost, accompanied by his wife and children. He counted out 20 Czarist gold rubles and asked that he and his family be immediately evacuated by air because they feared for their lives. He requested air transportation because he believed that partisan attacks made rail travel too hazardous.

In the summer of 1942 partisan attacks on the railway and highway west of Bryansk were executed by Force Ruda, so designated by the Germans because the village of Ruda was near its center of operation. This force was an extremely active group of 300 to 400 partisans under a particularly efficient and audacious leader who commanded the respect of his men and imposed strict discipline. In the course of time he acquired a reputation as a local hero.

Several German attempts to eliminate Force Ruda failed because the partisans were always able to vanish into the forests and swamps. Early in the autumn of 1942 the actual hideout of the group was discovered—a fortified camp deep in the forest, surrounded by several swamp belts. When the Germans attempted to take the camp their vehicles bogged down in the first swamp, and Major Stein, the German battalion commander, unwilling to proceed without heavy weapons support, decided to withdraw.

The intervening muddy period hindered both the Germans and the partisan forces. Stein used the time to organize five ski companies into an antipartisan battalion. Companies A, B, C, and D were rifle companies, each equipped to fight independently. Each company had 12 light machine guns, 3 heavy machine guns, 6 medium mortars which were transported on hand-drawn *akjas* [*Ed:* A Finnish boat-type sled], and a number of machine pistols. Company E, the heavy-weapons company, had four 75-mm. mountain artillery guns and six Russian heavy mortars. The artillery and mortars were carried on horse-drawn sleds, as was the ammunition. The battalion was equipped with several radio sets.

When the first heavy snows fell in November, the battalion was used to protect the rail line. Because of their greater mobility, the ski units had a decided advantage over the partisans, who made their attacks on foot. On several occasions the ski troops were able to overtake partisan groups that had staged raids against trains.

The partisans, however, were not long in taking appropriate countermeasures. Whenever a ski company occupied billets in a village, large-scale attacks against the rail traffic in the vicinity of the village would cease, and the partisans would restrict their activity to isolated demolitions by small teams. Obviously an efficient intelligence system functioned between the partisans and the civilian populace.

Major Stein, who ordered a thorough search of the villages in the immediate vicinity of the railroad and highway, was amazed at the number of radio sets found there. These were all identical to the model issued to his battalion and must have been taken from German supply trains by the partisans. The recapture of the radio sets failed to produce the slightest effect on the activities of the partisans, who apparently had still other means of communication. Stein then decided to stay out of inhabited localities, even though this meant spending the midwinter nights out in the open. The troops were issued supplementary winter clothing and Russian-type felt boots to be worn

SMALL UNIT ACTIONS

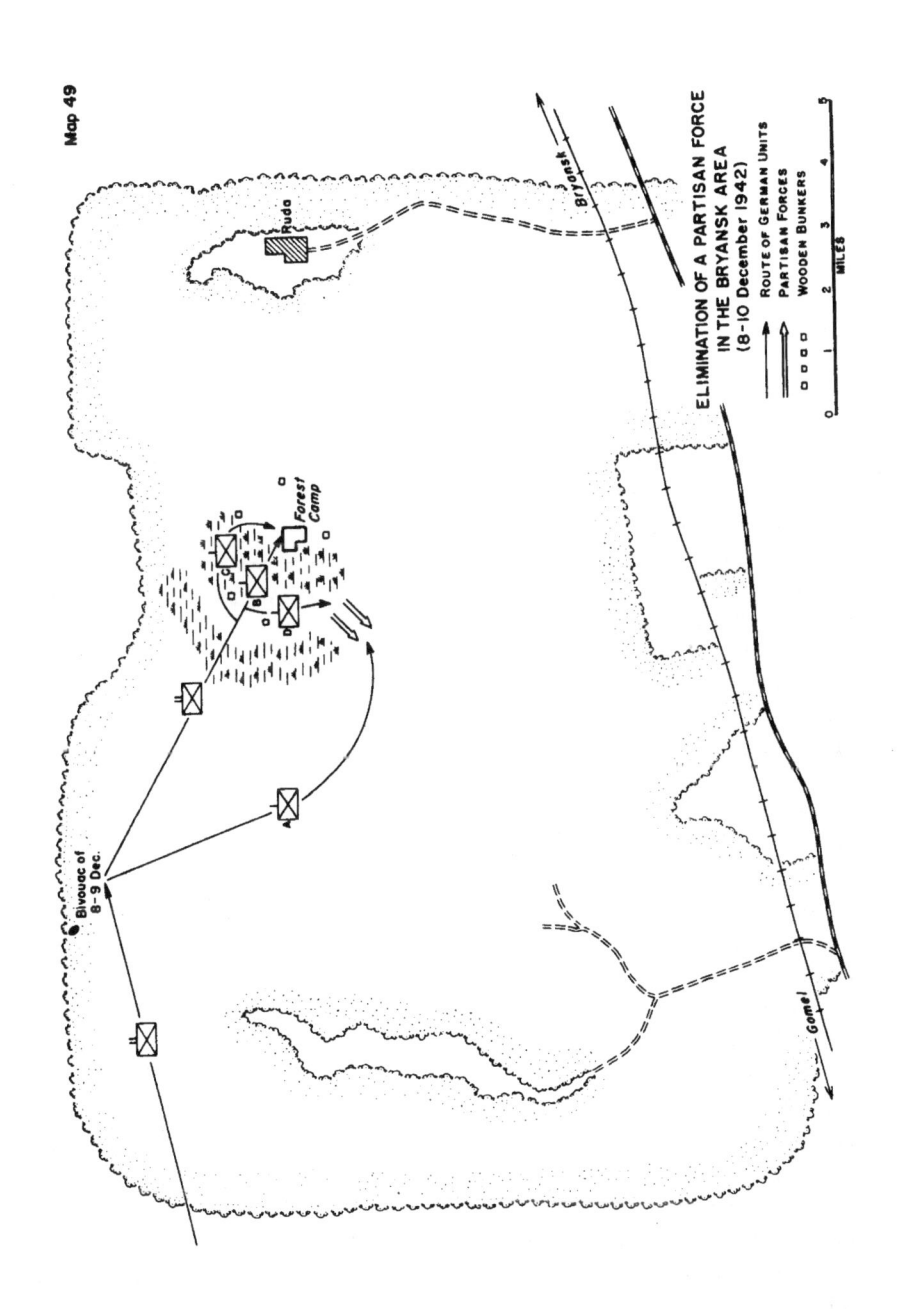

Map 49

ELIMINATION OF A PARTISAN FORCE
IN THE BRYANSK AREA
(8–10 December 1942)

ROUTE OF GERMAN UNITS
PARTISAN FORCES
WOODEN BUNKERS

at night. By the end of November the newly organized ski battalion became quite accustomed to spending the night in snow huts.

The swamps that had foiled the summer attack on the partisan camp were frozen over by early December. Stein drew up a plan for an attack against the forest camp of Force Ruda.

On 8 December the battalion moved out of its bivouac and entered the forest adjacent to the camp (map 49). Reconnaissance patrols were detailed to observe whether the column was being followed. One after another they picked up four farmers hauling firewood, but found no evidence to justify their suspicion.

When well into the forest the battalion suddenly turned eastward in the direction of the forest camp, which was then approximately 15 miles away. Stein estimated that an attack would be least expected through the desolate swamp area northwest of the camp, and on the evening of 8 December the battalion bivouaced in the forest about 6 miles northwest of the partisan camp.

At dawn on 9 December Company A proceeded into the area just southwest of the camp to establish the camp's exact location. Stein planned to lauch the attack on 10 December.

On the afternoon of the 9th Company A reported by radio that a partisan force taking ski training had been sighted at a point presumed to be about 2 miles southwest of the camp. The coordinates of the camp's location were reported around midnight following a reconnaissance mission.

On the basis of the two messages Stein concluded that the approach of Company A had not been observed by the partisans. He was completely surprised when, even before dawn, the company reported that it was engaged in heavy fighting with a partisan force. At 0800 the company sent another report indicating that the intensity of the attack was increasing, and 30 minutes later it radioed that the entire Force Ruda was participating in the action. The company was under intense mortar fire, and partisans were enveloping its right flank. At 0900 the company reported that it was withdrawing westward in a delaying action.

Faced with the necessity of relieving Company A, Stein considered three possible solutions to his problem: the battalion could join forces with Company A, or turn against the partisan camp, or effect a compromise, committing some elements against the camp and sending the rest to the asistance of Company A.

To move the entire battalion to the scene of the fighting was not feasible because Company A was about 3 hours away, and it was doubtful whether the partisans would make a stand since their tactics called for withdrawal whenever faced by superior forces. Even if the partisans did decide to make a stand, the battalion could achieve only a local success at most, and the element of surprise in the main attack against the camp would be lost.

To divide the battalion would be effective only if Company A's commander was correct in his assumption that he was engaging the entire Force Ruda. If this was true, then the partisans were probably holding the camp with few, if any, defense forces, in which case the camp could be quickly occupied and Company A relieved. However, the actual strength of Force Ruda was unknown to the Germans. If the camp was strongly held, splitting up the German forces could only lead to failure of the principal mission.

Stein reasoned that he could achieve a decision only by employing all his forces in one direction, that the main objective of the battalion was the partisan camp, and that, if the bulk of Force Ruda was engaged with Company A, an attack on the camp would divert some of the pressure from that company. Even if the garrison of the camp was stronger than expected, a delay in the attack would offer no greater chance of success than an immediate operation. He therefore decided to concentrate his entire force in a thrust against the partisan camp.

Shortly after 0900 the battalion started its advance toward the camp, Company B in the lead, reinforced by the four mountain artillery guns of Company E. The movement proceeded without incident until 1130 when the forward elements drew submachinegun fire from five wooden bunkers, which constituted the outer defenses of the camp. As the battalion moved forward, the bunkers were evacuated. Company B was about to advance over a second snow-covered swamp when it came under intense machinegun fire from the forest, about 150 yards distant.

Stein ordered Company B to seize the northwest part of the camp; Company C, reinforced by the six heavy mortars of the weapons company, was to attack the camp from the north; Company D was held in reserve. Company A was ordered by radio to go over to the offensive in order to pin down as many partisans as possible.

At 1300 Company B approached the immediate vicinity of the camp while Company C fought for the bunkers along the northern perimeter. Shortly thereafter Company D was committed to intercept partisan elements that had broken off the battle with Company A and were attempting to move toward the camp.

Toward 1400, with the aid of the mountain artillery, the last resistance in front of Company B was crushed, and the first elements broke into the camp. The advance of Company B brought relief to Company C, attacking from the north. Company B fought its way to the center of the camp and mopped up the remaining nests of resistance.

By 1500 the struggle was over. Both sides had suffered heavy casualties. Company A lost 25 percent of its strength and was unable to encircle the remnants of Force Ruda, thereby preventing their escape. The partisan leader was killed in Company D's sector.

Interrogation of prisoners brought to light the fact that the camp had been held by 150 men, and that a force of about 350 men had attacked Company A. The Germans also learned that the area around the camp, except for a few lanes, was heavily mined. The ski battalion was fortunate in that heavy snowfall had covered the mines, making them ineffective.

The dimensions of the camp and the amount of supplies it contained amazed Stein and his men. In addition to quantities of small arms, there were tons of ammunition and sufficient rations for several months. Moreover, the Germans recovered a great variety of items looted from supply trains, including binoculars, telescopes, and the most recent models of radio sets.

The example shows how an aggressive antipartisan unit, trained and equipped for winter warfare, successfully carried out an operation in forest and swamp over terrain impassable at other seasons of the year.

IV. Attack on a Partisan Headquarters (June 1943)

By early 1943 the partisans were directing their activities mainly against the major railway lines used to move supplies from Germany to the Russian front. Partisan attacks on moving trains and extensive demolition of tracks, bridges, and tunnels at times almost halted traffic on the railway routes Warsaw-Gomel-Bryansk and Minsk-Borisov-Smolensk.

German antipartisan operations had developed a definite pattern. As soon as the location of a partisan force became known, it would be attacked simultaneously from several sides. Dawn was the preferred time for such raids. However, these tactics were successful only if the partisans did not learn beforehand of the Germans' intentions. After Stalingrad, the partisans increased in numbers and improved their organization and intelligence system. More and more frequently the Germans, when closing in on one of their strongholds, would find no partisans at all.

Early in June 1943 the Germans obtained information that the partisan staff planning the attacks against the rail line in the Borisov sector had its headquarters at Daliki, about 10 miles south of Lepel

SMALL UNIT ACTIONS

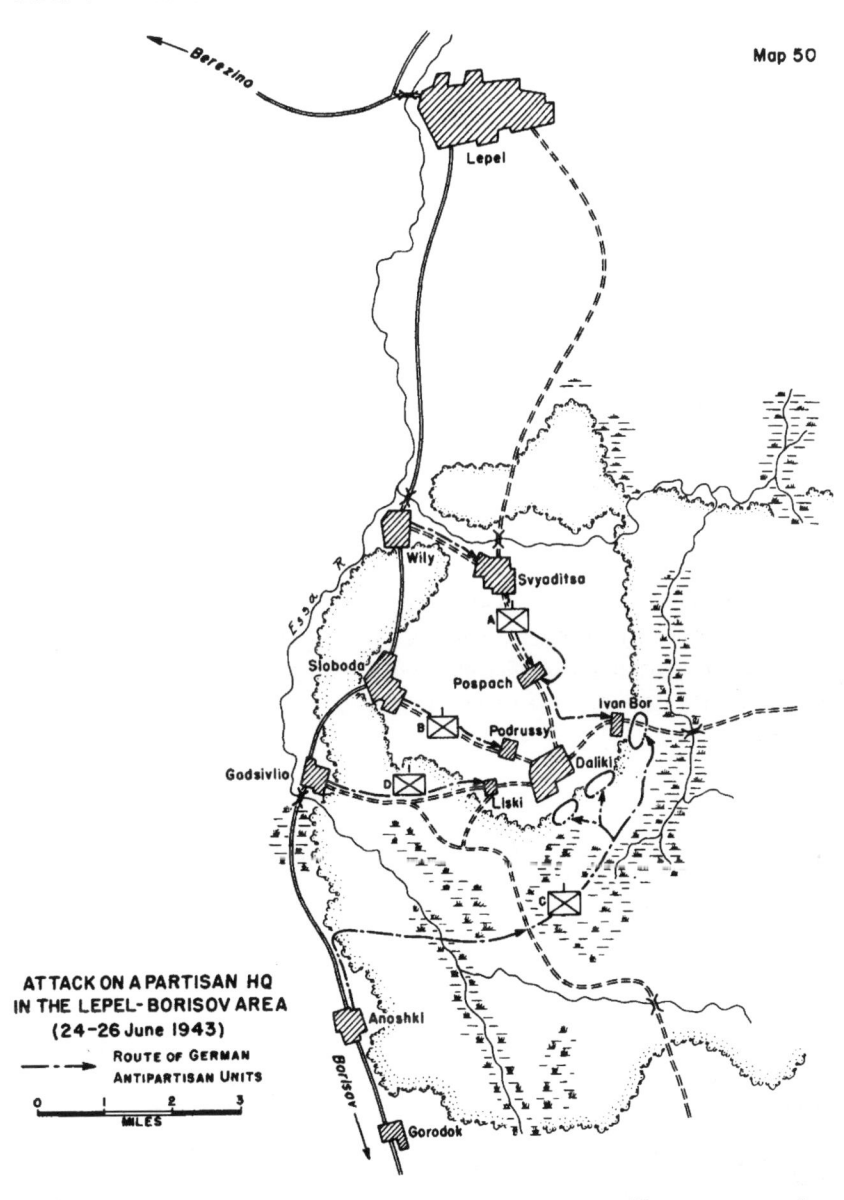

ATTACK ON A PARTISAN HQ IN THE LEPEL-BORISOV AREA (24-26 June 1943)

Map 50

(map 50). The partisan force at Daliki was no ordinary group, but the nerve center for a large partisan area of operations with a well-organized system of communication. It was unlikely that the Daliki staff would not learn about a German advance from several sides.

The German commander in charge of the Borisov district therefore decided to entrust the destruction of the partisan headquarters to a bicycle-mounted infantry battalion that had been temporarily withdrawn from the front and made available for antipartisan operations. The reinforced battalion consisted of four companies, a headquarters with attached signal platoon, and a motorized supply column; Companies A, B, and C were equipped with bicycles, 12 light machineguns, and 6 light mortars each; Company D, the heavy weapons company, was motorized and had 12 heavy machineguns and six 37-mm. antitank guns.

On 24 June Major Beer, the battalion commander, issued the following order to his subordinates:

1. The battalion will carry out an antipartisan operation in the Berezina Valley, 20 miles west of Lepel.
2. The battalion, less Company C, will move out at 0700 on 25 June and proceed toward Berezino. On the night of 25 June battalion headquarters and the signal platoon will establish a command post at Wily; Company A will stop in Sloboda; Company B in Gadsivlia; and Company D in Anoshki.
3. Billeting parties will precede the march columns. After the units have arrived at their new quarters (about 1600), billeting parties will report to the battalion command post in Wily at 1900 and proceed via Lepel to Berezino where they will obtain billets for 26 June from the local commander.
4. At 0700 on 26 June the battalion will assemble just north of Wily and proceed via Lepel to Berezino.

The first day's march went according to plan, and at 0700 on 26 June the battalion crossed the initial point north of Wily and drove on toward Lepel. At the first house on the outskirts of Lepel the battalion executive officer met the column, ordered a 2-hour halt and an issue of rations, and directed the company commanders to report to battalion headquarters at the northern edge of the town.

As the last company commander arrived at the command post, Major Beer stated blunty: "I want you to know right now that I have played a trick on you. Our battalion was never ordered to fight the partisans in the Berezina Valley. That was a fabrication on my part to hide our real objective: a raid on the Borisov area partisan headquarters, reportedly located in Daliki."

The company commanders were not too surprised. If the true objective had been stated in battalion orders, partisan agents would have informed their headquarters in Daliki long before the Germans could have reached the village. Beer continued:

> Let's look at the map. When I was ordered to capture the partisan staff, I tried to develop a plan that would achieve surprise. In this situation I believed that to bring up my four companies

during the night and then attempt to break into Daliki from four sides would be impractical. I am convinced that the partisans would have learned of our movement—the distance from Borisov to Daliki incidentally is about 30 miles—and I am even more certain that they would have found out about our assembly at night. We would have found Daliki deserted.

I would have liked to use a small motorized force of one or, at most, two companies, moving at top speed from Borisov to Sloboda. From there they could have turned right and driven along the cart road to Daliki. The advance elements could have raced right into the center of Daliki, while the rear elements sealed off the village from the south and east, toward the swamp area. That would have been a real surprise! For such an operation, however, we would need cross-country vehicles.

The solution, therefore, was to simulate a normal march movement, such as is frequently made from Borisov to Lepel, with the partisan center in Berezino as the obvious objective. In order to strengthen the impression of a routine movement, I ordered the battalion to spend last night at a stop-over point on our march route directly opposite Daliki. For the same reason I requisitioned billets in different villages in the usual manner, whereupon the billeting parties were ordered to proceed to Berezino. They are arranging for billets there right now, and not until tonight will they know that their efforts were for nought. All these measures are calculated to prevent the partisan leaders from becoming suspicious, and to induce them to remain in Daliki. I am convinced that they were informed last night that the battalion is moving into the Berezina Valley.

Beer looked at his watch and said:

It is now 0900. Rest your men until 1100. Nothing must point to the fact that we have a different objective. Until that time our objective continues to be Berezino. At 1100 the battalion will turn around and drive back over the same road we followed this morning, maintaining the same order of march. The three cart roads leading to Daliki will be assigned as follows: Company A will take the road from Wily through Svyaditsa, Company B will turn off at Sloboda, and Company D will take the road from Gadsivlia. Battalion headquarters will proceed with Company D. There will be no intermediate halts, no reconnaissance. The common objective is Daliki.

I believe that the partisan leaders will try to escape into the swamps south and east of the village. Therefore I have ordered

Company C to take up positions at the adjacent edge of the swamp at 1100. Yesterday, as you know, this company remained in place when the battalion moved out and in the afternoon Company C was loaded—without its bicycles—onto six tarpaulin-covered trucks and moved to Gorodok, where it remained overnight. Company C is carrying only small arms such as pistols, carbines, submachineguns, and rifles equipped with silencers [*Ed:* These were captured Russian rifles that used special ammunition, the report being barely audible at a distance of 100 yards]. Early this morning the company left Gorodok for Lepel. About 1½ miles north of Anoshki, at a point where the forest borders on the road, the column stopped, allowing the personnel to detruck, whereupon the empty trucks were driven on through Lepel to Berezino. My orders to the company commander were to stop for only 30 seconds and keep the motors running.

Beer spread an aerial photograph of the Daliki area on the table and continued:

Using this photograph as a map, Company C was ordered to march by compass due east through the woods and moors, and, after crossing the Essa River, to advance—or rather wade—into the swamp southeast of Daliki. It will hide in the middle of the swamp. No patrols will be sent out since the company must remain unnoticed. At 1100, when the battalion turns around, Company C will occupy the fringe of the swamp facing Daliki and a portion of the forest just east of Ivan Bor. However, when the other companies enter Daliki, it will refrain from attacking, its mission being to capture the partisan leaders when they try to escape. Everything else is secondary.

I would gladly have spared Company C the march through the wet forest and moors, the crossing of the Essa, and the stay in the swamp, where they will be half-devoured by insects. There is a cart road running north toward Liski about 5 miles east of the Borisov-Lepel road, but I believe that this cart road is used as a route of communication between the partisan headquarters and its subordinate units in the forest around Borisov. I have no doubt that an advance along this road would have been reported immediately to partisan headquarters. That is why I ordered Company C to take the more difficult route.

In my estimate, we shall encounter our first resistance at the farm houses in Liski, Podrussy, Pospach, and Ivan Bor, which form a semicircle around Daliki. I am certain that an important partisan headquarters such as this one would not depend solely on close-

SMALL UNIT ACTIONS

in security. Any resistance encountered at these farms must be crushed without delay, and for this purpose Company D will detach two antitank guns each to both Companies A and B. At 1200, gentlemen, I want to see you and your companies enter Daliki. Are there any questions?

After asking a few questions the company commanders returned to their respective units in order to brief their platoon leaders.

GERMAN SOLDIER searching a captured Russian partisan.

At 1100 the battalion turned around and retraced its route of 3 hours earlier.

At Wily Company A turned off and proceeded through Svyaditsa. The leading elements were almost in Pospach when a machinegun opened fire from there, forcing them to take cover. As the company's antitank guns were being brought up, a second machinegun in Pospach opened fire. While one platoon, together with the antitank guns, delivered frontal fire on the partisan machine guns, the two other platoons moved through the woods just east of the village in order to envelop it from the rear. Despite the Germans' attempts at encirclement, the partisans managed to get out, but most of them were cut down as they fled across the open terrain toward Ivan Bor.

It was close to 1300 when Company A resumed its advance. Company B, too, was delayed by resistance in Podrussy. Company D was the only one to enter Daliki according to plan.

Company C's platoon nearest Ivan Bor became heavily engaged with the partisans withdrawing from that village. Meanwhile, Company A pushed on, but before reaching Daliki it received an order to turn off toward Ivan Bor and to take it from the west. The company used its entire fire power including 12 machineguns, 6 mortars, and 2 antitank guns, but the partisans in Ivan Bor held out to the last man, very few having been able to get away. It was subsequently learned that when the Germans attacked Pospach, about 20 members of the partisan staff withdrew southward from Daliki and ran up against some Company C men hiding at the edge of the swamp. When asked to surrender, the partisans opened fire with their submachineguns, and in the ensuing hand-to-hand fighting the entire group was killed.

No top-echelon partisan leaders were taken alive. The manner in which they probably met their deaths is suggested by the following account: Soon after the firing around Pospach had started, members of the Company C platoon east of Ivan Bor spotted a horse-drawn carriage coming from the direction of Daliki. In the carriage were the driver and what appeared to be four women, wearing the customary large shawls. Having passed through Ivan Bor, the carriage came to the platoon position. When the driver was asked to stop, the women suddenly opened fire on the platoon. All five occupants of the carriage were killed in the brief exchange that followed. The four "women" were found to be men—probably the core of the partisan staff. However, no documentary proof of this supposition was found.

An attack against the headquarters of a partisan force is always hazardous because a headquarters has a more extensive intelligence system, including closer contact with the local populace, than the ordinary partisan group.

If a large force is assembled for an attack on a headquarters, it can be expected that the partisans will learn about the impending operation and will avoid an encounter by timely withdrawal. If the unit to carry out the attack is small, its approach may remain unnoticed. Nevertheless, it will lack the strength to overcome even the partisans' security and covering detachments, and will furthermore be unable to seal off the area to prevent the escape of the leaders. If the leaders of a partisan force are able to escape, the operation must be considered a failure, even if all the other personnel are captured or killed.

A possible solution may be found in the employment of a flexible force organized for swift and effective action. Such a force needs vehicles that can move rapidly over long distances and across difficult terrain. It must have self-propelled guns and sufficient machineguns to knock out security and covering forces, and an assault echelon to raid the headquarters proper and seize the staff personnel. The force should have armored vehicles, flame throwers, mortars, and ground-support aircraft, and, finally, enough troops to seal off possible escape routes.

In many areas the terrain of European Russia is not suitable for motor vehicles and self-propelled guns. The attack on the partisan headquarters described in the preceding pages occurred in a sector where forests, swamps, and waterways interdicted movements of strong forces. In general, partisans preferred to rely on natural terrain obstacles that could not be surmounted at any season of the year, rather than on customary military security measures.

V. Operation QUARRY (January–March 1944)

The last example of German antipartisan operations indicates the disturbing effect Russian partisans had on the weakened Axis forces in early 1944. Lacking manpower at the front, the Germans were struggling desperately to extinguish the flames of insurrection that threatened their rear area security. Sensing the decline of Germany's military might, the partisans grew ever more audacious. The following story illustrates the desperateness of the struggle.

At the eastern end of the Crimean Peninsula lies Kerch, its white stone houses gleaming in the sun. This city of 50,000 inhabitants, strategically located along the Strait of Kerch, which connects the Black Sea with the Sea of Azov, has had an eventful history since

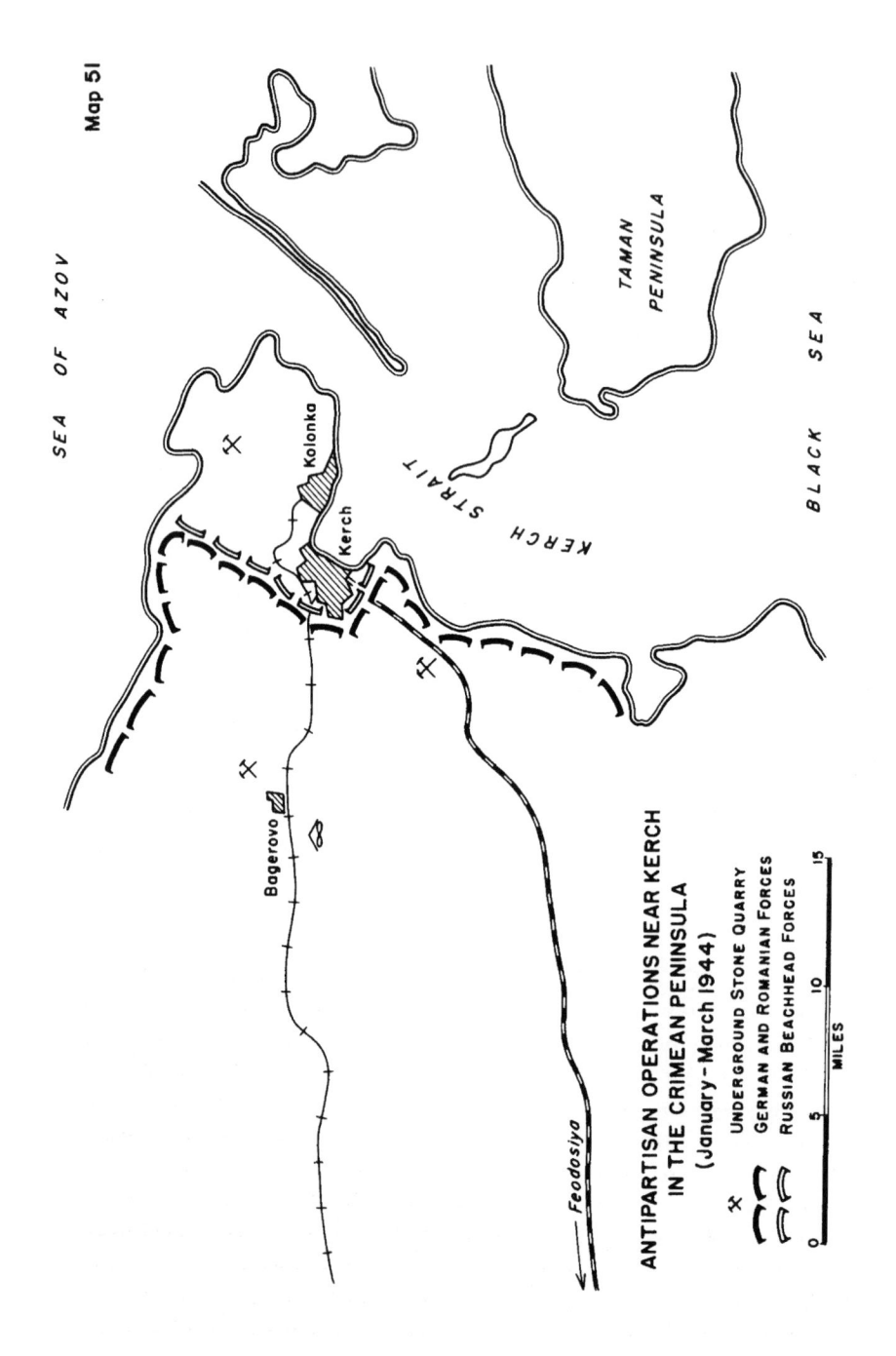

Map 51

ANTIPARTISAN OPERATIONS NEAR KERCH
IN THE CRIMEAN PENINSULA
(January–March 1944)

it was founded as a Greek trading post more than 2,000 years ago (map 51).

After the Germans occupied Kerch in World War II, the city played an important role as a transloading point for shipments to the Kuban area. Early in October 1943, when the German Seventeenth Army evacuated the Kuban bridgehead and withdrew across the Strait because of a Russian advance in the Don area, the city of Kerch was once again in the combat zone.

The Seventeenth Army was composed of German and Romanian divisions. After the retirement from the Kuban bridgehead all but two German divisions and some Romanian units were transferred to Sixth Army, then fighting north of the Sea of Azov. Despite these reinforcements, Sixth Army was unable to halt the Russians westward drive to Kherson, which cut off the Crimea late in October 1943.

During the night of 31 October–1 November the Russians carried out an amphibious operation across the Strait and established a beachhead in the mountainous terrain northeast of the city of Kerch. The German forces opposing the beachhead included the 98th Infantry Division and another division that was brought in by air; Romanian troops meanwhile were protecting the coast on both sides of the beachhead against further landing attempts.

For the next 6 months the Germans succeeded in preventing a Russian breakout. During that time the Russians gradually built up a force of 12 divisions in their lodgment area.

Since the very beginning of the German occupation partisans had operated in the Crimea, although usually only in the woods of the Yaila and Yalta Mountains. During November and December of 1943 the civilian population in the Kerch area caused the Germans no difficulties. Early in 1944, however, this situation changed.

Kerch is connected with Feodosiya, a Black Sea port to the southwest, by the only paved road in the area, which was therefore the main supply route feeding the defensive battle around Kerch. The countryside between Kerch and Feodosiya was completely barren; even in the inhabited localities, trees were rare. The monotony of the steppeland was broken only by occasional hills with rocky slopes and naked summits. Visibility was excellent, and thus the villages could be easily kept under control by the German rear area elements.

Suddenly a number of attacks on German trucks and personnel carriers took place along a stretch of the road about 3 miles southwest of Kerch. Vehicles were ambushed and set afire; their drivers and passengers killed. Initially the attacks occurred only at night, but before long, officers and soldiers proceeding alone were shot down in broad daylight.

After a short time the attacks spread over a larger area. A German soldier was shot and killed near the Bagerovo airfield, west of Kerch. North of that same airfield a German battalion marching toward the front was engaged by a partisan force that appeared out of nowhere at its front and flanks and then disappeared a few minutes later, as suddenly as it had come.

One afternoon some Romanian troops armed with submachineguns were loaded on a truck covered with a tarpaulin. The truck started out from Kerch for Feodosiya. About 5 miles from Kerch the truck was ambushed, as expected. The Romanian troops returned the fire and, jumping off quickly, pursued the ambush force over the open terrain. Suddenly the Romanians found themselves alone. The fleeing partisans had disappeared as if swallowed up by the ground.

A systematic search of the area revealed numerous holes in the ground that looked like shell craters. Closer examination, however, proved that these holes were entrances to a huge underground quarry. Quarries in this region were the source of the stone used to build the white houses in Kerch. When freshly cut this stone was so soft that it could be sawed. Once exposed to the air, it became hard and durable. In the course of 2,000 years the inhabitants of Kerch had worked almost a dozen of these underground quarries, the largest of which had multistoried galleries several hundred yards long, as well as numerous side galleries.

The partisan headquarters was located in a quarry just southwest of Kerch. Knowing this to be the case, the commander of the Romanian division charged with the defense of the coastal area south of the Russian beachhead decided to wrest the quarry from the partisans as soon as possible and liquidate them in the process.

Should the partisans decide to make a stand, it was recognized that a savage and most unusual struggle would undoubtedly ensue in the dark underground labyrinth. The troops selected for the initial assault—a reinforced company—were therefore issued appropriate equipment. In addition to pistols, submachineguns, flamethrowers, and portable searchlights, they carried large quantities of hand grenades. Two companies were to be held in reserve.

The plan of operation called for all entrances to the quarry to be sealed except one. The assault unit was to use this one entrance, enter the galleries, and overcome the partisans in close combat.

When members of the advance element passed through the entrance, they were sharply silhouetted against the light background and came under heavy fire from the darkness of the quarry. With admirable determination the Romanians advanced about 100 yards into the main

SMALL UNIT ACTIONS

gallery and were attempting to break down the resistance in front of them when they were suddenly attacked from the side galleries. Reinforcements were committed but, unable to turn the tide of battle in the underground darkness, the assault troops had to fight their way back to the daylight, leaving behind numerous casualties. The surrendered terms offered to the partisans were rejected.

A second attempt by specially trained Romanian assault troops, who entered the quarry simultaneously through several passages, also failed.

The two abortive assaults with their heavy losses led the local command to conclude that the partisans could not be driven out by force; accordingly, all entrances were sealed off in the hope of forcing the partisans to surrender through lack of air, food, and water. However, the raids in that area did not cease. One night late in January the troops guarding a sealed entrance were attacked from open terrain. Romanian reserves responded quickly, routing the partisans and capturing some of their wounded.

Interrogation of the prisoners revealed that there were in the quarry

GERMAN SUPPLY DUMP in Russia.

about 120 well-armed partisans and a number of women who did the cooking and took care of the sick and wounded. Their leader was an engineer who had been employed in the steel mills located in the vicinity of Kerch. A group of partisans had expressed the wish to comply with the Romanian surrender terms. The engineer, however, had their spokesman shot and established the death penalty for anyone who might harbor such thoughts in the future. The filling-in of the entrances had not cut off the air supply. In fact, this measure proved completely ineffectual, since the partisans had dug new air shafts. During the day these shafts were carefully camouflaged; at night they were used as exits for raids. Food was rationed, but adequate. There was no real water shortage. A pit filled with water was available and, in addition, dripping water was collected.

On the basis of this information, the Romanian commander asked the Germans for further instructions. To make the correct decision was far from easy. It was, of course, desirable that this partisan stronghold, so close to the German front and astride an important supply line, be quickly and completely liquidated. But it appeared doubtful that a third operation, for which the Romanians requested German aid, would meet with greater success, even if stronger forces were used. Moreover, the Germans were under such heavy pressure from the Russian beachhead that no troops could be made available for the operation and, given a continuation of the Russian attacks, even the Romanian units securing the coast would probably have to be used to help contain the beachhead. Under these circumstances a large-scale operation resulting in heavy losses could not be risked.

The Germans therefore ordered that no all-out attack be undertaken, but that the quarry area be completely surrounded by wire. As soon as the wire was in place, the Romanian combat troops were to be withdrawn and replaced with personnel drawn from rear area service troops.

However, the order to set up the wire obstacle was not carried out in full. As soon as the Romanians started building it, the partisans recognized the impending danger and broke through the lightly manned cordon at night, moving bag and baggage to another underground quarry near Bagerovo.

Located 6 miles west of Kerch, Bagerovo with its airfield and railhead was the most important supply point behind the German front in the Crimea. The new partisan base was an even more serious threat than the recently abandoned one southwest of Kerch.

The Germans immediately ordered Romanian units to surround the Bagerovo quarry, an area of approximately 250 acres, and to work around the clock on the construction of a continuous wire obstacle.

A Romanian officer was placed in charge of the guard and labor units.

In addition, the Germans provided the Romanian commander with so-called alert units, which were made up of personnel drawn from transportation, signal, and supply units, as well as from kitchens and orderly rooms. One German searchlight battalion was also made available. The force constituted for the main phase of Operation QUARRY was such as was rarely assembled for a combat operation in this isolated theater, where manpower was at a premium. Two Romanian infantry battalions, German and Romanian alert units, two construction battalions, and a searchlight battalion—altogether some 2,000 troops—were tied down by a partisan force hiding underground and numbering little over 100 men.

Within 5 days an effective continuous wire obstacle was constructed. The Romanian infantry battalions and the construction battalions were relieved, and the German and Romanian alert units took over the guard. During daylight hours the number of guards was small. At night, sentries were posted along the wire obstacle and patrols kept the entire area under observation with the aid of searchlights placed on elevations overlooking the quarry.

During the first weeks of their forced isolation the partisans made several attempts to break out at night, but these were frustrated by the machinegun fire of the alert units. Toward the end of February, 3 weeks after the beginning of Operation QUARRY, the first deserters appeared at the wire obstacle. They stated the food stocks were almost exhausted, that contact with the outside had been cut off, and that their leader, the engineer, was preparing for a breakout in order to move to another quarry. On the basis of this information, the alert units were reinforced by two companies. If the partisans made an escape and succeeded in establishing themselves in another quarry, the Romanian and German forces would have to be spread so thin that there would be no end to this unwelcome diversion.

The expected breakout attempt did not take place until late March. Although the partisans displayed their characteristic skill and daring, most of them were killed and the rest taken prisoner. The leader, however, was not among the prisoners or the dead. A Russian radio message subsequently intercepted by the Germans revealed that he had succeeded in slipping through the German lines and had arrived safely within the Russian beachhead. For 3 months he had been the driving force of an operation that had tied down a considerable number of German and Romanian forces and cost them much time and many casualties. Here was an underground operation in the literal sense of the word.

Hunger alone had driven the partisans to attempt the breakout. Had they held out for only a few more days, they would have been liberated, because on 8 April Russian troops pierced the defenses of the Perekop Isthmus and advanced on Simferopol, the Crimean capital. On the night of 9 April the German troops who had contained the Russian beachhead for 6 months were compelled to make a hasty withdrawal across the peninsula.

Although it does not lend itself to generalizations, this example of a force that held out for months in underground quarries is characteristic of Russian partisan warfare. Among other things, it demonstrates that partisans conceal themselves anywhere.

That the initial assaults against the quarry force failed was due in no small measure to the partisans' familiarity with the ramifications of their underground stronghold. This advantage compensated for the numerical superiority of the attack force. Subterranean caves, galleries, and shafts are difficult to locate, and their extension cannot be accurately gaged. It is doubtful whether a third attempt to ferret the partisans out of the first quarry by force would have been successful. The advantages to a defender familiar with every corner of the quarry and accustomed to moving in darkness were too great, particularly in view of the fact that the partisan force had an exceptionally resolute and aggressive leader.

The wire obstacle built around the second quarry at Bagerovo might easily have proven ineffective. The partisans had started to dig an escape tunnel through the soft stone and failed to achieve their objective only because they were physically exhausted from lack of food. The problem of destroying a tenacious force hiding below the surface of the ground other than through starvation, the use of gas, or by suffering excessive casualties among one's own troops thus remained unsolved.

Immediately after Operation QUARRY had been brought to a successful end, the Germans investigated the underground system at Bagerovo and found that it was much larger than the one southwest of Kerch. The Bagerovo system, moreover, was thoroughly organized for a section-by-section defense, principally through the use of built-in demolition charges and machineguns strategically placed to cover the passageways. Every provision for a successful defense had been made; there was a command post with numerous telephone circuits, an aid station, an infirmary, emergency assembly areas, depleted ration and ammunition dumps, a reservoir for collecting drip water, and directional signs in luminous paint. At the beginning of the siege the partisans had at their disposal a small herd of cattle which had been hidden in the caves by local residents. The animals were slaughtered one by one to provide fresh meat.

According to local inhabitants, these same quarries had been used during the Russian Civil War in 1917. After the Bolsheviks occupied the Crimea, White Russians were said to have lived in them for years.

Printed in Great Britain
by Amazon